A Place at the Nayarit

The publisher and the University of California Press Foundation gratefully acknowledge the generous support of the Lisa See Endowment Fund in Southern California History and Culture.

A Place at the Nayarit

*How a Mexican Restaurant Nourished
a Community*

NATALIA MOLINA

UNIVERSITY OF CALIFORNIA PRESS

University of California Press
Oakland, California

© 2022 by Natalia Molina

Library of Congress Cataloging-in-Publication Data

Names: Molina, Natalia, author.
Title: A place at the Nayarit : how a Mexican
     restaurant nourished a community / Natalia
     Molina.
Description: Oakland, California : University of
     California Press, [2022] | Includes bibliographical
     references and index.
Identifiers: LCCN 2021029639 (print) | LCCN
     2021029640 (ebook) | ISBN 9780520385481 (cloth)
     | ISBN 9780520385498 (epub)
Subjects: LCSH: Barraza, Natalia, -1969. | Nayarit
     (Restaurant : Los Angeles, Calif.) | Restaurants—
     California—Los Angeles. | Mexican American
     neighborhoods—California—Los Angeles—Social
     life and customs. | Mexican Americans—
     California—Los Angeles. | Immigrants—California—
     Los Angeles. | Echo Park (Los Angeles, Calif.)
Classification: LCC TX909.2.C22 N39 2022
     (print) | LCC TX909.2.C22 (ebook) | DDC
     647.95794/94—dc23
LC record available at https://lccn.loc
     .gov/2021029639
LC ebook record available at https://lccn.loc
     .gov/2021029640

31 30 29 28 27 26 25 24 23 22
10 9 8 7 6 5 4 3 2 1

For Michael

CONTENTS

ILLUSTRATIONS

MAPS

ACKNOWLEDGMENTS

My grandmother used to say, "Dime con quién andas, y te diré quién eres": "Tell me with whom you walk, and I will tell you who you are." That dictum applies to my writing as well as my life. I am not a close-hauled writer. I depend on conversations and colleagues to help the writing grow and mature. Throughout this project and the ones that came before, I shared my work at different stages and in different ways. Thank you to George Sánchez and George Lipsitz, who have been my frontline readers for three monographs now. We would meet at a downtown Mexican restaurant (where else?) where we drank pots of coffee and talked until I had a plan to get what I had on the page to look something like the narrative that was in my mind. I am also grateful to live near the Huntington Library, which is an unofficial coworking space for academics in the Los Angeles area. I talked through many ideas with experts who work there regularly or were passing through. A special shout-out to Bill Deverell, Miriam Pawel, Eric Avila, Veronica Castillo-Muñoz, Wade Graham, Tom Sitton, Oliver Wang, and Richard White. I was fortunate as well to have a short-term Huntington fellowship at the same time as José Alamillo, Rosina Lozano, and Jerry González, and I regularly bounced ideas off them during long lunches and walks in the gardens. Josh Kun generously brought me into the Southern California Food-ways Project, a warm and generative community.

I am grateful for many opportunities to present parts of the in-progress manuscript, including invitations from the Latinx Project and the Food Stud-ies Program at New York University; the Newberry Library's seminar in Bor-derlands and Latino/a Studies; the Department of Ethnic Studies at the Uni-versity of California, Berkeley; the University of California, Irvine; the University of Iowa's Mellon Sawyer Seminar, "Imagining Latinidades"; the American Studies Program at Yale University; and the U.S. History Workshop at the University of Chicago. A special thanks to Merry Ovnick and Josh Sides, who invited me to deliver the annual W. P. Whitsett Lecture at California State University, Northridge, which served to kick off this book. It was espe-cially meaningful to share my work on migration with audiences outside of the United States, taking my findings on the Cuban experience in Los Angeles to the Casa de las Américas in Havana, Cuba, and to Chinese historians of the United States at Northeast Normal University in Changchun, China. I also gained much from presenting to public audiences at the Autry National Center, the Huntington Library, and the Los Angeles Plaza de Cultura y Artes.

It does not matter how many books you've written, each new one is just as difficult. But I have learned to make it fun whenever possible and to always have some company. Thanks to Alina Méndez and Jorge Leal, who were my graduate students when this project started and are now professors and with whom I wrote the first draft of this book. Also, every writer needs a writing accountability group like my WAGettes Evelyn Alsultany, Neetu Khanna, and Kyla Wazana Tompkins. They kept me focused and were there to celebrate the milestones, not just the big ones. I owe a special shout-out to Evelyn, who kept me going as I finished this book in the "zoom where it happens."

I have been blessed to find two intellectual homes: first in the University of Californa, San Diego (UCSD), Department of History and since 2018 in the

Department of American Studies and Ethnicity at the University of Southern California (USC). In both places I have been graced with many interlocutors among my students and colleagues. In addition, conversations with friends and colleagues via email, at conferences and invited talks, and over shared meals and coffee served to light my way, about the book and about how to make time to write. Thank you to Meg Wesling, Nancy Postero, Cathy Gere, Hildie Kraus, Sara Johnson, Simeon Man, Pamela Radcliff, Danny Widener, Nayan Shah, Juan de Lara, Miroslava Chávez-García, Kelly Lytle Hernández, David Roediger, John Carlos Rowe, and Heather Maynard.

Thank you to those who took time from their own writing to give insightful feedback on mine: Ramón Gutiérrez, Vicki Ruiz, Luis Alvarez, David Gutiérrez, Nancy Kwak, Kathleen Belew, Rebecca Kinney, Alan Kraut, Judith Smith, and Alyssa Smith. Genevieve Carpio, Laura Barraclough, and Mark Padoongpatt generously served as reviewers for the press. It's a special thrill to get the feedback of people whose work you are in conversation with in your research and teaching. Last, I thank Isabella Furth, David Lobenstine, and Megan Pugh for their sharp editorial skills and gifts for bringing clarity to complex ideas.

For my first two books, I worked in archives, gathering evidence of worlds I did not personally know; the challenge was crafting those shards into a story that told us something about what it meant to be Mexican in the United States and why we think about race the way that we do. But this is a book about a place and a people that have no archives—what I call the "underdocumented." And so the challenge was the complete opposite: I had the story or at least a piece of it: I had grown up in this place (Echo Park), with many of these people, and I knew that being raised by placemakers in a cultural crossroads had shaped my own experience, my identity. But the shards were much harder to find. I'm especially grateful to the many people who shared their experiences with me in oral interviews. I also called on talented and knowledgeable librarians for help in my ongoing search for information,

Acknowledgments

including Kelly Smith at UCSD and Christal Young at USC. Andy Rutkowski, also at USC, made me a better spatial thinker with his GIS expertise. I must give special thanks to research guru Harold Colson at UCSD. Whenever I was at a dead end in a genealogical or city directory search, he would find another angle and unearth another fragment, helping make the details in this book sharper and fleshed out. And on top of it all, telling this story required rummaging through a lot of haystacks in hopes of finding a needle. Thanks to Alina Méndez, Jorge Leal, and Laura Dominguez for their research assistance on that quest.

All of this work takes time and resources. A National Endowment for the Humanities Public Scholar Award provided me with a yearlong fellowship. Short-term fellowships from the Huntington Library and the Research Network for Latin America at the University of Köln, Germany, provided key time for intensive research and writing. Academic Senate grants from UCSD during my tenure there were crucial to funding research trips and research assistance. I received the MacArthur Fellowship as I finished this book. I have been touched by how deeply the foundation's staff know the work I do, care about it, and work to share it.

My editor at the University of California Press, Niels Hooper, cheered me along the entire journey, skillfully balancing my autonomy with his advice. Along with Niels and his editorial assistant, Naja Pulliam Collins, I would like to thank Francisco Reinking and the extraordinarily resourceful and helpful staff at University of California Press.

My family—*las familias* Tavares, Taylor, Porras, Pack, Molina, and Perea-Lugo-Maese—makes L.A. much more than a place of study. They make it my home. My brother, David Porras, the unofficial mayor of Echo Park, always has my back; my mom, María ("Mary") Molina, offers unconditional support. My husband, Ian Fusselman, is my everything, offering both love and the most pragmatic support: tech assistance, looking up court cases, editing and proofreading, attending my talks, and keeping me well fed while I am writing. And finally thanks to my son, Michael Molina. I wrote my last book in fifteen- to twenty-five-minute spurts, if I was lucky, because then-adolescent Michael interrupted so much. It's strange to now be thanking him for his support. He consistently asked about this project, accompanied me on oral interview trips, connected the ideas in the book to what he was seeing around him in the world, and overall showed unflagging interest and enthusiasm. His questions pushed me, and his support deeply touched me.

Introduction

Placemaking in a New Homeland

In 1965, Natalia Barraza placed a full-page advertisement in her hometown paper, *El Eco de Nayarit*. She wanted to spread the word about her two restaurants, the Nayarit and the Nayarit II, where customers could count on excellent service and delicious, freshly prepared food. They would just need to travel some thirteen hundred miles, to Los Angeles, where the restaurants were located.

I saw the ad decades later, when I paged through leather-bound volumes of old issues of *El Eco* at the Hemeroteca Nacional de México, National Newspaper Library of Mexico. As a historian of race and immigration, I wasn't surprised to see ads for businesses like the Nayarit run by *los de afuera*, particularly in Los Angeles.[1] A large number of immigrants from Nayarit had settled there, and many stayed tethered to their homeland. But the ad for the Nayarit restaurants still took me aback. It was so much bigger than the others, and—beginning "Cuando Visite Usted Los Ángeles, Calif." (When You Visit Los Angeles, Calif.)—it seemed to promote the city itself, suggesting that the restaurants were on par with other, not-to-be-missed attractions.[2] That took some chutzpah. So did the inclusion of Natalia Barraza's name, in large, confident letters at the bottom of the page.

Yet the column of stock photographs running down the right-hand side of the ad would give most Angelenos pause. The top photo shows Los Angeles City Hall and the bottom one, Wilshire Boulevard along MacArthur Park—lovely municipal sites but not exactly tourist attractions. The middle photo does show the famous intersection of Hollywood and Vine, including the iconic Capitol Records Building, designed to resemble a stack of records on an autochanger, with a tower whose light blinks out the word *Hollywood* in Morse code. The caption, however, reveals an unfamiliarity with the area, and with the English language. "La famosa South on Vine Street de Holly-wood, Calif.," it reads, neglecting to mention Hollywood Boulevard. It is not clear what "South" refers to, perhaps the direction from which the photo-graph was taken. Neither of the Nayarit restaurants was particularly near to or had any identification with the landmarks pictured. The larger restaurant, the Nayarit, was located between downtown and Hollywood, in Echo Park. The Nayarit II was located two miles east, on the northeast edge of down-town Los Angeles. The ad suggested that these restaurants catered to insid-ers but revealed that their owner was an outsider, navigating multiple cultures.

She was poised to help others do the same. "**NAYARIT PRIMERO Y NAYARIT SEGUNDO**," the text proclaims, are "bellos rinconcitos de nuestra patria que le brindan comidas y cenas de lo mejor atendidos por personal netamente Mexicano" (beautiful little corners of our homeland that provide the best lunches and dinners served by a clearly Mexican staff). The ad goes on to read, "visite usted estos restaurantes y estará como en su propia casa, en un ambiente elegante y distinguido" (visit these restaurants, and it will be like you are in your own home in an elegant and distinguished environ-ment). Clearly, the ad plays on the concept of *patria chica* (literally, "small country"), which refers to the highly localized loyalty an immigrant has to their hometown, village, or region.[3] By evoking the visitor's connections to a particular home state, the restaurant would satisfy that feeling of patria

Figure 1. Doña Natalia's ad for the Nayarit in *El Eco*, August 1965.

chica. Mexican visitors could feel safe at the Nayarit, a space where they could speak their native tongue, be served only by fellow nationals, and escape whatever prejudice they might fear having to face in the city as a whole. Analyzing the operation and extent of those prejudices and dangers— from daily slights to large-scale terror campaigns like mass deportation— has been at the heart of my work as a historian over the past twenty years. That work has shown how thoroughly being Mexican shaped people's access to space, including where they could live, work, worship, play, go to school, and even be buried.

I have a unique connection to the Nayarit. Natalia Barraza is my grand-mother. I never met her, but I was named after her, and my mother, María, was her right-hand assistant in the business. I grew up surrounded by people who worked at the Nayarit or had been regular customers, listening, fascinated, to their stories about the restaurant and about Doña Natalia. They all spoke of her with admiration for her strength, her talent, and her generosity with relatives in Los Angeles and Nayarit. She had come to the United States on her own, on the heels of the Mexican Revolution, and worked through the Great Depression. She could not write, read, or speak English, but she ran a successful business, sponsored dozens of immigrants—many of them single women and gay men—gave them jobs and places to stay, and encour-aged them to venture out and explore L.A. Sometimes she would loan the women clothing and jewelry for the occasion. No one, however, described her as a warm person. She was formidable and removed. My mother never called her "mom"—only the more formal "my mother"—and everyone else referred to her with a title: *Tía* (Aunt) Natalia, Doña Barraza, or Doña Natalia. "Doña" conveys a bit more respect and a higher rank than "Mrs." or "Miss," and it captures my own sense of my grandmother. I think and write about her as Doña Natalia.

Over the course of her life, Doña Natalia started three restaurants called the Nayarit. The earliest, which I call the original Nayarit, was at 421 Sunset

Figure 2. The Nayarit in 1966. Edward Ruscha, Edward Ruscha photographs of Sunset Boulevard and Hollywood Boulevard, Getty Research Institute, Los Angeles, CA, 1966.

Boulevard, between Broadway and Spring Streets, and was in operation from 1943 to around 1952. What the ad in *El Eco* refers to as the "Nayarit Primero" was founded in 1951 at 1822 Sunset Boulevard. In 1964, she opened what the ad calls the "Nayarit Segundo," and what some people called the "little Nayarit," at 640 N. Spring Street, around the corner from where the original Nayarit had stood. It catered mainly to downtown office workers and closed in 1968. But it was the main location, in Echo Park on Sunset, that I grew up hearing about. It was the largest and the longest-lasting, and the place where Doña Natalia spent most of her waking hours. My cousin, Doña Natalia's granddaughter, told me that when her family visited our grandmother, they rarely did so at her home. Instead, they came to the restaurant. The Nayarit was the center of the community Doña Natalia helped build, and she was there seven days a week, ensuring it ran smoothly.

At the time, Echo Park was something of a cultural crossroads, a haven for gays, liberal whites, ethnic Mexicans (referring to both Mexican Americans and Mexican immigrants), and an abundance of other immigrants.[4] Living alongside one another made it easier for people to develop comfort with those outside their racial and ethnic communities, and while the Nayarit's largest customer base was ethnic Mexicans, it catered to a diverse clientele and became a fixture in the community. Alexis McSweyn, whose ethnic Mexican parents had begun taking her to the Nayarit when she was nine, told me years later that she was shocked if she ever met someone in the neighborhood who *hadn't* been to the Nayarit: "You'd think, 'What?!' The Nayarit *was* Echo Park."

Doña Natalia died in 1969, two years before I was born. María ran the business for a few more years while caring for me and my older brother, David (born in 1965), but sold the lease in 1976 to new owners who kept the old name. I have scant memories of the Nayarit from those first few years of my life, but I grew up in the neighborhood it fed, in a home Doña Natalia purchased, in a place she helped make. By the time I was five years old, I felt perfectly safe venturing out from the restaurant where my mother was busy with work to walk a couple of doors down to the corner to get a Cuban *pastelito* at El Carmelo Bakery. The regulars there knew one another, had known my grandmother, knew my mother, and knew me. The neighborhood was an extension of home. A number of former Nayarit employees went on to open their own restaurants nearby, including Barragan's and La Villa Taxco and El Conquistador and El Chavo, which were havens for gay clientele. When my family and I would eat at these restaurants, we were also visiting fictive kin. I played with the children of Nayarit workers and customers, attended christenings and weddings and funerals of family and friends with ties to the restaurant, and learned from them to be curious about the wider world. Even now, when we go out together, they are eager to see how restaurants approach decor, menu planning, plating, and service. They go to all sorts of restaurants, all across the city. To get more information about both restaurants and the experiences of workers, they tend to find a Latinx immigrant server or busboy whom they pepper with questions. What is in the *mole* that gives it that distinctive taste? Where are you from? Do they treat you well here? Sometimes they end up getting off-the-menu extras, like salsas made for staff meals in the back, shuttled to our table.

The Nayarit has taken on renewed prominence in my life over the past few years, as I see the ways Echo Park is changing. When I attended college at UCLA in the early 1990s, I grew accustomed to classmates dismissing my neighborhood as a "bad part of town." One wrong turn on the way to a Dodgers game, they would say, and you risked ending up in the barrio. If I told them that was my 'hood, they would fall into uncomfortable silence. I knew their viewpoints were shaped by a lifetime of seeing barrios and ghettos depicted as dangerous places inhabited by dangerous people. They had been given no historical understanding of how these places came to be, or what they meant to the people who lived there. In the ensuing years, though, Echo Park has undergone remarkable levels of gentrification. Hipsters have replaced homeboys, high-end coffee shops have pushed out *mercaditos*—and some of the "pioneering" new businesses have now been priced out themselves. Echo Park is no longer the subject of urban decline but of urban renewal. Ironically, it's the diversity of the neighborhood, its "authenticity," that makes it attractive, and yet this is what is most threatened as those with higher incomes move in.[5] Similar changes are afoot in the traditionally Latinx neighborhoods of Boyle Heights and Highland Park and in cities across the country.

Echo Park and neighborhoods like it are often perceived as lacking a rich history, as though nothing much happened before the arrival of wealthier newcomers.[6] People who have built their lives in such places know otherwise. So as the neighborhood has become less and less familiar to me, I kept circling back to this place, and these people, because I recognized that they get at something important, something that history books, popular media, and landmark timelines rarely capture: how marginalized people can create their own places in ways that reclaim dignity, create social cohesion, and foster mutual care. This book is meant to call attention to such creative actions, to the ways communities can define places on their own terms, sometimes as a direct challenge to the existing environment and sometimes as an alternative.

PLACEMAKING AT RESTAURANTS

The ethnic Mexicans who worked and ate at the Nayarit were not just putting food on the table or into their mouths. They were creating meaning, establishing links with one another, and tending to roots both old and new. They were also asserting their place in a nation that often seemed intent on pushing them to the margins: the fields, the barrio, the kitchen, or back across the border altogether. The subjects of this book knew firsthand that, as the theorist Henri Lefebvre wrote, "Space is not a scientific object removed from ideology or politics. It has always been political and strategic."[7] The politics of space include the politics of race, which can become codified in public policy, cemented by institutions, and bound up with public perception and presumption.

Throughout this book, I use the term "racialized group." Terms like "race" and "ethnicity," although useful, tend to reify the categories they describe rather than underscore their constructedness. In addition, these categories can and do change over time based on a host of factors, including time period, region, skin color, class, language, and generation.

Following George Lipsitz, who writes that "social relations take on their full force and meaning when they are enacted physically in actual places," I explore how race "takes place," not just figuratively but also literally.[8] Just think of how labeling a part of the city a "barrio" or a "ghetto" suggests that certain types of people live there. Consider, too, how people's lives unfold in place. Their sense of connection to—or alienation from—their home is often about feeling rooted to a particular place: a neighborhood, a park, a news-stand, a restaurant. The subjects of this story, most of them working-class immigrants who did not arrive in the United States speaking English, endeavored to make places their own. They went to work, worshipped in church, attended school, ate out, and, in Doña Natalia's case, opened a restaurant where people could come together for labor, leisure, and access to a ready-made social network. I call them placemakers.

In my work here, I mobilize a rich scholarship on placemaking in order to center the question of *who* gets to define a place and *how* they do so.[9] Public spaces can be hostile to marginalized, racialized people like the ethnic Mexican immigrants whose lives this book chronicles. Semipublic spaces like restaurants provide a safer and no less vital site to host and shape community life, and a more capacious definition of the term "placemaking" can encompass this other, important work by racialized people. To see how racialized people are placemakers, we need to turn to such semipublic spaces, beauty salons and barbershops, bars and coffee shops, bookstores and bowling alleys, places where community members congregate on a regular, sometimes daily basis and sometimes for hours at a time.[10] Though such businesses are certainly economic actors, the placemaking that goes on in them is social and cultural, sustained by countless small acts of everyday life that build and sustain affective relationships in a particular time and place: eating, laughing, gossiping, debating, celebrating, claiming space, bonding, forging community. If we treat placemaking more expansively, we can see the city not just as it might look from a bench in the park or on a city planning map, but as people used it.

Placemaking has worked in distinct ways for racialized groups. The kinds of spaces created, how they were used, the relationships that sprang from them, and the nurturing of collectivity and inclusivity they enabled resulted in a placemaking that could be resistant and oppositional—a counter to dominant spatial formations and imaginaries. The ethnic Mexican immigrants who congregated at the Nayarit were attempting to carve out a niche for themselves in their new homeland. Their story is not simply about struggling to gain access to urban space by grabbing a slice of the existing pie; it is an expression of challenge that, in its own way, works to remake the existing city altogether.[11]

At the Nayarit and places like it, immigrants lived out values of mutuality, public sociability, and collectivity. The restaurant provided immigrant workers and customers with the familiarity of home and a ready-made social network, offering local history, introductions, and information about how to navigate the system—all invaluable assets for newcomers attempting to negotiate a large, daunting foreign city. The resources and networks available there allowed working people to assume full identities that went beyond who they were as laborers. At the restaurant, immigrants might not feel any more American (nor was that necessarily their goal), but they were insiders.

The spaces that marginalized and racialized placemakers have cultivated—including restaurants, bars, jazz clubs, music stores, and performance spaces—help communities find their moorings. I call them urban anchors. They are different from what urban planners describe as "anchor institutions": large public or semipublic institutions such as schools, universities, and hospitals that are vital to community growth. Some anchor institutions, like libraries, nonprofit organizations, or cultural institutions, can also function as urban anchors of a sort, if they serve as important sites for community building. (I don't know what I would have done as a kid without my local library where adults helped me track down what felt like an endless supply of books that served as my gateway to all things I was curious about.)[12] But on the whole, urban anchors tend to be smaller, built by the community for the community. If we fold them into our accounts of urban history, we can broaden our conceptions of who creates meaningful public places, what those places look like, and how community dynamics take shape.

Restaurants like the Nayarit reflect the cultural politics of a wider society as it plays out in everyday life.[13] They influence the rhythm of people's days,

Figure 3. Placemakers: a celebration at the Nayarit, April 1968. Clockwise from top left: María Perea; unknown woman; Ofelia Encinas (customer); Natalia Barraza; María del Rosario ("Chayo") Díaz Cueva; Pedro Cueva; Salvador ("Chavo") Barrajas; Ramón Barragan; Ramón's sister Dolores ("Lola") Barragan (in profile); unknown woman and man. Photograph provided by María Perea Molina.

their feelings about their surroundings, the way they claim space or are pushed out from it, and the ways they conceive of race.[14] They can also be sites of political resistance. Consider what happened on the other side of the country from the Nayarit, at a Woolworth's in Greensboro, North Carolina, when, on February 1, 1960, four African American students sat down at the whites-only lunch counter. The Greensboro Four, as they came to be called, did not move when they were asked to leave or when patrons began yelling at them and throwing food at them. Joined by fellow students and community

Placemaking in a New Homeland

members, their actions became a template for nonviolent protest across the South, throwing segregationist policies into stark, ugly relief. After a summer of intense struggle, the South reluctantly began to integrate its dining facilities, thus marking an early victory of the Civil Rights Movement and a crucial step on the path that would lead to the passage of the Civil Rights Act of 1964, which outlawed racial segregation in public facilities.[15]

But resistance also takes quieter, less well-documented forms, in what the political scientist and anthropologist James Scott described as the struggles "waged daily by subordinate groups," which can be more subtle, "like infrared rays, beyond the visible end of the spectrum."[16] Bars and restaurants were where people held their strategizing meetings, met before protests, and debriefed afterward. Just as important, they were where individuals came into contact with others to discuss and debate the politics of the day or simply to hang out with people who perhaps, like themselves, felt excluded from other places because of citizenship, language, skin color, or sexuality. The Nayarit played host to all these activities, and the lives of residents in Echo Park were better for it.

COCINA CONFIDENTIAL

Los Angeles has long been known for its robust restaurant scene. As early as 1910, it was declared the number three "Top Restaurant City" in the country.[17] Today, Los Angeles is a foodie mecca, renowned not only for the work of celebrity chefs but also for a broader gastronomic landscape characterized by racial, ethnic, and immigrant diversity. For those who have moved to the city from elsewhere—and these days, it can be hard to find someone who isn't a transplant—restaurants are often first points of contact with a new neighborhood or even a new culture. Perhaps it is no surprise, then, that much of the public, printed discussion of the L.A. restaurant scene focuses on novelty: diners and critics eat at new (to them) restaurants in new (to them) neighborhoods. Ethnic restaurants, in particular, entice residents who might not otherwise visit working-class neighborhoods to brave the freeways and patronize what are, to them, new places. Such encounters can be tutelary, or even generative, as food brings people together across divides of race, class, or politics. But being a culinary tourist is different from being a regular at a neighborhood restaurant. And it would be wrong to see restaurants as necessarily neutral or democratic meeting grounds. Ethnic cuisine is often exoticized, and everything about food—who farms it, prepares it, serves it, is able to consume it, and is lauded for it, as well as where it is sold and how it is assessed and valued—is inescapably enmeshed with the larger politics of race, class, gender, and sexuality.[18]

Awareness of the politics surrounding food has grown steadily over the past few decades. When Jonathan Gold, restaurant critic for the *L.A. Weekly* and later the *Los Angeles Times*, came onto the food journalism scene in 1986, it was immediately clear that he cared not just about the dishes he ate but also about the people who prepared them.[19] Chef Anthony Bourdain also helped make visible and humanize the working-class back-of-house *cocina* (kitchen) staff. They were often Latinx immigrants, many of them undocumented, at the lower rungs of the kitchen hierarchy, but they made meals everywhere, from humble eateries to five-star restaurants, possible. Bourdain wrote, "In nearly 30 years of cooking professionally, just about every time I walked into a new kitchen, it was a Mexican guy who looked after me, had my back, showed me what was what."[20]

Mexican workers have always been part of the Los Angeles gastronomic landscape, as has Mexican food—though it did not achieve mainstream popularity until the 1990s, when as the *New York Times* wrote, salsa "took the condiment crown" from ketchup.[21] Historically, Mexican food was working class, often sold at mom-and-pop establishments or out of carts that specialize in inexpensive and filling meals—think of tamales or tacos—that are easy to eat on the go.[22] For the first half of the twentieth century, a smaller group of Mexican restaurants catered to a primarily middle-class, white clientele, as well as to some Mexican patrons. To attract a wide public, they often simplified the food: adding more cheese and fewer chilis, frying instead of roasting or grilling, making tastes more predictable. Restaurateurs have always been faced with such economic choices, as the institutions of the Chinese chop suey house and the Italian red sauce joint make clear.[23] But simplifying the cuisine can sometimes homogenize not just the food but the people who make and serve it as well, turning them into standardized "types"—predictable, appealingly "spicy!" In L.A., that standardization also meant connecting Mexican food with what the historian Carey McWilliams called the "Spanish fantasy past."[24] Beginning in the 1880s, Southern California boosters who wanted to downplay the region's violent recent history in the wake of the US war with Mexico (1846–48) replaced it with a romantic account of Spanish colonialism.[25] It erased the region's indigenous histories and transformed Mexicans from conquered subjects into picturesque denizens. Mexican restaurants followed suit, selling "Spanish rice" and beans out of buildings modeled on Spanish missions.[26]

Doña Natalia took a different approach. As a Mexican immigrant, she would have been at least somewhat skeptical of the Spanish fantasy past. She named her restaurant after the region in Mexico where she grew up and made sure that the Nayarit served fresh, well-prepared dishes that she refused to whitewash for Anglo-American palates. It was an implicit declaration about what kind of place the restaurant was and whom it served—a quiet but important act of political contestation.

Mexican immigrants to L.A. faced a fluctuating racial hierarchy in a city that was highly segregated. In the early twentieth century, Harry Chandler, the *Los Angeles Times* publisher, famously referred to Los Angeles as a "white spot." He meant that it was an anti-union city (i.e., not "red"), but the phrase was soon taken up to refer to the city's preferred racial makeup.[27] Groups like the Los Angeles Chamber of Commerce promoted an idyllic image of the city in the hope of attracting desirable residents and visitors: white, financially secure Easterners and Midwesterners. But other people came too and found that their search for opportunity was rife with racism and discrimination. African Americans, Mexicans, and Asians all faced systematic legal and social barriers that prevented them from bargaining freely over wages and working conditions, from owning land or accumulating other assets that might appreciate in value and be passed on to subsequent generations, and even from moving freely about the city in search of housing, employment, and business opportunities.[28] Those who tried to cross these boundaries were met with violence, from mob assaults on ethnic neighborhoods and businesses to lynchings, cross burnings, and Klan intimidation.

However, each group was racialized in different ways depending on many factors, including their demographics, whether they were needed as laborers or seen as labor competition, their citizenship status, and global politics, such as who the United States was at war with.[29] For example, in the early twentieth century, the African American population in Los Angeles County was small, and African Americans enjoyed somewhat more autonomy in L.A. than in the South, where, the historian Douglas Flamming writes, racism "had them by the throat." But Los Angeles was only a "half free environment," and African Americans lived largely segregated lives.[30] California's anti-miscegenation laws prevented marriage between whites and nonwhites, including Asians, and these laws stayed on the books until 1948 and the California Supreme Court's ruling in *Perez v. Sharp*. It was also not until that year that the US Supreme Court ruled in *Shelley v. Kraemer* that racially restrictive covenants—private agreements that barred people from owning or living in property on the basis of their race—were not enforceable by states. (The case was argued by Loren Miller, a prominent civil rights attorney from Los Angeles, and Thurgood Marshall, then at the NAACP, who would go on to argue *Brown v. Board of Education* before the Supreme Court and later become the first African American Supreme Court justice.) But the court did not find that racially restrictive covenants that did not involve

Placemaking in a New Homeland

government action or enforcement were unconstitutional outright; thus, private parties could abide by them. It thus remained commonplace for private parties to voluntarily execute racially restrictive covenants, which, even if they were not enforceable by law, were nonetheless difficult, expensive, and sometimes dangerous to challenge, as well as a clear and unambiguous statement that racial (and religious) minorities were not welcome. That would not change until 1968, when Congress adopted the Fair Housing Act, prohibiting discrimination in the sale and rental of housing; however, the act did not require removal of the covenants from existing deeds. What's more, the law only affected future discrimination; it did nothing to reverse the segregation the government had effectively enforced over the previous thirty-five years.[31]

Though Mexicans were legally classified as white, the dominant public still saw them as racialized subjects, and they were subject to considerable everyday racism, as well as both de facto and de jure segregation at schools and public facilities. Nor did Mexicans' legal classification shield them from discriminatory real estate practices and racial covenants when people wished to enforce them—which white realtors and property owners often did, though not as universally against Mexicans as they did against Blacks.[32] Ethnic Mexicans walked a color line that both overlapped and diverged from that of African Americans. Take, for example, *Mendez v. Westminster School District*, a 1946 school segregation case fought at the federal level. The case was initiated when Soledad ("Sally") Vidaurri took her children, along with those of her brother, Gonzalo Mendez, to enroll in a white school. The school was only willing to enroll Sally's children because they were lighter-skinned; her brother's children were turned away. The court found for the plaintiffs, ruling that school segregation did not provide equal protection and, thus, violated the Fourteenth Amendment, though it stopped short of challenging the "separate but equal" precedent famously established by *Plessy v. Ferguson* (1896). *Mendez* was an important precursor to *Brown v. Board of Education*, and the NAACP filed an amicus brief for the plaintiffs co-authored by Thurgood Marshall. But *Mendez* also showed the limits of whiteness for Latinx who could be deemed legally white and still be treated as racially other. After *Mendez* and even after *Brown*, Mexican Americans were locked into their position as unequal citizens for generations to come.[33] And along with the rest of Los Angeles, they faced an increasingly segregated city. In 1950, a Latinx family had a 55 percent chance of having white neighbors. By 2000, that likelihood had dropped to 18 percent.[34]

Ethnic enclaves had their own placemakers, and as Earl Lewis elegantly puts it, they allowed for "segregation to become congregation."[35] Central Avenue, for example, was for decades the center of African American life in Los Angeles, its jazz clubs and other businesses true urban anchors.[36] But Echo Park, multiethnic and multicultural, allowed Doña Natalia and other ethnic Mexicans a different way of living, where congregation could be cosmopolitan. For while the Nayarit's core customer base, and its employees, were mostly ethnic Mexicans, it still drew in other customers from the neighborhood and beyond. Movie stars, athletes, musicians, and singers—some Latinx and some not—were regulars. Their frequent, casual presence helped connect the immigrant workers and working-class customers to what the historian Anthony Macías calls the "multicultural urban civility" of mid-twentieth-century Los Angeles.[37] In turn, these Mexican restaurants, with their Spanish-speaking owners and workers and the foods they cooked, provided these famous personalities with a sense of comfort and casual joy. The larger landscape of L.A. was deeply segregated, but spaces like the Nayarit allowed for cross-racial and cross-ethnic interaction and communion.

DOCUMENTING THE UNDERDOCUMENTED

During the 1950s and 1960s, when Doña Natalia owned and operated the Nayarit, Mexicans accounted for more than 15 percent of all immigrants to the United States. Between 1957 and 1966, more people arrived in the United States on visas from Mexico than from any other country. Most were manual laborers, mainly men, who came to *el Norte* seeking jobs and better wages that, in many cases, they planned to save and take with them when returning home to Mexico. Between 1942 and 1964, the Bracero Program permitted an estimated two million to three million Mexican men to come to the United States as guest workers for agriculture and other industries with limited contracts providing for room, board, and health insurance.[38] Many US employers preferred to hire Mexicans through other, cheaper channels, and Mexican immigrants knew that they could secure work not just without a Bracero Program contract but also without papers. The sociologist Kitty Calavita has estimated that for every authorized Mexican entry during this period, there were three unauthorized ones.[39] Unauthorized immigration grew even more after 1964, when the Bracero Program ended, and 1965, when the Hart–Celler Act, also known as the Immigration and Nationality Act of 1965, was enacted, limiting the number of visas available for Mexicans to immigrate to the United States.

Even with the rise in immigration from Mexico, the population of ethnic Mexicans in the United States at this time was largely native born. By the 1960s, many Mexican American families had been in the United States for generations, had shared in a history of struggle for civil rights and workers' rights, but were still excluded from the American dream. The Chicanx movement that came to the fore during this time demanded a fundamental reordering of power structures in the United States. Groups and causes proliferated— from student organizations, such as Movimiento Estudiantil Chicano de Aztlán (MEChA), to those that fought on behalf of agricultural workers, such as the United Farm Workers (UFW)—but they all challenged assimilationist models that viewed Chicanx as second-class citizens and insisted on full rights. Cultural nationalism lay at the heart of this varied movement, which embraced Mexican heritage and a "brown pride" identity.

The Bracero Program and the Chicanx movement dominate historical accounts of Mexicans in the United States in the 1960s, and for good reason: they are visible, they are well documented, and they provide rich insights into the interplay of race, ethnicity, immigration status, democracy, equity, and civil rights. But if we focus only on the relatively small percentage of ethnic Mexicans who participated in formal organizing efforts, particularly the immigrant farmworkers, usually men, demanding higher wages and decent working conditions, we limit our understanding.[40] We lose sight of the many other ethnic Mexicans who did not fight for civil rights or decent labor conditions but still sought dignity and belonging in the country in which they settled.[41]

Immigrants and native-born Mexican Americans occupied many of the same physical and cultural spaces, but occupying the same space did not mean that immigrants who settled in cities were automatically pulled into the Mexican American orbit. Just as today immigrants to the United States from Chile or Argentina do not automatically think of themselves as Latinx, Mexican immigrants who migrated immediately before or during the Chicanx movement did not necessarily adopt a Chicanx identity or feel an affinity with it. Nor did they necessarily feel compelled to mount legal challenges, sign petitions, join unions, or participate in strikes and protests. Perhaps they feared unwanted recognition or even retribution. Perhaps they felt they had a better chance of being heard at their own local institutions, like restaurants and bars. Yet their experiences still matter, and their lives have still shaped history. They made sense of their settlement, supported themselves and each other, and conceived of their attachments to home in different ways. They contested the prevailing order in the course of their daily lives, by belonging, mutual support, and placemaking. They too were making history. This book tells their stories.[42]

When trying to paint a picture of a community, as I am doing here, historians rely on documents, using their training to scour official records and the personal papers of people deemed important enough to have their papers deposited in an archive. They read the correspondence of mayors and city council members, compile census records to paint a picture of an area's demographics, read through years of old newspapers to have a sense of what was going on during the period being studied, and investigate the records of any people and institutions residents might have come in contact with, including social workers, police officers, schoolteachers, and public health officials.

This methodology worked for me in the past. My first book, *Fit to Be Citizens? Public Health and Race in Los Angeles, 1879–1940*, which demonstrated how both science and public health shaped the meaning of race in the early twentieth century, was propelled by documented stories of how Chinese, Japanese, and Mexican immigrants fought back in court, petitioned the city council, stalled enforcement of city legislation, resisted and refused to attend health clinics, practiced alternative health practices, refused to let housing inspectors into their homes, and wrote letters to state and national officials protesting unfair treatment. But the lives of Doña Natalia and her fellow placemakers in Echo Park were comparatively underdocumented, meaning that their own individual stories are not well served by printed records. (Being underdocumented is not the same as being undocumented—a term used to describe an immigrant who is in a country without official permission—although the legally undocumented are often historically underdocumented.) I still consulted archives kept by the City and the County of Los Angeles, combed through local and national newspapers, pored over Federal Housing Administration maps and reports, and examined census records in order to understand Echo Park's demographics and how they changed over time. At the Hemeroteca Nacional de México, I studied a twenty-year run of *El Eco*, the hometown paper of Nayarit. Remarkably, it told me more about the lives of Mexicans in the United States than any US papers, including *La Opinión*, Los Angeles's Spanish-language newspaper. *El*

Eco reported on people's comings and goings, the postcards they sent home, and the nature of their work abroad.[43]

In general, though, daily life is poorly served by the archives. As George Lipsitz has observed, official archives are structured in dominance. To avoid replicating the narrowness of the archive in our own narratives, we need to study communities alongside—not inside—archives.[44] So to learn about the Nayarit and Echo Park, I turned to the community and its members, making an effort to eat at restaurants like my grandmother's. (That was not a difficult task.) I wanted to understand how such places functioned and how they could transform into urban anchors. What drew in regular customers? What was it like to eat there alone versus in a group? Why did immigrants choose to work there for years? As often as I could, I would ask my mother, the best cultural liaison for the project, to accompany me. When we went out to a restaurant, whether Mexican or not, she often would bump into former customers and workers, whom I would recruit as interview subjects. I conducted interviews with all the former workers from the Nayarit I could locate, as well as some former Nayarit customers and other residents of Echo Park.[45]

Oral histories helped fill in the details, the vibrancy, and the texture of my subjects' lives: how they met their spouse; what their first apartment was like; tales of nights out on the town; how they hid things from their sponsor (Doña Natalia), how much their feet hurt after a long shift; the waitstaff's territorial claims to tables and regulars; the best tables for tips; how much they laughed and joked at work. They also reminded me that what I, as a historian, might think of as major events were not necessarily how other people experienced their daily lives. For example, I asked several interviewees about the Watts uprising, five days of upheaval in a predominantly African American neighborhood in August 1965. Watts is some twenty miles from Echo Park, but given its historical significance and the impact that images of police violence had on Chicanx youth in their own organizing, I was curious to hear people's memories about it. I was normally met with a puzzled look and some version of this answer: "I don't know. I was working."[46]

Other questions went unanswered because people were unwilling, or unable, to discuss painful events in their lives openly. When an otherwise bold and outspoken interlocutor told me, in response to one of my questions, that she did not know why her parents had divorced, I persisted: "You don't know because your mother wouldn't tell you?"

"No," she replied matter-of-factly, "you knew not to ask about those things."

Another time, at a Mexican restaurant, my mother introduced me to an employee whom she identified as the daughter of a former Nayarit employee. When the woman had left, I double-checked my understanding of who it was she had just introduced me to.

"In my interviews, people said [that former employee] was gay," I said.

My mother stared at me blankly, then answered, "Yes, he was."

I was perplexed. "But you just introduced me to his daughter and said he was married and had several children!"

"Yes," she replied. "We all knew that he was gay but that he was also married with a family and that he was different when he was with his family."

I tried to pursue the question further, asking if he was out at the restaurant but not at home, but in this instance, as in so many others, I found myself at an impasse. Some subjects simply were off limits. These moments could be frustrating, but they were also revealing: they told me about cultural mores and taboos, about conceptions of public and private life. And, having spent many years analyzing what we call "silences in the archives," I was accustomed to working with and around biases, contradictions, and silences.[47] As the oral historian Alessandro Portelli has argued, the researcher must work in the intersection of the factual evidence and the collected narratives, the referent and the signifier, the past and the present, and from the spaces between all these areas.[48] That is what I have endeavored to do here.

I begin, in chapter 1, with Doña Natalia's immigration to the United States and her eventual settlement in Echo Park. Located in the shadow of downtown Los Angeles and along the symbolic lifeline of Sunset Boulevard, Echo Park served as a geographic and cultural crossing point for multiple communities, including artists, gay men, left-leaning and radical white residents, and immigrants. I show that, contrary to what we find in many urban histories, these residents were less likely after World War II to succumb to the white flight that led to disinvestment in the urban core and an increasingly segregated society. As a result, Echo Park continued to attract diverse populations even after the war, when cities across America were becoming less, rather than more, diverse. The result was a racially mixed neighborhood stamped by its progressive politics, an inviting place for a Mexican immigrant like Natalia Barraza to open her restaurant.

In chapter 2, I turn to the story of placemaking at the Nayarit. At a time when Mexicans were routinely discriminated against in public spaces, Doña Natalia's restaurant was a safe and familiar space for working-class Mexicans, who made up its core clientele. But the restaurant's regulars included other Latinx groups (particularly Cubans), as well as movie stars, athletes, and musicians from well beyond Echo Park. Those who worked at and frequented the restaurant did not have to cross boundaries to have encounters across lines of ethnicity and class; it was a part of their everyday lives, and I argue that it helped them feel more at home in the city as a whole, as they developed comfort with difference and imagined new opportunities for themselves.

Doña Natalia sponsored and employed dozens of immigrants, many of them gay men and single or divorced women. Their stories make up chapter 3. Because the Nayarit was located outside of an ethnic enclave, it provided more freedoms for those who did not fit conservative norms. More than just a place to work, the restaurant was a place where immigrants developed attachments with one another that shaped the course of their lives. Of course, life happened outside the restaurant, too, and Doña Natalia encouraged people to lay claim to their new city. Chapter 4 describes the way that, bolstered by the cosmopolitanism of their workplace, Nayarit employees ventured into places where other working-class or ethnic Angelenos would not. In this way, these employees became not just placemakers, but *place-takers*, crossing racial, class, and sexual boundaries in a largely segregated Los Angeles.

Even as they put down roots in Los Angeles, Nayaritas retained links to home that were based not on national identity or transnational institutions but on the highly local idea of patria chica. They wrote letters, sent gifts home when people from their hometown visited, and, if they had the opportunity, visited their hometown themselves. Chapter 5 tracks such translocal placemaking efforts through the pages of *El Eco* and in the establishment and operation of a Nayarit hometown association in Los Angeles.

This book is meant to capture those aspects of life that lie beneath the official timeline of events, the minutiae and joys and frustrations that are rarely manifested in formal histories focused on major events: people dissatisfied with their jobs, fed up with being judged based on the color of their skin, angry at being stopped by the police when driving in an affluent neighborhood, humiliated by the suspicious looks they get at a nice restaurant. These moments are nearly always transient, often banal. They are emotionally significant but also ephemeral and do not make it into archives. This is particularly true of moments concerning immigrants and, even more particularly, immigrant women.[49] Even the richest repositories of immigrant lives mainly reflect the lives of men.[50] So while I have come up against the absence of details in my research again and again, I have also been struck by how fortunate I am to know as much about Doña Natalia and the Nayarit's story as I do.

Many immigrant communities have their version of a Nayarit restaurant, a place that helped sustain them when they were far from home in both culinary and communal terms. And in many communities, their Nayarit is closing, if it hasn't already. In addition to offering a history of one particular place, this book is also an exploration of what is at stake if we do not begin to capture these stories, as well as a demonstration of how to do so.

CHAPTER ONE

Finding a Place in Echo Park

Natalia Barraza immigrated to the United States in 1922. She had grown up in Tecuala, in the coastal state of Nayarit, though in later years she considered Acaponeta, ten miles away, her adopted home. They were small cities, most of whose residents earned a living by farming, fishing, or hunting. Doña Natalia lived through the Mexican Revolution, married at age seventeen, and was newly divorced when—just twenty-one years old and alone—she crossed the border. We don't know where she crossed or exactly when. She likely wanted to get away from her former husband and knew that Los Angeles was a place of reinvention for immigrants and transplants alike.

Men comprised the majority of Mexican immigrants at this time, and most of them did not bring their families with them: they hoped to work, make money, and return to Mexico. Women like Doña Natalia who tried to cross on their own, *solas*, were suspect. They frequently came under the scrutiny of immigration officers who declared them ineligible to enter the United States on the grounds that they would not be able to support them-selves and would become public charges; they could be turned back at any stage of their journeys.[1] Immigrating alone must have posed challenges for Doña Natalia, but it may have had advantages too. As a single woman, Doña

Natalia was neither beholden to nor constrained by anyone else.[2] She quickly found work in a small Los Angeles restaurant whose owner, learning that she was newly arrived and knew no one, took pity on her. Besides, she was already a skillful cook.[3]

If Doña Natalia had waited even two years to immigrate, she likely would have had a much harder time. The Immigration Act of 1924, also called the Johnson-Reed Act, established strict quotas for immigrants entering the United States based on their country of origin, drastically reducing the entry of southern and eastern Europeans and excluding Chinese, Japanese, and other Asian immigrants altogether. Thanks to the lobbying power of industries that relied on low-wage Mexican labor, the law did not establish a quota for Mexican immigrants, but it did reduce the number of visas issued to Mexicans. That same year, Congress created the Border Patrol, whose presence on the border made it much harder for Mexicans to cross into the United States without authorization.[4] Many Mexicans who had depended on easy crossings now had to decide which side they would settle on permanently or if they decided to migrate, whether they would do so without visas, undocumented.

We know virtually nothing about what happened to Doña Natalia for the next eight years. There are no oral interviews, family lore, newspaper clippings, or photos to turn to. But we do know that she was a Mexican in the United States: her skin was dark, she spoke only Spanish, and thus she faced the same discrimination as millions of her country people. A few decades later, those facts were unchanged, but she was running a thriving business in Echo Park. I want to underscore here the importance of the neighborhood—rather than the city as a whole—as a unit of analysis.[5] Los Angeles County encompasses four thousand square miles. Its racial politics can vary by zip code or even by block, and had Doña Natalia settled in a predominantly Mexican ethnic enclave, her life would have been very different. Echo Park, however, was diverse and progressive, a welcoming place for Doña Natalia to live and run her business. It allowed her workers and customers to make bonds across the color line and to achieve social and geographic mobility as they left their own mark on the neighborhood.

WHERE SHE ARRIVED

When Doña Natalia arrived in Los Angeles, she entered a landscape that had been shaped by centuries of race-making practices, beginning when Europeans first settled on land that had been home to the Chumash and Gabrielino-Tongva peoples for thirteen thousand and twelve thousand years, respectively. Spanish explorers came to the area in 1769 and by 1781 had formally established Los Angeles as Nuestra Señora la Reina de los Ángeles de Porciúncula (Our Lady Queen of Angels of Porciúncula). They imposed a mission system, forcibly converting Indigenous peoples and taking their lands for agriculture, and a presidio system, to counter "savage" Indigenous resistance with law and order. The mission system was supposed to be temporary, to convert Indigenous peoples to Catholicism and "civilize" and acculturate them in order to help them transition to a Spanish system in which they would be productive members of society. But even after Mexico won its independence from Spain (1821) and the secularization process was largely completed, few Indigenous people were given back their land.[6] Instead, the government gave land to Mexican administrators and military officials. Mexico's geographic reach encompassed all of present-day California, Nevada, Utah, Arizona, New Mexico, and Texas, along with parts of Colorado, Kansas, and Wyoming.

In 1846, fueled by the imperialist ideology of Manifest Destiny, the United States declared war on its southern neighbor over a border dispute. The conflict ended on February 2, 1848, with the Treaty of Guadalupe Hidalgo. The treaty ceded a huge swath of Mexican land—55 percent of its territory—to the United States and also laid out the terms of citizenship for the roughly 75,000 to 100,000 Mexicans living there. They could choose to move south of the new border or stay in what was now the United States, where they could choose between Mexican and US citizenship. If they stayed in the United States but did not declare a choice within one year, they would become US citizens automatically.[7] With few opportunities for advancement in the United States, immigration from Mexico stagnated, and the Mexican population dwindled.

Taken in the aggregate, Spanish colonial rule (1781–1821) and US conquest (1848) were overlapping empires, a palimpsest of racialized power. The power brokers who laid claim to the land changed, but racialized power structures themselves remained intact. For example, the carceral systems from one era were transferred to the next in ways that kept the racial hierarchy of the region undiminished and showed who those in power considered legitimate members of this new society. Often these dynamics emerged in contestations over who could legitimately occupy space: as Kelly Lytle Hernández has demonstrated, public order charges, like "vagrancy, disorderly conduct, and public drunkenness, systematically penalize[d] the landless, homeless, and underemployed," thereby punishing those who lived their lives in public.[8] Conquest is never fully past. It continues to reverberate in the racial and spatial inequities we see today.

By the turn of the twentieth century, Los Angeles was a sprawling metropolis.[9] It had become the terminus of two cross-continental railroads in the 1880s, and it sometimes seemed that every train brought new residents to the city. The population soared from slightly over 11,000 in 1880 to more than 100,000 by 1900, with an additional 70,000 residents in the county.[10] Mexican immigration was rising too. One wave came because President Porfirio Díaz, whose tenure, on and off, encompassed the years between 1876 and 1911, used the Vacant Lands Law (Ley de Terrenos Baldíos) to increase foreign investment in Mexico's countryside, denying Mexicans access to land on which they had depended for generations.[11] A larger wave headed north as a result of the combined forces of the Mexican Revolution (1910–20) and US employers' increased demand for low-wage labor, as factories embraced mass production and water projects spurred the rapid

Finding a Place in Echo Park

expansion of large-scale agriculture. Between 1910 and 1930, over one million Mexicans immigrated to the United States. Their main port of entry was El Paso, Texas, but many moved farther west after crossing the border and settled in California, where employers sought low-wage laborers to build railroad lines, plant and harvest crops, and work in the city's newly developing industries. In 1910, Los Angeles's Mexican population numbered 5,000; in 1920, it was 30,000; and in 1930, it was 97,000. By 1930, Los Angeles could claim a Mexican population second only to Mexico City.

Los Angeles, like many other parts of the Southwest, had a history of welcoming immigrants as laborers but restricting them socially, culturally, and geographically through laws and practices. The city and surrounding county were the sites of persistent struggles between the white elite and the racially diverse remainder of the population, as people sparred over politics, civil rights, housing, employment, and the distribution of city and county services.[12] Before 1910, Mexican newcomers had often settled in La Placita, an area near the original Chinese settlement. Increased demand for housing in that section of the city resulting from commercialization and continued immigration crowded out residents and prompted resettlement of the Mexican population after 1910.[13] Many Mexicans moved outside the city limits, especially to rural and unincorporated East Los Angeles.[14]

By 1930, the Depression had set in, jobs were disappearing, and the marginal acceptance of Mexicans and Mexican Americans as a source of cheap labor evaporated. The US government funded repatriation campaigns, ostensibly to encourage or coerce Mexican nationals to return to Mexico. By 1935, one-third of Mexicans living in Los Angeles had been repatriated, and over the course of the decade, an estimated one million people had been repatriated, many involuntarily.[15] Only now are historians (including myself) able to show that up to 60 percent of those who "returned" to Mexico were in actuality Mexican Americans with US citizenship, many of them children. Instead of the innocuously termed "repatriations," the scholar

Marla Ramírez has come up with a more accurate way to refer to the forced removal of American citizens: "banishments."[16]

Doña Natalia never shared her memories of these years with my mother, María. I do not know whether her friends and associates were among the banished, whether she feared the loss of others, or how she made sense of the era. But census records show that in 1930, Doña Natalia was living with Alberto Perea, who was four years her senior, on the northeastern edge of downtown Los Angeles. Alberto was also from Mexico and had immigrated to the United States in 1910. According to the census, they both worked at a restaurant, he as a manager and she as a waitress; perhaps this is where they met. The census lists them as married, but there are no corroborating records such as a marriage certificate, and family stories maintain that they married later. Perhaps one or both of them told the census taker that they were married to avoid judgment. Or there may have been a language barrier. Certainly, the census taker (Mike Schmalzgruber, himself the son of German immigrants) got many details wrong: he noted that Alberto was a citizen (he was not), that the couple spoke "Mexican" (which was crossed out and replaced by "Spanish"), and that they could read, write, and speak English, which they could not. How it was possible to misunderstand this last point when the couple could not have understood or answered his questions in English remains unclear.[17]

Doña Natalia next appears in official records in 1934, when, in the depths of the Depression, she leased her own restaurant. All that we know of this restaurant is what we can glean from one-line entries in city directories and a couple of business records archived by the city: it was located in the northern part of Echo Park, and Doña Natalia made minor improvements, installing an awning outside and fixing her boiler, in accordance with a city ordinance and an inspector's direction, respectively. It closed in 1938, for unknown reasons, and its name is lost to us. Alberto might have been able to remember, for though his name is not listed anywhere on the business-related documents, he was still in and out of Doña Natalia's life during these years, but he passed away in 1988, long before I thought to ask him, and my mother, María, does not know.

But María has other important information about the restaurant. Doña Natalia was good friends with one of the waitresses, Petra, who became terminally ill with tuberculosis. Petra asked Doña Natalia to adopt her two children after her death, and Doña Natalia agreed.

Because Petra had tuberculosis, she was almost certainly receiving municipal health care, which put her at risk of deportation. According to California's particularly harsh interpretation of the Immigration Act of 1924, any medical care provided by the city or county was considered charity, and recipients of such care, who were labeled public charges, were subject to deportation. When "repatriation" efforts picked up during the Depression, the Los Angeles County Department of Charities created a "transportation section" or "deportation section" (the names were used interchangeably), tasked with identifying and then deporting any Mexican immigrant receiving county-sponsored medical aid. Between 1931 and 1933, the department deported "to their former homes" over thirteen thousand Mexicans deemed guilty of receiving county medical or financial aid.[18] Petra's children were US citizens, born in California, but had Petra been identified as a public charge, the children would have been deported along with their mother.[19] Instead, Petra lived her last days in Los Angeles, and when she died Doña Natalia prepared to fulfill her promise.

María maintains that although the 1930 census records Doña Natalia and Alberto Perea as married, it was Doña Natalia's promise to Petra that prompted the marriage, in 1935 or 1936. As a single woman, Doña Natalia was not able to adopt, María says, and the marriage was platonic. Indeed, it was not Alberto but Doña Natalia's good friend, Cecilia, who accompanied her to pick up the children 150 miles north of Los Angeles in Lompoc, California, where they had been born and were staying with family. The adoption papers

Figure 4. Doña Natalia, María, and Carlos, on the day the children came to live with Doña Natalia. Photograph provided by María Perea Molina.

no longer exist, but an undated photograph, taken by Cecilia that day, shows Doña Natalia with the two children, who were about four and three years of age: my *tío* (uncle), Carlos, and my mother, María.

Regardless of when and why the marriage to Alberto came about, Doña Natalia continued to live a relatively independent life. She used her maiden name instead of her married name. The couple lived in the same home at various times over the years, but they were also apart for long periods. Though Doña Natalia employed large numbers of relatives, Alberto was not among them; he worked at a brass factory and later a pillow factory. Sometime in the late 1930s, around the same time Doña Natalia's first restaurant closed, she and Alberto must have separated. By 1940, according to the census, Alberto was working as a laborer at a brass factory and living in a boardinghouse for immigrant workers run by an Italian couple on the northeastern edge of downtown Los Angeles, not far from the home he had shared with Doña Natalia in 1930.

After the restaurant closed, Doña Natalia, Carlos, and María moved to Fresno, 230 miles north of Los Angeles, in California's Central Valley, so that she could take a job as a cook at an agricultural camp—a job that allowed her to keep her children close. Migrant camps were notoriously difficult places to live and work. The housing for farm laborers was often subpar, letting in cold in the winter and heat in the summer, when the temperatures could soar to over one hundred degrees. Toilet facilities tended to be shared, insufficient, and poorly maintained, if at all, by employers. Working conditions in the fields were so terrible that in 1939–40, the US Senate's La Follette Civil Liberties Committee (1936–41), headed by Senator Robert M. La Follette Jr., investigated the plight of migrant farmworkers in California as part of its larger investigation of employer violations of workers' rights to organize and bargain collectively. They found agricultural workers living in deplorable circumstances: underpaid, badly housed, poorly fed, and exploited by the contractors in charge of staffing and supervising field operations.[20] And as many historians have documented, the color lines in rural areas were even less malleable than in Los Angeles.[21] According to María, after six months, her mother declared, "This isn't a life for us." Doña Natalia and the children returned to Los Angeles, and she began plotting to open another restaurant.

Her drive was remarkable. As late as 1960, according to the census, only 1.4 percent of managers and proprietors of all businesses in the nation had Spanish surnames, and these were almost exclusively men.[22] The fact that Doña Natalia did not speak English and was unable to write in Spanish did not deter her. She used to say, "Si Dios nos da un centavo, nosotros podemos trabajar y hacer dos" (If God gives us one cent, we can work and turn it into two). Perhaps the very boldness of Doña Natalia's dream sprang from the recognition that for someone with limited education and English-language skills, entrepreneurship might be her only way to get ahead.[23] There were limited options available to women at this time—laundress, seamstress, live-in housekeeper, nanny—and she likely did not want to be separated from her children. When I asked María for insights into Doña Natalia's motivations—what compelled her to start her own business, even though one had already closed—she refused to speculate. "We just did it," she said.

Doña Natalia opened her new restaurant, called the Nayarit, in 1943. This time, her timing seemed right. While the economic context of the Depression may have brought about the closure of her first restaurant, World War II brought an economic boom to Los Angeles. What's more, the growth in war-related industries led to another increase in migrants from Mexico who were hungry for a taste of home.

The restaurant was located on Sunset Boulevard, between Spring and Broadway, northeast of downtown.[24] It sat at the edge of Chinatown, just a few blocks from La Placita, which had been home to a large Mexican immigrant population a few decades before. By this time, however, the area had been transformed into a tourist destination, with businesses up and down Olvera Street trading in popular images of Los Angeles's Spanish past. Once the center of a Mexican neighborhood, Olvera Street was redeveloped in 1930 under the leadership of Christine Sterling, who oversaw its transformation into a tourist-friendly, premodern Mexican fantasyland. There were antique shops, art galleries, studios, and bookstores, as well as outdoor market stalls (which Sterling called "puestos") selling Mexican handicrafts. That, as the historian Phoebe Young has noted, the more lucrative brick-and-mortar spaces were leased by whites while the puestos went to Mexicans reinforced the segregated geography of the street: whites as core businesses, Mexicans as local color.[25]

It was a stark contrast to the modern, forward-looking city Los Angeles portrayed itself as and left little room for the voices and viewpoints of contemporary, living Mexican Angelenos. The famed Mexican muralist David Siqueiros was commissioned to paint a mural there, which he titled *América Tropical* and unveiled in 1932. Its explicit anti-American iconography and anti-imperialist images, such as an Indian peasant crucified under an American eagle at the center of the mural, were too controversial for Sterling's vision; within a year, city workers painted over it.

Even so, the church at La Placita, Nuestra Señora la Reina de los Ángeles, continued to draw Mexican immigrants to the area. The church offered daily mass in Spanish, and many Mexican Angelenos, no matter how regularly they attended mass, considered it the only suitable place for important ceremonies, such as baptisms, marriages, and funerals.

The Nayarit may have benefited from spillover from Olvera Street, but its steadiest clientele were Mexican workers who lived or worked in the area. They appreciated the authenticity and freshness of the food, including the handmade tortillas. The Nayarit also served green stuffed peppers, *patas de puerco* (pigs' feet) *en salsa*, and *lengua* (tongue) *en salsa*—economical proteins that may have reflected Doña Natalia's limited resources—as well as *costillas de puerco* (pork ribs) *en colorado*, and a few items like tacos and enchiladas that would have been more familiar to non-Mexican customers.

Figure 5. Facade of the original Nayarit restaurant, which closed around 1953. Left to right: Doña Natalia's friend Cecilia Torres; Carlos Perea (Doña Natalia's son); Ramón Barragan. Photograph provided by María Perea Molina.

When the journalist Paul Coates reviewed the restaurant in 1949, he declared it "one of the best Mexican dining rooms [he had] ever visited." He also emphasized its foreignness, sprinkling his review with Spanish, which he claimed to "*hablo* [talk] a little," joking about what his opinions might mean for "Pan-American relations," and bringing along a guide named José Antonio Rivera y Betancourt to help interpret the menu. (Coates called this "caballero" a "disturbing type of Mexican" because he "spoke English with all the unique charm of a native of Van Nuys." Presumably, he was a Mexican American who had grown up in the San Fernando Valley.) Coates seems to have gone to the Nayarit with the same exoticizing lens that drew visitors to nearby Olvera Street, but he made clear that the food at the Nayarit was not the standard, Spanish-fantasy-past type of fare. He warned readers about Doña Natalia's hot sauces ("Apply the chili with an eye dropper and all you get is a third-degree burn of the palate. Any larger amount is sheer arson!") and declared dishes like the patas, lengua, and chorizo and eggs suitable for the more "experienced diner."[26]

The restaurant was sparsely furnished but would have been even more spartan had Doña Natalia not been befriended by Isaac Ranger, who owned the Phoenix furniture store next door. Ranger provided her with chairs at no interest, asking only that she repay him when she could afford to do so. They maintained a strong friendship for years.

For eight years, Doña Natalia lived upstairs from her business, in four small rooms, with her two children and occasionally also with relatives who came from Mexico to work in the restaurant. María remembered how poor they were at this time. They had one bed, which the three of them took turns sleeping in; the other two, and any guests, would sleep on mattresses lined up on the floor. During the week, Doña Natalia sent Carlos and María to Methodist-run boarding schools for ethnic Mexican youth. She was not after the religious education—she was Catholic, though the church would not have welcomed her after her divorce—but wanted to know that the children would be safe and supervised. Had the children gone to a local school and lived with her, they would have been unattended after classes while she was working long hours. Carlos attended the Spanish American Institute for Boys, located ten miles south of Los Angeles, for one year, then went to live with Alberto. He joined the army at eighteen. After he finished his service, he married Raquel Picasso, a Mexican immigrant, and initially settled down near her family in San Jose, California. María, though, remained close to Doña Natalia. For middle and elementary school, she attended the all-girls Frances De Pauw School, located on Sunset Boulevard in Hollywood, six miles west of the restaurant, boarding there during the week. When World War II rations were still in effect, Doña Natalia would save sugar cubes and pack María off to school with them so that she could enjoy something sweet while she was away.[27] On the weekends, María returned home and worked at the restaurant, standing on a crate in order to reach the sink to wash dishes. By the time María graduated from middle school, Doña Natalia had developed rheumatoid arthritis in her hands; as it worsened, she relied on María more and more. For high school, María transferred to Sacred Heart, an all-girls Catholic day school, northeast of downtown Los Angeles, often working at the Nayarit after school and on the weekends.

Doña Natalia's business grew, but in 1951, her landlord, for personal reasons that had nothing to do with the Nayarit, let her know that he would not be renewing her lease the next year. It was time to search for a new location, for both her business and her residence.

One obvious move would have been to reopen her restaurant in East Los Angeles, where she would have been in the company of many fellow Mexican nationals, easily conducting her business almost exclusively in Spanish, her only language. But she had already been living and working outside an ethnic enclave, forming ties with people outside her own classed and racial social networks. In addition to being her friends, some of these individuals acted as her cultural brokers. Cultural brokers did more than help with transactions and translations; they helped an immigrant obtain the cultural capital they needed to thrive.[28] Isaac Ranger, the furniture-store owner, had been one such cultural broker. Carlos Armario, Doña Natalia's real estate agent, was another.

It is not clear why Doña Natalia decided to move two miles west and re-open the Nayarit in Echo Park. Perhaps she wanted to return to the neighborhood where, during the Depression, she had established her first restaurant. Perhaps she was drawn to the area's diversity and its openness to immigrants. Perhaps she sensed that there was room, and a customer base, for a new restaurant there, at a property she liked and could afford. Whatever her motivation, it was a bold decision. She had developed a loyal following at the original Nayarit, but most of the clientele worked downtown, stopping in for a gracious but by necessity quick meal. It was not clear if they would, or could, follow her to the new location. But something made her sign the lease. That two-mile move would change her life as much as the 1,400-mile journey from her hometown in Mexico to Los Angeles had done thirty years earlier.

Carlos Armario helped her navigate the English-speaking neighborhood and locate and lease the property. Their business relationship and friendship lasted for years, and he helped her invest in property and develop financial literacy. During the next two decades, she would go on to purchase three houses in Echo Park. Her own home, which she purchased in 1951, the same year she leased space for the restaurant, was built in 1912, had three bedrooms, one bath, and a two-bedroom apartment over the carport that served as a landing pad for a series of newly arrived Mexican relatives. It was six blocks from the restaurant, close enough that she and María could work long hours and still return home easily. Later, she bought two modest two-bedroom, one-bath homes in Echo Park and rented them to recently immigrated family members until they could afford to purchase them from her. She was transplanting Nayarit into Echo Park, and it proved to be fertile ground.

PLACEMAKING IN ECHO PARK

The new restaurant, which seated seventy people, was larger than the original Nayarit. Doña Natalia leased the space from Joseph Nahama, a Jewish immigrant who would become another cultural broker and friend. Nahama was born in Thessaloniki—Greece in the present day but at that time part of the Ottoman Empire, which had a vibrant Jewish community—and fled in 1910, during the tumultuous dissolution of the Ottoman Empire. As a Jewish immigrant, he would have known what it meant to live on the margins of US society. Like Mexicans, Jews were legally classified as white and could naturalize, which Joseph did in 1931. Also like Mexicans, Jews were often seen as not-quite-white and experienced discrimination. Into the twentieth century, Jews along with Poles, Italians, and other groups we tend to think of as "white" today were considered distinct groups. David Roediger calls them "inbetween people," because they were "inbetween hard racism and full inclusion—neither securely white nor non-white."[29] Many were first- or second-generation immigrants, with memories of immigration inspectors who checked them or their families for signs of the diseases it was assumed they carried. As Roediger points out, the discrimination they faced under Anglo-Saxon Protestant exclusionary practices was not the same type of racism that African Americans have experienced but was nevertheless "an experience of racialization."[30]

Joseph and Doña Natalia were contemporaries: he was two years her senior, and his son was a few years older than María. Over the years, Joseph learned some phrases in Spanish to communicate with Doña Natalia, and Doña Natalia and María attended his family parties at his home. While he owned and leased three properties in Echo Park, he lived on Los Angeles's wealthier Westside, where many Jews had moved after World War II.[31] But his warm relationship with Doña Natalia was typical of the types of connections that Echo Park, as a neighborhood, engendered—part of an atmosphere that would shape and be shaped by the Nayarit.

Echo Park lies just a couple of miles northwest of downtown Los Angeles, close enough that you can see the downtown skyline from various areas. The neighborhood itself is small, roughly 2.4 square miles, and when Doña Natalia moved there, the Hollywood Freeway (US 101) had recently been constructed across its southern border. Today, Interstate 5, Route 110, and Route 2 bracket the neighborhood as well. The neighborhood's central artery—and the place where Doña Natalia opened the new Nayarit—was, and is, the 21.75-mile-long Sunset Boulevard. Sunset runs from downtown to the Pacific Coast Highway. It bisects Echo Park and connects it to the rest of Los Angeles: take it east, and you are downtown in minutes; go west five miles, and you'll be in Hollywood; keep going, and you'll reach the Pacific Ocean in a single, if long, bus ride. The twenty-one-acre Elysian Park, home to Dodger Stadium since 1962 and the Los Angeles Police Academy since the 1930s, sits in Echo Park's backyard. The neighborhood is a geographic crossroads, which positioned it to become a cultural crossroads as well.

Residents who have lived in the area for decades talk about Echo Park as having a different sensibility from the rest of Los Angeles, of it being a place where one could "just be." Jake Zeitlin, who owned a series of bookstores around Los Angeles and was at the heart of the city's cultural and artistic scene, lived in Echo Park from 1926 to 1938. He described the live-and-let-live attitude of Echo Park: "The rents were low, the shacks on the tree-filled hills afforded more privacy than flatland apartments did, and people could conduct their individual lives in peace."[32] Similarly, the artist Billy Shire, son of the labor organizers and activists Hank and Barbara Shire, described why his parents moved to Echo Park in the 1950s: "There were kind of bohemian and politically active spots in L.A.—Topanga Canyon, Laurel Canyon, or Echo Park. Echo Park was I think the cheapest, or something. It was a really nice mixed neighborhood [and] they had a lot of friends there."[33] How did it get this way? We can piece together a story.

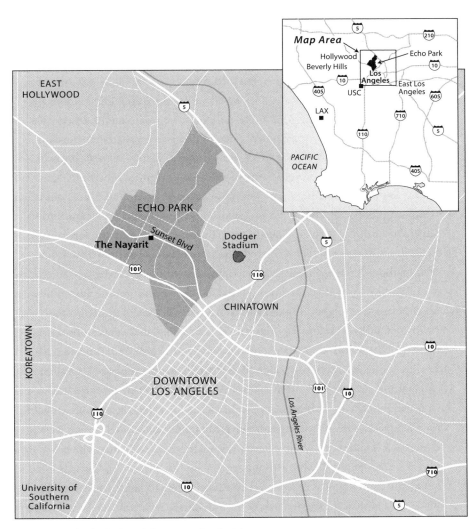

Map 1. Map of Echo Park and the greater Los Angeles area.

Unlike other parts of Los Angeles, Echo Park did not develop as a racially segregated neighborhood. The official record is mostly silent as to why.[34] There are no city council minutes or filed petitions discussing anything related to segregation in the area, but it likely helped that Echo Park had not experienced planned development. When real estate developers purchased large plots of land, subdivided them, and built houses, racially restrictive covenants were often written into the deeds of sale as a way to keep developments segregated and thus protect home values. Racial segregation was, therefore, woven into the very fabric of many communities. Restrictive covenants kept African Americans, Jews, Mexicans, Asians, and others out of white neighborhoods, both rich and blue-collar; South Gate and Huntington Park, for example, both employed them. The 1948 US Supreme Court ruling in *Shelley v. Kraemer*, which declared that states could not enforce such covenants, did not strike them down outright, allowing private parties to continue excluding or discouraging people of color from moving into white neighborhoods. Neighborhood associations sought to keep would-be buyers out by defending deed restrictions in court, working with real estate agents to "steer" prospective buyers of color away from the area and imposing different conditions, including much higher prices, for people of color. Unofficial methods, like intimidation, harassment, and violence, were also used to keep neighborhoods white. In 1948, for example, when the famous singer Nat King Cole moved into the moneyed neighborhood of Hancock Park, which had had restrictive covenants written into its deeds since the neighborhood was established in the 1920s, a cross was burned on his family's lawn, and their dog was poisoned.[35] The Shorts, an African American family who moved into a segregated part of Fontana, in San Bernardino County, in 1945, faced even worse. When they did not heed warnings to move out, their house was firebombed, killing the family of four, which included two young children.[36] But as a rule, such aggressive policing of the color line did not take place in Echo Park.

Figure 6. A member of the Hollywood Protective Association puts her support for residential segregation on display, ca. 1920. Courtesy of the National Japanese American Historical Society.

When Doña Natalia moved into Echo Park, 79 percent of its population was white, including many immigrants from Italy, Germany, and Eastern Europe (specifically, Czechoslovakia, Hungary, Lithuania, Poland, Romania, Russia, and Yugoslavia). Latinx people, most of whom were Mexican, made up another 16 percent (by 1970, that number increased to 52 percent). In addition, there was a small Asian population, including a Filipino community that had lived in southwest Echo Park since the early twentieth century. This area, known as Little Manila, was officially designated Historic Filipinotown in 2002.[37]

This racial and ethnic diversity helped many of Echo Park's residents feel comfortable crossing what were, in other parts of the city, starker color lines. Carol Jacques, who grew up in Chavez Ravine and moved with her family to Silver Lake in 1951, felt very connected to nearby Echo Park, where she spent a good deal of time. As an adult, she realized that growing up in a multiethnic area had deeply shaped her identity and viewpoint. "We had a meeting at a coworker's home," she reflected. "My friend, a *mexicana* who had grown up in East Los Angeles and was seated next to me, looked visibly uncomfortable. She leaned in and whispered to me, 'I've never been in a white person's home before.'"[38] Jacques, on the other hand, felt at ease.

Such comfort did not just stem from Echo Park's diversity; many of the people there could draw on shared experiences of being outsiders. Individuals differed along lines of citizenship status, racial and ethnic categorization, gender and sexuality, but their shared experiences of being marked as "other" promoted common cause. Even many white residents had lived experiences that complicated their white privilege, whether as socialists, communists, gays, Jews, or being read as a "foreigner." Rosemary Castillo, whose parents were from Nayarit and whose family often frequented the Nayarit restaurant in the 1960s, remembers their ethnic white neighbors fondly. "Our neighbors were a mixture of people—German, Jewish. They embraced people. Our landlord was Mrs. O'Connell. She helped us settle in the neighborhood and maneuver the city. She even took us to Bob Baker Marionette Theater!"[39]

Echo Park was an incubator that fostered relational notions of race, including my own. Growing up in a working-class neighborhood that was home to a large Mexican community but also to Vietnamese refugees, Filipino nationals, Chinese immigrants, and working-class whites shaped my academic work by showing me that when we make visible the connections among racial and ethnic groups, we can better understand the logic that underpins the forms of inclusion and dispossession they face. Living in Echo

Park allowed residents a relational space in which they could understand shared struggles. Echo Park attracted white residents with progressive and radical politics who were known for reaching across the color line and demonstrating a shared sense of struggle with racialized groups.[40] They had begun to move to the neighborhood soon after its inception.

Historically, Echo Park was part of a larger region called Edendale that included neighboring Silver Lake. Echo Park began to develop in 1887, when the speculator Thomas Kelley and his five partners purchased land across from the reservoir and divided it into lots, which he put on the market. When they found that the reservoir was a flood hazard that made building impractical, they entered into negotiations with the city. In 1891, Kelley and his partners exchanged thirty-three acres around the reservoir for the city's agreement that it would turn the area into a park (thereby raising the price of the partners' remaining land). Echo Park Lake was completed by 1895. Residents gathered on its banks with friends and neighbors, making it the neighborhood's first urban anchor. The arrival, around the turn of the twentieth century, of the electric railway cars that snaked through Echo Park and along major streets like Sunset Boulevard further connected Echo Park to downtown and to the greater Los Angeles and Orange County region; the streetcars remained a vital part of Echo Park's development until they were supplanted by freeways in the early 1950s.[41]

By the 1920s, Echo Park was developing into a downtown suburb, home to architects, Hollywood studio employees, printmakers, artists, and other creative people who were attracted in part by the neighborhood's affordable rents. These were often artists who prized self-expression over material possessions and career advancement. Gay men also found a receptive community there. According to the historian Daniel Hurewitz, it was some members of this gay community who founded the Mattachine Society, the first homophile group in Los Angeles, in 1950. Jake Zeitlin's description of bohemianism helps us see the attractions of Echo Park for these early residents.

Finding a Place in Echo Park

Bohemianism thrives on adversity. It's not a movement but a consequence of certain conditions. You have to have a concentration of people practicing their arts, people with superior endowments who don't necessarily fit into society, and who are, in fact, often engaged in rebellions against convention, creating a symbiotic society where not only can they go and eat at each other's houses when they're hungry, but where they can also spark each other and be each other's critical audiences. To such people, money is not the main motivation; they may like spaghetti and wine and women and conversation and not getting up in the morning to go to a job, but all believe in practicing something that is their justification for being, whether it be dancing, writing, sculpting or music.[42]

A handful of other people moved to the area—and millions of others from all over the country visited—to attend the nation's first megachurch, Angelus Temple. Founded by the Pentecostal evangelist Aimee Semple McPherson in 1923, Angelus Temple seats more than five thousand people beneath a 125-foot-wide concrete dome. It was a dramatic setting for McPherson's elaborately staged sermons, which she also delivered on radio broadcasts and in traveling revivals. Many in the congregation were new arrivals to California. According to the California historian and Echo Park resident Carey McWilliams, "She made migrants feel at home in Los Angeles, she gave them a chance to meet other people, and she exorcised the nameless fears which so many of them had acquired from the fire-and-brimstone theology of the Middle West."[43] Most of these new arrivals drawn to Angelus Temple were white. But a small proportion of African Americans and ethnic Mexicans worshipped there too, and for these parishioners (like the Echo Park bohemians) the temple provided a space for community in a larger world that pushed them to the margins. Congregants included the young Anthony Quinn, who joined McPherson's church as a teenager and would go on to achieve great fame as an actor. A group of parishioners going door to door in the Echo Park neighborhood had reached out to his ailing grandmother, and she believed her health had improved thanks to their prayers. Quinn joined the church, performed in the church band, and served as an interpreter for McPherson. He saw McPherson as a great ally to the ethnic Mexican community. During the Depression, when asking for charity from the county could brand one a public charge subject to deportation, McPherson offered assistance without questions or judgment. In an interview, Quinn recalled:

> I remember one Thanksgiving Day, actually and literally fainting on the street from hunger . . . and in those days if you called the government agency, you felt you could never recover your dignity from it. And the one human being that never asked what your nationality was, what you believed in and so forth, was Aimee Semple McPherson. All you had to do was pick up the phone and say 'I'm hungry,' and within an hour there'd be a food basket there for you. She literally kept most of that Mexican community alive for many years.[44]

McPherson died of an overdose in 1944 and was succeeded by her son Rolf, under whose leadership the temple continued to thrive.[45]

By the 1930s and 1940s, Echo Park had a reputation as a home for political leftists and Communist Party affiliates. Two miles north of Angelus Temple was a hilly area around Baxter Street and Vestal Avenue known as Red Gulch or Red Hill, because of the color's association with communism. Some residents of Echo Park attended the First Unitarian Church, a couple of miles west in the mid-Wilshire area, a spiritual community committed to social and racial justice. Labor organizers like Hank Shire, a member of the International Longshore and Warehouse Union, lived there, as did many activists.[46] Some Hollywood professionals who had been blacklisted for their suspected communism after the 1947 House Un-American Activities Committee (HUAC) investigations moved to Echo Park too.[47] Echo Park was also home to a chapter of the Communist-affiliated Civil Rights Congress (CRC).

Nationally, the CRC was active from 1946 to 1955, and though the exact dates of the Echo Park chapter's existence are unknown, it was active from

1952 to 1954. Its mostly white membership, including many ethnic whites and Jews, fought against McCarthyism and racial injustice. After the sentence of Wesley Wells, a Black man imprisoned in San Quentin, was increased to the death penalty for a minor assault on a guard who was taunting him, the CRC led a national campaign seeking justice on Wells's behalf. (Wells's execution was stayed at the eleventh hour; he was eventually released, in 1974.) The Echo Park CRC's 1954 Christmas party, attended by over five hundred people, served as a fundraiser to fight "negro genocide."

The Echo Park CRC chapter also campaigned on behalf of ethnic Mexican victims of police brutality. In a 1951 incident known as "Bloody Christmas," police officers took seven young men into custody, five of whom were ethnic Mexicans. It's not clear what the charges were since the officers had originally suspected them of underage drinking at a bar but the men had provided identification to show they were of legal drinking age. The men's arrival at the city jail coincided with the Los Angeles Police Department's (LAPD's) Christmas Eve party, which was attended by over one hundred officers, many of them drinking alcohol in violation of the department's policy. When a false rumor spread that one of the officers had lost an eye in an altercation with the young men, the police stormed into the men's cell and over fifty of them viciously beat the young men while the rest stood witness.[48] A few months later, in 1952, the police forced their way into the home of a Mexican American family without a warrant and arrested five youths, including one who had recently returned from military service. The CRC protested the arrest, which they understood as part of a pattern of injustice, and spoke out against inflammatory press coverage too. Fearmongering headlines about "Rat Packs" and "Mexican hoodlums" were common.[49] A flyer the CRC distributed was titled, in bold capital letters, "**KNOW YOUR RIGHTS!**"[50]

Carey McWilliams and Alice McGrath, white leftists who would rise to almost heroic status in Mexican American history, lived in Echo Park too. McWilliams, a noted activist, journalist, and attorney, bought his home on

Alvarado Street in the 1940s. From 1939 to 1942, he served as director of California's Division of Immigration and Housing, which oversaw the living conditions of migrant laborers. In this capacity, he crisscrossed the state, visiting farms and interviewing workers of Mexican, Filipino, Japanese, and many other backgrounds. His criticisms of gubernatorial candidate Earl Warren, whom he saw as a pro-establishment, pro-business, conservative Republican, were so biting that Warren swore he would dismiss McWilliams immediately on taking office if he won. (Warren did win, and McWilliams left his post.) Returning to his legal practice, McWilliams worked on some of the most pressing civil rights cases of the time, including the Sleepy Lagoon trial.

The case was named for the reservoir where, in August 1942, the body of José Díaz, a twenty-two-year-old resident of East Los Angeles, was found dead, after an altercation that had broken out at a party. In the following weeks, police rounded up hundreds of Mexican youths and arrested twenty-two of them. At their trial, the judge blatantly discriminated against them, and they were the targets of racist, defamatory press coverage. Twelve of the young men were convicted of murder, five were found guilty of assault, and five were acquitted. Their treatment provoked a backlash of public support from both inside and outside the Mexican American community and led to the creation of the Sleepy Lagoon Defense Committee, a multiethnic coalition that provided support to the imprisoned men and raised funds for their defense. Alice McGrath was executive secretary, and McWilliams, along with other attorneys, launched a successful appeal of the case.[51]

McGrath later said that she fought on behalf of these Mexican American youths not just because she saw injustice, but because she understood it firsthand. Her parents were Russian Jewish immigrants, and she was well attuned to how race operated as a relational concept. Her archives include a timeline that records significant instances of racial injustice before and after the Sleepy Lagoon affair. She included events in which ethnic Mexicans were targeted, such as the June 1943 Zoot Suit riots, but she also noted that in

Figure 7. Alice McGrath (at right) with Sleepy Lagoon defendants and defense attorney Ben Margolis (seated). Alice Greenfield McGrath Papers (Collection 1490). UCLA Library Special Collections, Charles E. Young Research Library, University of California, Los Angeles.

April 1942, Japanese and Japanese Americans were relocated to internment camps.[52] Placing these events together in one timeline demonstrates her awareness that racism was not a single group's issue and could be deployed in the same period and the same area in very different ways, depending on the group. McWilliams showed a similar insight when he commented, "It was a foregone conclusion that Mexicans would be substituted as the major scapegoat group once the Japanese were removed."[53]

McWilliams was a prolific writer, and his books on race and racialization in America include *Prejudice: Japanese-Americans Symbol of Racial Intolerance*

(1944), *Brothers under the Skin* (1943), *A Mask for Privilege: Anti-Semitism in America* (1948), *North from Mexico* (1949), and *Factories in the Field: The Story of Migratory Farm Labor in California* (1969), which is often credited as the first book-length study of Mexican American history.[54] While all of these books provide detailed accounts of particular groups' unique histories in the United States, they also discuss how the experiences of one group affected others, even when separated by space and time. He argued, for instance, that the "modes of aggression tried against Indians and blacks easily transferred to the Chinese" and that the immigration policies and restrictions first directed at the Chinese were then directed at "brown" immigrants.[55] McWilliams's works are the first extended US histories to help us think through how the struggles of one group may affect another.

McWilliams moved to New York City in the early 1950s to work at *The Nation*; in 1955, he became its editor. For the next twenty years, he published dozens of articles and editorials, often on issues of social justice.[56] Much has been written about his contributions to Mexican American history, as well as Alice McGrath's, but no one has discussed their common connection to Echo Park. It seems safe to speculate that they were drawn to the neighborhood for its leftist politics and for the way its diverse population let them live in solidarity and connection with others.

Echo Park's legacy of progressive politics likely contributed to the fact that when my grandmother opened her restaurant, there was no "neighborhood committee" that greeted her to "suggest" she would be happier if she established her business elsewhere. No bricks were thrown through Doña Natalia's windows. No racial epithets were painted on the outside walls of the Nayarit. She did not face the types of discrimination that targeted African Americans or ethnic Mexicans in other Los Angeles neighborhoods. In 1949, just a few miles east, for example, a real estate agent told Los Angeles City Council member Edward Roybal, the first Mexican American to be elected to the council in the twentieth century, that he could not buy a home in a new housing development, located in the councilman's own District 9, because he was "a Mexican."[57]

My point here is not that Echo Park was a multicultural utopia. It was not. But it matters that the area did not have to contend with the great weight of a history of racial covenants and strictly enforced Jim Crow segregation (or "Jaime Crow," as the historian Albert Camarillo termed the racial segregation directed at Mexicans in the Southwest).[58] The absence of those burdens permitted more frequent and positive interactions among entrepreneurs, customers, and local residents, which in turn set the stage for the growth of meaningful bonds across the color line. The ways of living and being afforded by these diverse neighborhoods played a critical role in animating and sustaining political struggles. What's more, these dynamics were allowed to continue without the type of government intervention that in other working-class areas dramatically changed the texture of everyday life, or even existence.

For whatever reason, Echo Park managed to escape machinations by vast bureaucratic forces. Often stigmatized and overlooked when it came to government-provided resources and investments, Echo Park left only a faint presence in the institutional archive. Beyond an occasional story about fishing at the lake in the park or the lotuses blooming there, Echo Park rarely made it into the pages of the *Los Angeles Times* between 1950 and 1970. City council meeting minutes—the main record for municipal activity—and the files of representatives of Los Angeles City Council District 13, which includes Echo Park, barely mention it. The extensive searches I conducted in the files in the Los Angeles City Archives revealed only scant entries related to storm drains, parking, traffic conditions, tree planting, the replacement of streetcars with buses, and the problem of abandoned streetcar tracks. The official archives are also silent on how the community reacted to the construction of the Hollywood Freeway (US 101), which was built along Echo Park's southern border in the late 1940s. Given what freeways usually meant for the neighborhoods where they were typically sited, it is reasonable to expect that freeway construction brought "demolition, displacement and havoc."[59] Indeed, the lack of records is itself instructive, showing how top-down these projects were and how thoroughly the freeway's perceived benefit to Los Angeles as a whole eclipsed the community that bore the brunt of its construction. We don't know whether records on the construction of the freeway were lost as a result of poor archival preservation or never existed in the first place, but given the larger archival silence on Echo Park, their absence underscores the way that silence is yet another layer contributing to the devaluing of this place. Echo Park's only significant municipal project to speak of in the 1950s and 1960s was construction of a public swimming pool, for which residents had fought for years. In 1954, County Supervisor John Anson Ford committed county funds for a pool on the condition that the city contribute as well; when the pool was finally constructed four years later, it was adjacent to the Hollywood Freeway.[60]

During the 1950s and 1960s, Echo Park's city council representatives were not notable champions of the community. All three lived in other, more affluent parts of District 13: Ernest Debs (1947–59) and James Brown (1959–64) in Silver Lake and Paul Lamport (1965–69) in Hollywood Hills. Debs served on the board or was a member of over a dozen social clubs, but none was related to Echo Park.[61] Brown, who took office as part of a special election after Debs was elected to the Board of Supervisors, was at least slightly involved in Echo Park: in 1959, he commented that the district's recreational facilities had "fallen far behind." The next year, 1960, a new Senior Citizen Clubhouse was opened near the park.[62] Lamport, who replaced Brown when he left office for an appointment as a municipal judge in 1964, enjoyed yachting.[63] His 1969 reelection campaign asserted, in the words of one flyer, "He Gets Things Done." Yet none of the projects he described, including new street lighting, widening and resurfacing of streets, tree planting, programs for teenagers, and the creation of Head Start programs for low-income preschool children, had taken place in Echo Park. The campaign came under fire from the gay community and its supporters for his homophobic remarks and his willingness to support and direct police raids on gay bars and uphold anti-loitering ordinances used to keep gay men out of public places. The *Advocate*, a LGBT-interest magazine, established in 1967, accused Lamport of working "hand-in-hand" with the LAPD to harass gay bars in the district, which helped mobilize the gay community to campaign against and defeat him, the first time the gay vote was credited for swinging an election. ONE, Inc., founded in 1952 in L.A. with support from groups, including the Mattachine Society, rejoiced: "The Gay Vote had made its mark, and that mark had been hotly branded on the political skin of a man long reputed to have been back of police harassment and misconduct in the Echo Park/Silverlake/Hollywood District, probably the greatest single concentration of homophile population anywhere." That mark has been long lasting: every councilperson for the district since has supported gay rights.[64]

Still, being officially overlooked seems to have been a blessing of sorts. It is true that fewer resources were directed to Echo Park, but the community escaped having whole areas razed for "improvement" projects or having garbage dumps, prisons, or toxic incinerators built there, as they were in other Los Angeles neighborhoods that lacked the clout to block them. And Echo Park largely escaped the types of "urban renewal" that harmed or outright destroyed other working-class neighborhoods.[65] Neighboring Chavez Ravine, for example, was not so fortunate. It was a close-knit residential community, working class and racially mixed but predominantly Mexican and Mexican American, located just over the eastern border of Echo Park, in Elysian Park. Residents felt betrayed when, beginning in 1951, the city used the power of eminent domain to seize land for a public-housing project. In an infamous example of urban renewal at its worst, the city forced residents to vacate their homes and abandon the neighborhood. Home owners were bought out, purportedly at the market rate, but few could find equivalent properties for the low prices they had been paid. Renters were promised that they would be given first rights to the public housing that would be built over their razed community. Yet after the residents were displaced, the project languished. The Cold War intensified; public housing was deemed too much of a "socialist experiment" to build; and in 1959, to bring Major League Baseball to Los Angeles, the land was sold to Walter O'Malley, owner of the Brooklyn Dodgers, at a fraction of its worth.[66] Ground broke for the construction of Dodger Stadium in 1959.

The displacement still haunts the residents and their descendants, compounded by the fact that even though their story has been memorialized in scores of newspaper articles, books, music, and a play, no form of redress or acknowledgment has been forthcoming from the city. One man whose natal home was destroyed told the *Los Angeles Times* that his umbilical cord, buried in the house's yard by his parents, now rests under third base.[67] The history stands as a glaring example of how even when Latinx residents are placemakers, their communities remain vulnerable to the powers that be.

Echo Park also suffered from a different kind of government-driven disadvantage: redlining. Starting in the 1930s, the Federal Housing Administration (FHA) backed private loans offering low to no down payment financing. To determine which areas were appropriate for investment, the government relied on appraisals, in the form of city surveys, carried out by the Home Owners' Loan Corporation (HOLC). Around the country, HOLC bureaucrats used an area's racial diversity as a ready gauge of its desirability. If an area had a large proportion of "foreigners" or "negroes," the area received a low grade, which was color coded on the map in red (hence the term "redlining"). In Los Angeles, survey takers jotted down the percentage of Mexicans versus whites as unreflectively as they noted an area's proportion of home owners versus renters.[68] The HOLC surveys resulted in federal mortgage assistance loans being disproportionately awarded to whites seeking to buy homes in areas deemed worthy of investment, namely, the suburbs. The result was "white flight," in which white families abandoned the often-diverse core urban areas for less diverse suburbs. The decisions of individuals, in other words, were prompted and supported by the racist policies of the government.[69] Most Americans hold the majority of their wealth in their homes, so the ability to buy a home that could go up in value and be passed down to one's children made a significant difference in shaping the opportunities of not only that generation but also the next.[70]

The HOLC survey maps from 1939 show that Echo Park and parts of the broader Edendale area were deemed high-risk investments because of "foreign" and "racial elements." The area just south of Echo Park Lake was given a "high red grade," the worst mark possible. The area was described as "blighted," with a "concentration of negro families," "a large population of Russian and Polish Jews," a "settlement of Mexicans," and an overall trend toward greater numbers of "subversive racial elements and lower income groups." Another part of Edendale on the hillside was described as having only 10 percent foreign families and being dominated by "small business men, white collar workers, skilled and unskilled artisans, laborers," yet it too was given a "high red grade." Even though the surveyors declared this area "not entirely blighted"—there were relatively few "subversive racial elements," and it was geographically separate from the more problematic area near the lake—they concluded that the neighborhood's "trend of desirability will continue downward." The implication is clear: mere proximity to racialized groups could influence how an area was assessed.[71] The lowest grades resulted in redlining, which made obtaining an FHA loan for a property in this area virtually impossible. Over time, the government's designation of Echo Park as a "poor risk" became a self-fulfilling prophecy, manifesting in lower home-ownership rates and home values and less civic investment. Although these ills were often blamed on the residents themselves, they were in fact created by the powers that be—whether through benign neglect or the heavy hand of government—and concealed by the convenient moniker "bad neighborhood."

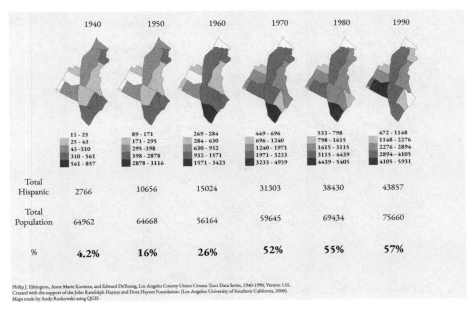

	1940	1950	1960	1970	1980	1990
	11 - 25	89 - 171	269 - 284	449 - 696	533 - 798	472 - 1148
	25 - 43	171 - 295	284 - 630	696 - 1240	798 - 1615	1148 - 2276
	43 - 310	295 - 398	630 - 932	1240 - 1971	1615 - 3115	2276 - 2894
	310 - 561	398 - 2878	932 - 1571	1971 - 3233	3115 - 4439	2894 - 4105
	561 - 857	2878 - 3116	1571 - 3423	3233 - 4939	4439 - 5405	4105 - 5931
Total Hispanic	2766	10656	15024	31303	38430	43857
Total Population	64962	64668	56164	59645	69434	75660
%	**4.2%**	**16%**	**26%**	**52%**	**55%**	**57%**

Philip J. Ethington, Anne Marie Kooistra, and Edward DeYoung, Los Angeles County Union Census Tract Data Series, 1940-1990, Version 1.01.
Created with the support of the John Randolph Haynes and Dora Haynes Foundation. (Los Angeles: University of Southern California, 2000).
Maps made by Andy Rutkowski using QGIS

Figure 8. Echo Park's Hispanic demographics over time.

Echo Park was not immune from white flight. By the 1950s, when Doña Natalia moved to the neighborhood, its white population was declining steadily: from 93 percent in 1940 to 79 percent in 1950, 64 percent in 1960, and 33 percent in 1970.[72] As these white residents relocated, Mexicans and some Asians, attracted by affordable housing, replaced them. But many whites who could have traded in their 1920s Craftsman bungalows for larger ranch houses in new suburban developments instead chose to remain in Echo Park, with its progressive politics and multicultural vibe. These individuals, and the generally progressive politics that characterized Echo Park before World War II, helped establish a legacy and identity for the area that would attract like-minded newcomers over the decades to come.

Finding a Place in Echo Park

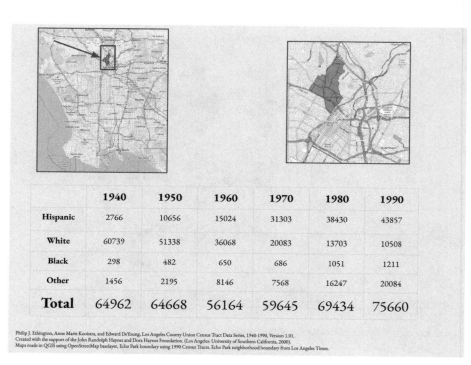

	1940	1950	1960	1970	1980	1990
Hispanic	2766	10656	15024	31303	38430	43857
White	60739	51338	36068	20083	13703	10508
Black	298	482	650	686	1051	1211
Other	1456	2195	8146	7568	16247	20084
Total	64962	64668	56164	59645	69434	75660

Philip J. Ethington, Anne Marie Kooistra, and Edward DeYoung, Los Angeles County Union Census Tract Data Series, 1940-1990, Version 1.01.
Created with the support of the John Randolph Haynes and Dora Haynes Foundation. (Los Angeles: University of Southern California, 2000).
Maps made in QGIS using OpenStreetMap baselayer, Echo Park boundary using 1990 Census Tracts. Echo Park neighborhood boundary from Los Angeles Times.

Figure 9. Echo Park's shifting demographics, 1940–1990.

Some of these newer residents formed organizations to protect the neighborhood. One was the Citizens Committee to Save Elysian Park, established
in 1965 by Grace E. Simons, a former reporter and editor for Los Angeles's oldest African American newspaper, the *California Eagle*. Simons originally
organized the group to fight a proposal to establish the Los Angeles Convention Center on sixty-two acres in the heart of the park. Over the years, the
organization went on to fight off many other proposed "enhancements,"
including plans for a small airport, oil drilling, and condominium projects.
While this committee was organized to preserve Elysian Park, large numbers
of its members, including Simons and her husband, Frank Glass, lived in

Echo Park.[73] As the historian Andrea Thabet has argued, Simons viewed preservation as an act on behalf of the area's working-class residents who had little disposable income to spend on leisure. Thus the park was of special importance to them as it was a place that they could picnic, play, and think of as their backyard.[74]

Art Goldberg, a self-described radical, was also fighting for Echo Park's working-class residents when he opened the Working People's Law Center on Echo Park Avenue, just off of Sunset. It served those who made too much to qualify for a free clinic but not enough to be able to hire an attorney at their normal rates. Goldberg described the rates as operating on a "sliding socialist fee scale." Echo Park was also home to the Echo Park Food Conspiracy, an "anti-Establishment" food cooperative. In 1970, self-described progressives opened the People's Child Care Center with the goal of teaching their children political and social awareness. While civil rights and human rights were on the lesson plans, the center also showed commitment to social change by making sure it was accessible to working-class families of color in the neighborhood: it charged an affordable tuition, as little as $20 a month.[75]

The actions of individuals and organizations like these may not have had the same magnitude of impact on people's quality of life or opportunities to advance as did the discriminatory government home-loan-lending practices or the uneven allocation of government resources across city neighborhoods and racial groups. But our understanding of the history of Los Angeles would be incomplete without examining the legacy of the placemakers who worked to better race relations in the city, even if their efforts did not directly translate into policy. The bonds they developed and their affective relationship to this space opened up opportunities for Mexican immigrants who moved into the area in larger numbers after World War II. As these newcomers entered the cultural crossroads of Echo Park, they could develop a sense of belonging and have opportunities that Mexican immigrants living and working elsewhere at this same time—in agricultural field work in the Southwest, for example, or even in isolated ethnic enclaves in L.A.—could not. The choice of a neighborhood could have powerful ramifications in a city like Los Angeles, where segregation, de facto and de jure, operated unevenly.

In the 1950s and 1960s, most businesses owned by ethnic entrepreneurs were located in such ethnic enclaves, primarily served community residents, and often made only enough profit to meet the needs of the owner and their family. In Echo Park, however, the Nayarit attracted both locals and diners from other parts of town, developing into a successful business that allowed Doña Natalia to support and create opportunities for dozens of other family members and employees. Locating the restaurant on Sunset Boulevard, Echo Park's central artery, made it easy to find and to reach by streetcar or car or on foot. It also put the Nayarit in the company of other owner-operated urban anchors.

If you lived in Echo Park, you could get what you needed without leaving the neighborhood: groceries at Pioneer Market, opened in 1925 by Leonard Lum and later operated by his son, Michael; and clothes at Finer's, a haberdashery that opened in 1923 and stayed in business for the next seventy years.[76] Walking down Sunset, you would likely see the owners sweeping the sidewalk before their stores opened, greet one another as you passed by, and know that whenever you went in to make a purchase a familiar face would help you find what you needed and ring you up. Farther east, a few blocks from where the main entrance to Dodger Stadium now stands, you could eat dinner at Nikola's, which opened a few years after the Nayarit, in 1955. Nikola Rasic, a Yugoslavian immigrant, cooked in the back with his wife, Eva, while his three sons ran the front. Nikola's served hearty dishes like steaks, ham, and spareribs, accompanied by mixed green salads and soups du jour, all offered in a dark, wood-paneled restaurant with booths you could sink cozily into. It became a hangout for politicians and police officers—City Hall and the Police Academy were close by—as well as USC Trojan fans and, after Dodger Stadium opened in 1962, anyone heading to or from a Dodger game. Dodger's owner, Walter O'Malley, became a regular; his standing order was White Label on the rocks, with a splash of water.[77] My family went there too, for special occasions, until it closed in 1988.

Les Freres Taix, known simply as "Taix" to locals, moved to Sunset Boulevard in 1962, a block from the Nayarit. Family-owned and family-run since 1927, when it opened in downtown Los Angeles, Taix served traditional French family-style meals at affordable prices. Taix had a loyal customer base, including a number of white-collar workers in the downtown office building who followed the restaurant to its new location, and also attracted a celebrity crowd. A black-and-white photo displayed at the restaurant shows the actor Doris Day being served by a waiter. For decades, Hayward "Kelly" Fong, who worked as a county engineer, would come to the Echo Park location with his wife, Dorothy, always requesting their favorite waiter, Bernard Inchauspe. Over the years, Inchauspe had turned down numerous job offers from Taix's competitors. An article in the *Los Angeles Times* described his perspective: "Taix is his second home. . . . And its staff and customers are his second family." In 2012, Inchauspe, along with waiter José Fragoso and bartender Fernando Gómez, celebrated fifty years of working at Taix. Over a dozen of their fellow employees had been there for at least thirty years. That kind of stable workforce, people who recognize and connect with a business's clientele, is an integral element of an urban anchor, and Doña Natalia fostered it too.[78]

Opening the Nayarit in 1951 in the absence of other restaurants that drew people into the neighborhood may have felt like a risk to Doña Natalia. But as other immigrants like the founders of Taix and Nikola's opened their own establishments, they formed a cluster of urban anchors that customers could travel easily between, hopping from one place to another and stamping the area with the intimate feel of a neighborhood nestled in the heart of a sprawling metropolis.

We know nothing about the first day of business at Doña Natalia's new restaurant. There are no stories told by my family members about that day, no surviving newspaper ads, and no photos. From what I know about Doña Natalia herself, though, my guess is that she treated the day like any other. She was fifty years old. She likely dressed in her usual work attire, with her black hair in a relaxed upsweep. She favored fashionable dresses made of practical, hard-wearing fabrics: a 1950s swing dress, a form fitting top, and a flowing tea-length skirt, nothing too constricting or flashy. Her makeup and jewelry would likewise have been simple and tasteful, appropriate for facing the public but not elaborate enough to disturb her when working in a hot kitchen. She probably arrived well before the restaurant opened and made sure that the sidewalk was swept, the chairs were precisely in place, and the vegetables were properly chopped. Then she propped open the doors, letting in the fresh air, confident that customers would come.

CHAPTER TWO

Tasting Home

When Doña Natalia first opened the Nayarit in Echo Park in 1951, she did not have money for anything more than a modest space. A few simple and inexpensive decorations from her home, Nayarit, adorned the walls, such as *Ojos de Dios* (Eyes of God), made by weaving colorful yarn on wooden crosses. María and other people who worked there remember it having five high-backed wooden booths lining opposite walls, with about five freestanding tables in the center of the room. Nailheads stuck out of some of the booths, sometimes snagging women's stockings. For its first several years of operation, the Nayarit's appearance could be described as rustic at best.

The new location got off to a slow start, but it received a boost in publicity in its first year of opening after two famous boxers—the Mexican Lauro Salas, who would go on to win the World Lightweight Championship title the next year, and the Mexican American Art Aragón, another top-ranked lightweight, nicknamed "the Golden Boy"—got into a fistfight in the middle of the dining room. Aragón was a ladies' man who had dated the actress Mamie Van Doren and could claim friendships with a string of starlets, including Marilyn Monroe, Jayne Mansfield, Sophia Loren, and Betty Martin (Dean Martin's former wife). His fight with Salas was over a woman, of course, though not one of these celebrities.[1] The no-holds-barred brawl lasted forty-five minutes and ended when the police broke it up, though many declared Salas, who knocked Aragón to the ground five times, the winner. When the two met the next year, in a sold-out match at Olympic Auditorium in Los Angeles, Aragón beat Salas. For years, Salas would remind María that the Olympic Auditorium bout was not the definitive contest, asking, "But who won the night we fought at the Nayarit?" and then answering his own question: "Me!" The real winner that night, though, was the Nayarit. News of the fight spread quickly. The *Daily News* ran the story of the fight on the front page, complete with the Nayarit's name and address. (In fact, the brawl at the Nayarit was credited for the Olympic Auditorium deciding to schedule the fight; promoters knew the buzz it had created would bring in a sell-out crowd, which it did.)[2] Business at the Nayarit grew quickly as new customers came, eager to see where the fight had taken place. Both boxers remained regulars. While the spectacle might have drawn customers, much more kept them coming back. The Nayarit developed into an urban anchor that offered its ethnic Mexican customers a rare opportunity for belonging. It was likely what had attracted both boxers there to begin with.

As the Nayarit developed a solid customer base, Doña Natalia expanded. In 1957, when she learned that the store next door was closing—it was owned, like her own space, by Joseph Nahama—she approached Nahama to inquire about leasing it. He agreed to lease it to her and to allow her to knock down the dividing wall and merge the two spaces, thus expanding the restaurant by almost 50 percent. The larger space gave her more room for seating and provided a banquet space for special events. Doña Natalia also took this opportunity to remodel, swapping out the hosiery-snagging wooden booths for new cushioned booths upholstered with deep-red vinyl and hanging framed oil paintings depicting Mexico on the walls.

In a city where Mexican immigrants often lacked unfettered access to public space, the Nayarit offered a sense of safety and community. For many immigrants, Mexican and others, daily life—whether taking public transportation to work, buying a cup of coffee, or going shopping—was often a process of making themselves invisible, of trying to take up as little space as possible, in the hope of avoiding discrimination or confrontation. In spaces like the Nayarit, the opposite was true: customers could become visible, speak out, and claim space; they could unfold to their true dimensions. They could belong.

Doña Natalia's restaurant offered excellent food and hospitality, but it was more than a place to get a meal. The Nayarit was a refuge where working people could speak their own language, eat their own food, and live out identities that went beyond what the workplace usually allowed. A house-keeper would change her uniform for a pretty dress, come to the restaurant, and feel transformed. A bricklayer would dust off the residue of the day and go to the place where he was known as the fellow with the great voice who sang with a trio. Families would come to have their Sunday dinners, their children dressed in dignified Sunday best.[3] People would visit with friends, flirt, step into the fullness of their lives. The placemaking that went on at the Nayarit was both convivial and political, and as those qualities shaped the atmosphere of Echo Park, they helped make the city worth living in.

CULINARY PLACEMAKING

The Nayarit was a pioneering restaurant, but Mexican food has deep roots in Los Angeles, not least because the city, along with much of the rest of California and the Southwest, once belonged to Mexico. Mexicans and their foodways remained in the United States after the US takeover, and into the twentieth century, Mexican food was sold from carts in the plaza near Olvera Street in downtown Los Angeles. Merchants, laborers, farmhands, servants, and hotel workers taking a quick lunch break could eat hearty fare like tamales, made of stick-to-your-ribs corn masa with a meat filling, and wash them down with *atole*, a thick corn-based drink. The rise of the automobile, the move of Mexicans to the Eastside, and the availability of more sit-down restaurants led to the demise of these street vendors.[4]

Figure 10. Mexican laborers gathered at the Plaza, ca. 1911. Bancroft Library, University of California, Berkeley.

Yet, in keeping with Progressive Era ideas about immigrants, public health workers, reformers, social workers, and teachers derided both the diet of Mexican immigrants and the way they handled food as both inferior to American standards and outright unhealthy. Perpetuating the stereotype of the "dirty Mexican," these attitudes conflated the lack of health and hygiene with immorality and poverty.[5] For example, after the 1920 infantile diarrhea outbreak in a Mexican community, a Los Angeles County Health Department (LACHD) report blamed the outbreak in part on "the ignorance of the parents handling food" instead of addressing structural inequalities, like access to clean water, that produced the unhealthy environments that hosted virulent diseases.[6] LACHD officials held Mexican mothers responsible for high infant mortality rates more broadly, saying the mothers harmed their children with "improper feeding" techniques and "unkempt" homes. In response, the LACHD officials recommended the "training of foreign mothers, especially the Mexican group, in modern preventive medicine."[7] Such strategies were very much in keeping with the attitudes of the time. Pearl Ellis, who worked in the Americanization Department of the Covina City School District, wrote a book titled *Americanization through Homemaking* based on her experiences working with Mexicans. She advocated the same sorts of policies the LACHD did: training Mexican girls in food preparation, home nursing, parenting skills, and sewing. According to Ellis, such training would be a "safeguard to the community," not just as a matter of public health, but also assimilation.[8] When simply preparing traditional food was enough to mark someone as a "bad mother," with an "unhygienic" and insufficiently "American" family, holding to that tradition could be an act of defiance.

Given such views, along with class differences and widespread segregation, perhaps it is not surprising that well into the twentieth century Mexican food was still unfamiliar to many residents. The food writer Colman Andrews, for example, was born in 1945, raised on Los Angeles's Westside, and ate out regularly with his family when he was growing up. Yet he did not eat at a Mexican restaurant until college, in the early 1960s; he described his visit to El Cholo this way: "When I opened the menu, I recognized almost nothing—tamale, enchilada, tostada, chile relleno . . . these were another language to me, literally and otherwise. I did see my old friend chili con carne, but I ended up ordering what looked like the safest thing (and I quote): HAMBURGER STEAK, with Chile Beans, Spaghetti and French Fried Potatoes."[9] Andrews's father, a successful screenwriter, never embarked on even this level of culinary adventure. "Shortly before my father's death, in 1976," Andrews wrote, "he asked me in all seriousness, after noticing a sign at a Mexican fast-food place we were passing, 'Just what *is* a taco, anyway?' At that point, he had lived in Southern California for more than thirty years."[10]

As a matter of commercial strategy, many Mexican restaurants adapted their menus to suit American tastes. That meant embracing a kind of culinary conformity that sapped Mexican food of its regional specificity, watered down tastes to placate American palates, and—especially on Olvera Street,

Tasting Home

Figure 11. Councilman Edward Roybal worked to improve public health services and to combat stereotypes of Mexicans, such as in this campaign. "'Is the Mexican diet adequate?' asks the California Health Department. 'Yes,' says Councilman E. R. Roybal, first Councilman of Mexican descent in more than 70 years. To prove it, he is sending them a tasty open face taco. Tostadas have more health-giving qualities than the American counterpart of cokes, hamburgers and potato chips, according to Roybal." Ca. 1950. Herald Examiner Collection, No. 37026, Los Angeles Public Library.

the epicenter for such restaurants in Los Angeles—served food in the ambience of the Spanish fantasy past.

Olvera Street's restaurant scene was anchored by the enormously successful Casa La Golondrina Cafe, known simply as La Golondrina, opened in 1930 by Consuelo Castillo de Bonzo, an immigrant from Aguascalientes,

Mexico.[11] Olvera Street was a stone's throw from downtown offices and government buildings, and many of the city's power elite became regular customers: Christine Sterling, *Los Angeles Times* publisher Harry Chandler, the mayor and other politicians, and power brokers. In the 1940s, the restaurant added a nightclub, attracting Hollywood royalty like Humphrey Bogart and Lauren Bacall. De Bonzo worked alongside Sterling to curry favor with the city's political elite for the betterment of Olvera Street and hosted their banquets at her restaurant. Operating a restaurant in a space designed, as one historian summed it up, as a "homogenized presentation of Mexico in the middle of an American city" offered unique opportunities as well as pressures.[12] According to the historian Phoebe Young, de Bonzo was continually torn about the restaurant's identity. She both "used and undermined romantic imagery" of her home country, even hiring "dancing señoritas" to attract white clientele. At the same time, she hoped the restaurant could lead to a "better understanding with Mexico" and used her success to support others, fundraising on behalf of Tampico, Mexico, after it was devastated by a flood in 1933.[13]

One year after de Bonzo opened La Golondrina, Blanche and George March, a white couple, opened El Coyote Mexican Cafe on Los Angeles's Westside, a neighborhood where Mexicans tended neither to live nor to venture. Blanche had grown up in Thatcher, Arizona, northeast of Tucson, and the dishes she had eaten there inspired El Coyote's menu.[14] The restaurant served traditional Mexican dishes, such as tacos, enchiladas, rice, and beans, but they were not always prepared traditionally; for instance, ground beef replaced the more typical cubed or shredded beef; orange cheese, rather than *queso fresco*, was *de rigueur*; and a blatantly Americanized dish called "El Coyote Pizza" was perennially popular. The formula worked, and the restaurant has been an L.A. landmark for decades. As Andrews wrote, "Though . . . [it] didn't have much to do with what people actually ate in Mexico, it quickly became for me an emblem of what I loved about Mexican food: It was

Figure 12. Celebration in honor of Mayor Sam Yorty at Casa La Golondrina, 1965. Left to right: Elizabeth "Betts" Yorty, Mayor Sam Yorty, Consuelo Castillo de Bonzo, and US Rep. Edward Roybal. De Bonzo is wearing the traditional Spanish *mantilla y peineta* (veil and comb). Box C1918, Sam Yorty Papers, Los Angeles City Archives.

friendly, accessible, fare. . . . [B]est of all it was foreign, but foreign in a way over which I could claim partial ownership as a native and longtime resident of a city whose original name was El Pueblo de Nuestra Señora la Reina de los Ángeles del Río de Porciúncula."[15]

Though El Coyote was far from Olvera Street, it too embraced the Spanish fantasy past, as did El Cholo, another successful Mexican restaurant at the time. Andrews captured the similarities between El Coyote and El Cholo: "For decades, Mexican restaurants around Southern California, and probably beyond, called themselves 'Spanish.'"[16] Alejandro and Rosa

Borquez opened the original El Cholo, at first named the Sonora Cafe, on the edge of downtown Los Angeles, near the Coliseum, in 1923. Three years later, their daughter Aurelia met George Salisbury, an Englishman, at the restaurant, and they married. The couple opened their own restaurant, also named El Cholo, on Western Avenue, just west of downtown Los Angeles. Andrews noted that El Cholo and El Coyote established what has now become a norm, serving salty chips with salsa, chased down by margaritas. El Cholo's margaritas included pineapple juice—far from standard in Mexico. It was also known for its seasonal green corn tamales and nachos thanks to a waitress from San Antonio who brought word of a relatively new dish growing in popularity across Texas. Joe Reina, a chef for over fifty years at El Cholo, described the cooking as "California-style Mexican food," adding, "I have been to Mexico many times and I haven't learned anything I can apply here."[17] Lack of authenticity certainly did not hurt the restaurant, which has continued to thrive for over ninety years and now has six locations.

In such a context, Doña Natalia's unapologetic commitment to offering authentic Mexican food outside an ethnic enclave was a political act.[18] It was also central to the restaurant's success. The word *authentic*, of course, is vexed. Culture is permeable and changing, and dishes anywhere will eventually adapt—to new tastes, to available ingredients, to the market where they are sold, and to the pressures of conquest and appropriation.[19] This process of adaptation is similar to what the scholar Vicki Ruiz has described as "cultural coalescence," the process by which "immigrants and their children pick, borrow, and retain and create distinctive cultural forms."[20] Some immigrants have consciously changed their diets to distance themselves from their ethnic backgrounds or social class. But insofar as Doña Natalia was able, with the ingredients available to her, she offered a regionally based cuisine.[21] She refused to sacrifice distinctiveness in order to accommodate mainstream American palates.

Seafood is a staple of the cuisine in coastal Nayarit, including a variety of shrimp-based dishes: shrimp soup, shrimp empanadas, shrimp *albondigas* (meatballs), and shrimp tamales. But high-quality shrimp was difficult to procure in Los Angeles, as was good fresh fish in general. Still, when Doña Natalia could get the right ingredients, she served *pescado zarandeado*, a whole fish seasoned with sauces, wrapped in foil, and cooked on an open flame. (It's the type of dish you might eat at an open-air restaurant on the beach in Nayarit, but I had not seen it on offer on a Los Angeles menu until I went to Orange County's Taco María, which won a Michelin star for its adaptations of regional Mexican cuisine in 2019.)

Doña Natalia was able to buy some ingredients in L.A., such as queso fresco, a soft, curdlike, white Mexican cheese, which she would use to garnish her dishes rather than the orange, usually cheddar cheese that was a staple ingredient in more mainstream American Mexican restaurants. Whenever she was able, she would make the three-hundred-mile round-trip drive to Tijuana, Mexico, on the California border, to procure special ingredients that were not easily available in Los Angeles. She would stock up on dried corn husks for tamales, canned chilis (which lasted longer than fresh ones), and bars of Mexican chocolate to be used for making hot chocolate. She also purchased large jars of mole paste—a combination of chilis, peanuts, sesame and pumpkin seeds, cocoa, and cinnamon—to serve as the base for the thick mole she used for enchiladas or to stew chicken in. Making mole from scratch is a laborious and time-intensive process, involving dozens of ingredients and sometimes days of preparation. By starting with a paste, Doña Natalia could make a dish usually reserved for special occasions available as a regular part of her menu, with her own enhancements. When she reconstituted the sauce, she would add house-made chicken broth, tomatoes, and salt and other spices, including cumin, oregano, cloves, and star anise.

Other staple dishes at the Nayarit included *chile colorado*, tender pieces of beef stewed in a bright-red chili sauce; *chile verde*, succulent pieces of pork cooked in a tangy, green tomatillo-based sauce; and *machaca*, shredded beef with chili and spices, sometimes combined with eggs, making it a favorite for dinner, breakfast, a late-night snack, or any time in between. Doña Natalia also served specialty dishes, such as her famous *manchamanteles costillas* (tablecloth-staining ribs, an allusion to the delicious splattery sauce), cooked in a broth of spices, garlic, onion, and three different kinds of chili; *lengua*, beef tongue cooked in spices, garlic, and tomato or tomatillos; and *birria*, spicy goat-meat stew scooped up with corn tortillas. Many of these dishes were from other parts of Mexico, but she cooked them in her own, regional style. In Acaponeta, for example, cooks make *gorditas*—a thick corn pocket stuffed with ingredients—bathed in a light tomato sauce made from chicken broth, fresh tomato, and a little garlic. Doña Natalia did not have gorditas on the menu—she opted for the less time-consuming option of serving tacos, which could be quickly assembled with stacks of tortillas at the ready—but she still topped her tacos with the same Nayarit-style tomato-based sauce.

Doña Natalia made some concessions to American ingredients and tastes. *Jocoque*, a fermented cow's milk product whose texture is close to yogurt, was unavailable in L.A. She replaced it with sour cream—similar but richer and more decadent. While corn tortillas are typical in Nayarit, the restaurant served both corn and flour tortillas, the latter of which are more common in northern states like Sonora and Chihuahua. This may have been a strategic appeal to a non-Mexican clientele. But Doña Natalia made sure they were fresh and delicious: handmade in the kitchen, they were a hallmark of the restaurant.

In 1964, the *Los Angeles Times* lauded the Nayarit's food as "superb," especially their *enchiladas rancheras*. (The reviewer also mentioned Doña Natalia and María as "proprietresses" who "have been operating for years and know their business.")[22] An article on the restaurant in the Nayarit paper, *El Eco*, that same year described the food as "verdaderamente apegada a nuestra auténtica y variada comida MEXICANA."[23] This phrase can be translated as "truly close to our authentic and varied Mexican food." When I asked Vicky Tavares, who worked as a busgirl at the Nayarit from 1961 to 1969, to explain the restaurant's popularity, her reply was simple: "Well, the food, of course." Some variation of this answer came up in almost every interview I conducted, with Mexicans and non-Mexicans alike. Sherryl and Darryl Mleynek told me that the Nayarit was their go-to spot for dinner in the mid-1960s, when they were young newlyweds living in Echo Park. "It's still our idea of the best in Mexican food," Sherryl told me, and it remains the standard by which she and Darryl measure other Mexican restaurants. "'It's good,' we'll say. But it's not the Nayarit," she laughed.[24]

The food was more than an experience of texture and taste. For customers who had immigrated from Nayarit, Doña Natalia's dishes were a portal to a home that at times in their lives in the United States must have felt very far away. Mexican immigrants from other parts of the country—including the Central Plateau, which neighbored Nayarit and was home to the majority of Mexican immigrants to the United States in the 1950s and 1960s—would have been familiar with these flavors too.[25] Even customers who had grown up eating different regional Mexican cuisines recognized that this food was special, connected to specific histories, imbued with pride in local traditions, and offered up in a spirit of welcome.

Most of the former Nayarit workers I interviewed also spoke about Doña Natalia's *carácter fierce* (strong character), embodied in her eagle-eyed supervision of the kitchen. At the original Nayarit, Doña Natalia had been the main cook, but as her business grew in the new location and as her rheumatoid arthritis worsened, she cooked less, only three or four hours a day, and trained other cooks to meet her exacting standards. Every day, she ensured that the ingredients were fresh, that the vegetables were cut evenly, that the correct cuts of meat were used and cooked to perfect tenderness, and that the portions were consistent. When in the kitchen, she sat on a stool next to the swinging doors to the dining room, eyeing every dish and occasionally tasting them before the waitstaff carried them out to the customers. If the sauce on a dish spread onto the edge of the plate, she would declare the plate *sucio* (dirty) and send the food back to be replated. If she suspected the cooks of cutting corners in meal preparation, her response was uncompromising: "A mi no me engañan, aquí revolvieron el guisado de ayer, esto no está fresco, no lo vamos a servir, prepárenlo de nuevo" (You can't fool me. You stirred in yesterday's stewed meat here. It's not fresh, and we're not going to serve it. Prepare it again).[26]

When Doña Natalia was not in the kitchen, she often sat in a corner booth at the back of the restaurant and watched the service at the front of the house. She made sure customers were seated promptly by the hostess, greeted quickly thereafter by their server, and received their food in a timely manner. Once the customers left, she made sure the table was bused and turned over quickly for the next customer. "She seemed so tall to me," remembered Alexis McSweyn, who had begun to visit the Nayarit regularly with her parents when she was nine. "I know that is partly because I was a child, but it was also that she just seemed so in charge, constantly watching over everything from her corner booth."[27] Rodolfo Lora, a former dishwasher, remembered that at the end of the day Doña Natalia might invite employees, including him, to sit and talk about how the day had gone and sometimes share a meal.[28]

The restaurant was open seven days a week, from 10:00 a.m. to 4:00 a.m. the next morning, and either Doña Natalia or María was almost always there. Doña Natalia mainly worked the day shift, from about ten in the morning until seven at night. By the time the Nayarit's Echo Park location had opened, María was eighteen and a high school graduate. She would often go to the restaurant for a couple of hours midday, pitching in where needed and touching base with Doña Natalia, and then go home to rest for her evening shift, from 5:00 p.m. to 4:00 a.m. María did not cook. Her main role was to take over where Doña Natalia left off, supervising the front of the house (or "floor"). She closed the restaurant at the end of the night, making sure all the food was put away properly, all the dishes done, all the tables wiped down, and all the condiments refilled, so that everything was ready when the restaurant reopened in a few hours. She also closed out the register, ensuring it was balanced and that all of the servers' checks were accounted for. Every few days, María also prepared the bank deposit, deposited the cash, and got change for the registers.

Doña Natalia was religious, but she and María did not regularly attend church. As the owner of her business, Doña Natalia probably could have taken a few hours off from her seven-day-a-week schedule each week to attend Mass had that been a priority to her. She likely did not attend because she had divorced and remarried, but she did pray and wear a cross. And though the Nayarit, unlike other Mexican restaurants, did not display any Catholic iconography or art, Doña Natalia kept a statue of Santo Niño de Atocha, who is said to protect travelers, in her office. She said she did not want Jesus or the saints to witness the fistfights, drunkenness, and other shenanigans that went on in the restaurant, but, presumably, Santo Niño de Atocha's position away from the dining room kept him well shielded.

While Doña Natalia was reserved and dignified, surveying the scene from her corner booth, María could seem to be her polar opposite, smiling and chatting with customers as she led them to their tables. She would pepper them with compliments, ask after their families, remember details they had shared with her in the past, and help them feel not just welcome, but special. She was an extrovert's extrovert, wired for working with the public. In fact, when customers wanted to meet or speak with Doña Natalia, she sometimes sent María out in her place. When I asked María if she enjoyed this role, she responded, "I loooved it!" That did not surprise me. She was a natural.

Both María and Doña Natalia took special care with their appearances. María, young, pretty, and shapely, contributed to the feeling of excitement and energy that marked the Nayarit as a go-to spot. In the daytime, she might wear her hair down or in a chic headscarf. On the weekends, when her customers were sure to be dressed to go out on the town, she would have her hair done, sporting everything from a posh flipped bob to a skyscraping 1960s beehive. And she wore full makeup: brilliant eye shadow in aqua blue or shades of green, heavy black liquid liner, false eyelashes, and her go-to glossy satin pink lipstick. She wore contoured sheath dresses that hugged her hourglass curves. Every worker and customer I interviewed, even those who did not remember her name, commented on her appearance. Men in their eighties looked bashful as they remembered her, saying things like, "That was your mom?! She was quite a looker." In the early 1990s, when I lived in Boyle Heights and was a regular at another urban anchor, El Tepeyac Cafe, the owner, Manuel Rojas, also commented on María's good looks, though he added that she had rebuffed him, leading him to conclude she was "stuck up."[29]

As a woman and an entrepreneur, Doña Natalia, like generations of women of color before her, understood that dress was an important part of signaling a "politics of respectability" to her community and to the white public she wished to have among her base of customers. Such comportment was especially important for a single woman whose restaurant stayed open late into the night.[30] She shopped for dresses at upscale department stores like Bullock's on Wilshire Boulevard, the iconic art deco flagship store, and Robinson's in downtown L.A., and she had a weekly hair appointment on Friday mornings. When she came to work, coiffed and elegant, her appearance reflected her status as a business owner as well as her supervisorial role.

Doña Natalia's commitment to quality helped ensure the business's success, but it would be wrong to understand her leadership in purely economic terms. Her standards were part of an aesthetic and political commitment to running a restaurant that could sustain Mexican customers emotionally as well as physically. They may have come to the United States as laborers, experienced exploitation and alienation, and even found themselves unable to communicate. But at the restaurant they were guests, served by people who spoke their native language, able to savor food they craved that connected them with home. María, too, recognized the dignity of the Nayarit's customers. Her friendliness was of a piece with what the New Orleans civil rights leader Jerome Smith described as "the song of saying 'good morning' and 'good evening,'" the communal music of showing "that you care for the other, [that you] recognize the humanity of the other."[31] To this day, when María visits restaurants in Los Angeles, she is often recognized by employees and customers who greet her enthusiastically and reminisce about the Nayarit. Sometimes they even pick up her check as a way of thanking her for that "good morning" or "good evening" decades before and for the sense of place and community that she and her mother nurtured.

A RESTAURANT AT WORK

The Nayarit served a wide variety of people, and its neon sign advertised, in English, "lunches," "dinners," and "food to go." But its core customers were working-class Mexicans who often worked in subordinate positions, as construction workers, gardeners, nannies, bricklayers, and workers at other restaurants.[32] Some of them—especially young, single men—were unable to cook at home because they lacked knowledge and time or because they lived in boardinghouses without access to a kitchen, even the space to cook. They may not have been able to speak in their own language at work, either because it was not allowed or because those they worked for did not speak Spanish. (Lest such restrictions sound like the product of an older and less progressive time, keep in mind that in 1998, California voters passed Proposition 227, primarily an anti-bilingual-education measure that championed a legal definition of English as the official state language. It was not repealed until 2016.) The Nayarit was a place where Mexicans knew they would be able to relax, speak in their mother tongue, and readily bump into friends and fellow nationals. Here, Latinx presence was not the exception but the rule. Residents of ethnic enclaves can find all this at their local establishments, but it was unusual for such camaraderie to take place in a multiethnic neighborhood in central Los Angeles.

The Nayarit's location on Sunset Boulevard helped ensure a steady and diverse clientele. Admittedly, located just two blocks from Sunset's intersection with Alvarado Street, it was about ten miles east and a world away from the iconic Sunset Strip, a one-and-a-half-mile stretch of restaurants, clubs, and shops in West Hollywood. In fact, when the television show *Ralph Story's Los Angeles* (1964–70), which covered L.A.'s people, places, and history, shot an episode described as "a drive down the entire twenty-five-mile length of Sunset Boulevard," Echo Park—definitely a part of those twenty-five miles—was considered too insignificant to feature.[33] Still, the Nayarit was close enough to downtown for city hall workers to come to the restaurant for lunch; baseball fans could stop by after a game at nearby Dodger Stadium; art and culture lovers could eat at the Nayarit before or after performances at the downtown Los Angeles Music Center or the Pantages Theater in Hollywood. In addition, a major bus line, the Number 2, ran along almost the entire length of Sunset Boulevard, making it possible for people from farther away who did not own a car to get to the Nayarit.

When the restaurant opened at 10:00 a.m., things tended to be slow, since most would-be customers had already eaten breakfast and were at work. Lunchtime was busy with downtown office workers coming in on their midday break. Dinner was busy too, with Echo Park residents, people stopping in before performances at nearby venues, and, most of all, workers grabbing a bite at the end of their workdays on their way home. And since the Nayarit, unlike many other Mexican restaurants, offered a full menu until closing, it attracted a substantial late-night crowd. Ramón Pack, a regular customer, saw it as an essential bookend to an evening out, explaining, "It was the place that you started the night at or ended the night at." There were routinely lines down the block to get in, especially after 2:00 a.m. when most other places had closed.

For many workers, eating out at the Nayarit was a symbolic way to wash off the relative servitude of their days. Some customers came after wrapping up work at a building site, hungry from long hours of hard labor. Others stopped in for a nightcap after finishing their shifts at restaurants and businesses that often served a wealthier, whiter clientele. There were busboys who had clocked out at the historic Ambassador Hotel, home to the Cocoanut Grove nightclub; bartenders who had cashed out at the Beverly Wilshire, which catered to movie stars and dignitaries; waiters who had been taking orders at the Brown Derby, located across the street from the Ambassador (and actually shaped like a derby hat); as well as cooks and waitresses at other local restaurants whose kitchens had closed for the night.

Since most restaurants were closed on Mondays, Monday nights at the Nayarit were crowded with restaurant workers enjoying their time off. Aurelia Guijarro Preciado, originally from Jalisco, Mexico, a state that borders Nayarit, would come to the restaurant with her husband, Francisco Preciado, on his night off. They lived in West Hollywood, where Francisco worked at La Rue, an elegant French restaurant (and the place where Ronald and Nancy Reagan met) that was owned by Billy Wilkerson, who also owned the famous Ciro's supperclub. Francisco started at La Rue as a dishwasher. When one of the sous chefs was out unexpectedly, he filled in chopping vegetables and eventually filled the position permanently. Aurelia remembered their visits to the Nayarit as high points in her week. "I looked forward to dressing up, seeing other people dressed up, and being in the *ambiente* (the ambience)," she told me.[34]

For singles and couples, the Nayarit was the place to see and be seen, especially on Friday or Saturday nights. Francine Rodriguez and her friends, regular customers during the late 1960s, considered it the quintessential date night restaurant, starting when they were in high school.[35] But the restaurant also had something of the atmosphere of a family table. It was not unusual to see Mexican customers say grace and bless themselves with the sign of the cross before they ate, unselfconsciously performing a religious ritual just as they would at home.[36]

Sundays, too, were particularly busy. Women raising families and perhaps holding down other jobs could declare their own kitchens closed for the day, go to the Nayarit, and have someone wait on them for a change. Friends lingered over their meals, catching up with one another, sometimes moving from table to table. Alexis McSweyn recalled that while her parents hosted family and friends on Friday nights to eat, drink, and play cards, they came to the Nayarit on Sundays. Her parents were both ethnic Mexicans—her mother was from Metcalf, Arizona, an old mining town, and her stepfather was from Mexico—and they would stay at the restaurant for hours, joined by a constant flow of friends and relatives who were also visiting the Nayarit on their day off.[37]

Other customers, less eager to socialize or simply wanting to keep costs down, ordered takeout. Óscar López remembers his father, José, picking up food at the Nayarit on Sundays when he wanted to give his wife, Celia Leticia, a break from cooking for their seven-person family. José had grown up on a small ranch outside of Tepic, the capital of Nayarit, and Celia was from the neighboring state of Jalisco. José came to the United States as a bracero, found work in an orange grove in Santa Ana after the program ended, and was sponsored by his employer so that he could attain a green card and continue working as a foreman on the farm. It was strenuous work, and after friends advised him that restaurant jobs were less draining, he moved the family to L.A., eventually finding stable employment at the Beverly Wilshire in Beverly Hills. Óscar López recalls going with his dad to the Nayarit, toting a large kitchen pot from home. They would get the pot filled with a hearty soup, such as *cocido*, a Mexican beef stew, and pick up a stack of warm, freshly handmade tortillas.[38] It gave Celia some rest and helped the family maintain connections to home.

The restaurant did not obtain a liquor license until 1968. It was not uncommon for customers to discreetly take out a bottle of spirits to add to their soda or coffee, particularly late at night.[39] During these hours, the atmosphere was sometimes charged with a sense of romantic or sexual possibility, not unlike what patrons might experience at a nightclub. Vicky Tavares remembered that "there were always a lot of women" at the Nayarit, most of whom came with friends rather than alone. At the same time, women knew they could enjoy being out at the restaurant without having to navigate the types of sexually tinged encounters that pervaded nightclubs.

When I asked María who, apart from shift workers, would come to the Nayarit at 2:00 a.m. on a weekday, she replied, "There was always an event," and when it ended a fresh wave of customers would arrive.[40] Venue owners, particularly those who were not Latinx, and a few who were, were reluctant to take a chance by giving one of their lucrative Friday or Saturday spots to Mexican performers. So ethnic Mexican artists tended to perform midweek.[41] The Nayarit's central location made it a popular spot before or after a show or concert. Doña Natalia capitalized on this synergy, having her employees put flyers on car windshields just before the big Latin music dances held at nearby clubs ended for the night.

The name of the restaurant, the Nayarit, signaled Doña Natalia's love of patria chica, and served as a beacon for fellow nationals, whether they resided in Los Angeles or were visiting from Mexico. Guadalupe "Lupe" Reyes, a native of the Nayarit region, was living in East Los Angeles, which did not lack for Mexican fare, when she heard about the Nayarit and felt compelled to try it on the basis of its name. She first came to the restaurant as a customer in the 1960s and later worked there as a waitress. Nayaritas who still lived in Nayarit would come, too, on visits to Los Angeles, just as Doña Natalia's advertisement in *El Eco* had encouraged them to do.[42] In my interviews, people consistently said that when visiting Los Angeles, if you didn't visit the Nayarit, you didn't really visit Los Angeles. As a longtime waiter said, "Era un sitio obligado" (It was an essential site to visit).

The name could even have significance for non-Latinx customers; according to María, it sometimes served as a conversation starter about where the owner was from and questions about what Nayarit was like. In response, Nayarita employees could boast about their home state. Even though she had been born in the United States, María, too, responded to such questions with the pride of a native-born Nayarita. The close connections and affective bonds between Nayarit and Los Angeles, maintained through visits back and forth and the tight-knit community in Los Angeles—and especially at the restaurant—functioned for her as a source of what the sociologist Tomás Jiménez calls "replenished ethnicity."[43] Many years later, when she would take our family back to Nayarit, we understood that though Echo Park was home, Nayarit was too.

Doña Natalia also spread the word about the Nayarit to her fellow nationals by advertising on KWKW, one of L.A.'s oldest Spanish radio stations, thereby weaving her restaurant into the mental map of countless Los Angeles residents. The advertisements often were broadcast during Martín Becerra's daytime show. Becerra, a former music star, was known as the "housewife DJ," as women comprised his main listening audience.[44] He was a regular at the Nayarit and a friend of Doña Natalia. Even outside the paid advertising spots, Becerra would talk up the Nayarit on his show and when he emceed shows at the Million Dollar Theater, a popular Latinx nightspot, promoting it as his late-night go-to spot and praising specific dishes; he particularly loved "las costillas," the ribs.[45] Becerra was an esteemed figure in the Mexican community, so his personal endorsement carried a lot of weight.

Beginning in 1959, KWKW hosted the Spanish-language broadcast of Dodgers games, announced by Jaime Jarrín.[46] Jarrín, a native Ecuadorean and future baseball Hall of Famer, was also a regular at the restaurant. Years later he recalled, "It was a historic place in Los Angeles. Who didn't speak of [it]?" "For [Latinx] people in the 1950s and 1960s," he continued, "it was the ideal place to have a nice time, to 'saborear' [savor] delicious Mexican food, to 'saborear' the Mexican ambience." Whenever he visited the Nayarit, he said, he knew he would bump into friends.[47]

At a time when most established Latinx placemakers and urban anchors were Mexican, Mexican spaces became pan-Latinx spaces by default. The Nayarit drew a varied group of Latinx immigrants from different countries of origin who, despite historical, cultural, and religious differences, shared enough in common to feel comfortable together, eating and socializing in a shared space. This social comfort seems to reflect a version of the pan-Latinx identity scholars have termed *Latinidad*, "a collective sense of cultural affinity and identity deeply rooted in what many Latinos perceive to be a shared historical, spiritual, aesthetic, and linguistic heritage."[48] Scholars trace this phenomenon to the dramatic increase in immigration from Latin America and Asia that followed the Immigration and Nationality Act of 1965, which abolished the national quota system established by the Immigration Act of 1924. It was this rise in numbers and diversity of a Latin American population that made a pan-Latinx identity possible, at least from a demographic standpoint. To be clear, none of the patrons of the Nayarit would have recognized the term "Latinidad," which academics did not introduce until the 1980s.[49] Nor would they have considered themselves Latina/o, a term that came into wide use only in the 1970s and 1980s.[50] They would have called themselves Mexican, or Cuban, or Puerto Rican. Nevertheless, even before the Immigration and Nationality Act of 1965, a broader, more intertwined pan-Latinx identity was emerging, and spaces like the Nayarit helped nurture it.[51] For example, Angeleno Roberto Tejada, son of Colombian immigrant parents, remembered how after his parents settled in Los Angeles, they found in the Nayarit a welcoming site of sociability that provided them with a sense of pan-Latinx identity.[52]

The Spanish language, in particular, acted as a unifying force. Anyone whose language and culture are vilified knows the visceral reaction when out in a public space and hearing that language spoken. Your ears prick up and your head whips around to find the source, to feel connected. Your heart aches with relief or nostalgia, or both.[53] At the Nayarit, Spanish was a constant, allowing patrons a powerful sense of freedom and recognition. Speaking Spanish in public, speaking it loudly, proudly, even boisterously, being able to order your meal without having to have someone translate the menu for you or place your order, singing "Las Mañanitas" (the traditional Mexican birthday song)—all this felt empowering. It was a form of what the scholar Gaye Johnson calls "spatial entitlement."[54] Certainly, Latin American and Caribbean Spanish speakers use the language in different ways, and unofficial hierarchies judge some countries' Spanish to be more correct than that of others. But for this group of immigrants away from their homelands and finding solace at the Nayarit, differences in Spanish could become a source of enjoyment. Workers and customers playfully adopted each other's accents and slang. Ethnic Mexicans, for example, would try to imitate the dropped consonants of a Cuban accent.

The largest group of non-Mexican Latinx people in Echo Park were Cubans who had fled the island after 1959, when Fidel Castro took power. The first waves of exiles were predominantly middle-class people with educations and professions, but their degrees and certifications often were not recognized in the United States. These individuals found work where they could, former dentists and lawyers becoming busboys and waiters. Such jobs became another means for Mexicans and Cubans to meet and find common ground and pan-Latinx solidarity—both on the job and after work. Ramón Pack, who was born in Cuba, worked as a bartender and frequented the Nayarit when he was done with his shifts. He recalled, "To meet a Cuban in Los Angeles in the 1960s was something magical. Most of the Cubans I met, I met at the Nayarit." The Nayarit was particularly important for Ramón because he did not know many people in the city. He immigrated from Cuba to Miami in 1962 and then moved to Los Angeles under the US government's Cuban Refugee Program (started in 1961), which provided funds for resettlement, along with monthly assistance, temporary health benefits, and job training. Ramón chose Los Angeles because he had an aunt who lived there. He spoke of Doña Natalia with the gratitude of a guest to a generous host, crediting her with giving the Cubans who frequented the restaurant "una entrada muy bonito" (a very nice entrance, or start), something that included introductions to one another, as well as connections to a broader community.

Ramón recalled one of the Nayarit's waiters, Carlos Porras, as being especially helpful connecting him with other Cubans: "Nos reunió" (He brought us together), Ramón recalled. Carlos Porras eventually also played matchmaker to Ramón and his future wife, Evelia Díaz Barraza, the cashier at the Nayarit and Doña Natalia's niece. When I asked Ramón what he thought Carlos's motivation was for the introduction, he replied, "He knew what we were going through."[55] Carlos was not an immigrant himself but a migrant, originally from Kansas, whose family had moved to Texas for agricultural work. He knew the challenges involved in relocating to a new place with little or no family around to buffer the experience. And as a Mexican American, he could easily draw on a shared history of racism and discrimination, all of which allowed him to build affective bonds with his Cuban customers. The support Doña Natalia and Carlos Porras demonstrated allows us to see how Latinx did not operate exclusively within the immigrant networks of their own country, or need to be immigrants themselves, to play an important role in the settlement process. These pan-Latinx affinities were framed less by a shared country of origin, as they would be with immigrants, and more by a shared experience of movement and migration and resettlement in a country (and city) where both shared similar experiences and spaces.[56]

This is not to say that Cubans did all their placemaking in primarily Mexican spaces like the Nayarit. The churches in the neighborhood were especially good resources, providing English-language courses and meeting spaces for new arrivals from Cuba. St. Athanasius Episcopal Church, located directly across from Echo Park Lake, for example, was home to a Cuban club starting in 1962. A Cuban émigré also established a small newspaper, *20 de Mayo*, based in Echo Park and named for the date in 1902 when Cuba gained formal independence. With the support of the Cuban Chamber of Commerce, the Cuban community had the city install a bust of José Martí, a hero of the Cuban independence struggle, at the north entrance to Echo Park Lake along Glendale Boulevard. Cubans also established their own urban anchors like El Carmelo Bakery, where they and other Latinx people congregated for their *cafecito* (espresso with sugar) and *pastelitos de guayaba y queso* (puff pastries filled with guava and cheese); the legendary Porto's Bakery, which now has five locations across Los Angeles County and Orange County, got its start a couple miles east in neighboring Silver Lake.[57] These businesses were all within a few blocks of one another and of the Nayarit. Together, they helped stamp Echo Park as an entry point for people starting or rebuilding their lives.

The Nayarit offered another, somewhat more fraught form of safety: LAPD officers were regulars at the restaurant, lured not just by the good food but also by the comped meals offered if they were in uniform. In return, officers regularly drove by the Nayarit to send a signal that this was not a business to be robbed. Given the long history of tensions between the LAPD and the ethnic Mexican community this may be surprising.[58] But Doña Natalia sought cultural brokers to help her in areas where she lacked skills or connections, and a few comped meals were a small price to pay for protection of a business run by two women that operated into the wee hours of the night.

The restaurant also attracted famous actors, musicians, and athletes of both American and Latinx backgrounds. Occasionally, they would ask to eat in privacy, without the interruption of fans, and the restaurant staff would seat them out of public view in the small bussing station between the front of the house and the kitchen. Most of the time, though, they were in the dining room, contributing to the cosmopolitan atmosphere. Some could have been assured a welcome wherever they went, but many of the Latinx stars who visited, even though they had earned considerable fame, continued to experience and witness discrimination on the job and in their daily lives. Their welcome in the mostly white spaces in which they worked was limited to their role as performers and entertainers; metaphorically, and often literally, they had to use the service entrance, not the front door. They too needed somewhere where they felt they could belong.

The Puerto Rican actress and singer Rita Moreno, whose portrayal of Anita in the movie *West Side Story* gave young Latinas (including me) their first chance to see someone who looked like them in an important Hollywood role, came to the Nayarit occasionally during the several years she lived in Los Angeles. The Mexican cinema star Emilio Fernández, nicknamed "El Indio," also frequented the restaurant. In addition to acting, El Indio was a screenwriter and director. He won the Grand Prix, the highest prize then offered at the Cannes Film Festival, in 1946 for his direction of the film *María Candelaria*.

Musicians and singers came to the restaurant after they had finished their sets. Some were famous: Tito Puente, dubbed the "King of Latin Music"; Xavier Cugat, the Spanish American bandleader; Abbe Lane, the Jewish singer, dancer, and actress; and the Swedish American Latin jazz musician Cal Tjader. Other, less well-known entertainers stopped in after performing at local clubs like Club Virginia's in MacArthur Park or Club Havana in Silver Lake, helping the restaurant buzz with activity late into the night.[59]

The restaurant was just a mile from Dodger Stadium, and although the Dodgers had very few Latino ballplayers in the 1950s and 1960s, other Major League teams did, including a number of players from Puerto Rico and the Dominican Republic. The players who showed up at the Nayarit were mostly from visiting teams. Ramón Pack recalled, "You knew when the Dodger game was over because you would see the players at the Nayarit."[60] The Dominican brothers Felipe, Jesús, and Matty Alou, one of baseball's noted families, who for a short period in 1963 all played for the San Francisco Giants, were customers when they were in town. Giants player Juan Marichal, also from the Dominican Republic, visited the Nayarit frequently enough to become friends with María. He would sit and talk to her while she closed up. While Jackie Robinson had broken the color line in baseball, segregation was still legal in the United States, and Black and Latinx players, some of whom were Afro-Latinx, often had to stay in separate hotels and eat in separate restaurants from their teammates, as well as experience discrimination from both their opponents and their own managers and teammates.[61] Though the players had more money and social status than many of the Nayarit's working-class customers, their dark skin and accented English—if they spoke English at all—left them vulnerable to discrimination. Spaces like the Nayarit were an important haven for them, just as the restaurant was for many other Latinx customers, whether they were establishing themselves in Los Angeles or traveling through town. In the absence of a *Green Book*-type resource mapping out safe spaces for Mexican and other Latinx immigrants, word of mouth and the Nayarit's neon sign served as a beacon, announcing that this was a place where Latinx customers could experience a sense of belonging.[62]

Some of those who were attracted to the Nayarit were people who had crossed ethnic and racial lines in their personal lives already. At a time when mixed-race couples were often denied service at restaurants, the Nayarit welcomed them. Abbe Lane and Xavier Cugat found it a place of refuge. Marlon Brando, who enjoyed the company of Latinx women (and dated Rita Moreno on and off for several years starting in 1954) was a regular customer.[63] Brando was friendly with many of the staff at the Nayarit and always sat in the waitress Eva Díaz's section. Brando and María got along very well; the two would sit and talk when he visited the restaurant. Brando also occasionally asked out women he met at the Nayarit, including the restaurant's eighteen-year-old cashier, Evelia Díaz Barraza, who sometimes joined him at his table while he ate. Before she could accept the invitation, Evelia had to ask permission of Doña Natalia, who was not only her boss but also her aunt and guardian. According to an often-repeated family story, when Doña Natalia asked her niece what Brando wanted, Evelia replied that he said that "he wanted to make love," not understanding what the phrase meant. Doña Natalia made sure Brando went home alone that night. He remained a loyal customer. During the Christmas season, the Nayarit staff often distributed promotional keepsakes to their loyal customers; one year they gave out embossed leather wallets. Brando carried his Nayarit wallet for years, suggesting a sentimental attachment to the restaurant.

Doña Natalia and her workers did not try to whitewash Mexican culture to make it more palatable to a white clientele.[64] Unlike other successful Mexican restaurants in L.A. at the time, the Nayarit did not participate in culinary conformity or seek to perform a Mexican identity for a non-Mexican audience. Instead, it helped customers and workers alike counter the pervasive, degrading images of Mexicans in US society with a sense of pride and belonging. On September 16 every year, the restaurant celebrated Mexican Independence Day. The hostesses donned traditional Mexican dress from Nayarit, with colorful cross-stitch embroidery depicting designs such as flowers, eagles, and water. The staff proudly displayed the Mexican flag, and everyone partook in the "Grito," a long shout traditionally called out after eleven o'clock on the night of September 15, followed by cries of "¡Viva México!" These were not promotional undertakings to attract customers (as commonly happens at Mexican restaurants today on Cinco de Mayo). Instead, they were occasions for Mexican workers and regulars alike to connect with their history and celebrate together.

Sometime in the mid-1960s, the organizers of the Hollywood Christmas Parade, which had long been a mostly white affair, invited Doña Natalia to sponsor a float. The parade, held annually the Sunday after Thanksgiving, was a chance for local businesses to show themselves off and attract shoppers to the area. Doña Natalia agreed.[65] She paid $900 for the float and entrance fee—about $7,000 in today's dollars, not an insignificant sum—and was left to decide how it should be decorated to best represent the restaurant. As a rule, light-skinned metropolitan ethnic Mexican elites emphasized Iberian rather than Indigenous identity. A float from the 1957 annual Mexican Independence Day parade in East Los Angeles provides an example: ethnic Mexican participants atop it are dressed in traditional *charro* outfits with tight pants and short embroidered jackets—a style of dress that represents a more elite and "Spanish" Mexican identity. A woman who appears to be a beauty pageant winner rides at the front of the float. Symbols of cooperation and assimilation abound: a charro shakes hands with Uncle Sam beneath the Mexican and American flags. Across the front of the float is a banner that reads, "Latin American."

Doña Natalia chose instead to display the Nayarit's Indigenous heritage, which was already subtly present in the very name of the restaurant, which comes from a revered leader of the Indigenous Cora people.[66] Instead of charro outfits, the six staff and visiting family members on the float dressed in the attire of the Huichol, another Indigenous people from Nayarit and neighboring Jalisco. They wore white cotton, cross-stitched by hand with vibrantly colored designs that symbolized water and wildlife, as well as hats made with palm leaves with colorful beads that hung down from the brim. The decision to wear these clothes in the parade is noteworthy, given the emphasis on assimilation—either embraced by Mexicans or forced on them—that had dominated Mexican life in the United States for several decades.[67] Indigenous identity was not widely celebrated; in fact, it could be dangerous. Until just over two decades earlier, people claiming Indigenous roots could be barred from naturalizing—or could have their citizenship revoked, as evidenced by generations of legal cases challenging Mexicans' rights to naturalize.[68] Not until the Nationality Act of 1940 were "descendants of races indigenous to the Western Hemisphere" recognized as groups eligible for

Figure 13. Float for the 1957 Mexican Independence Day Parade. Los Angeles Times Photographic Archives (Collection 1429). UCLA Library Special Collections, Charles E. Young Research Library, University of California, Los Angeles.

naturalization. For parade-goers in the know, the Nayarit's float would have signaled both patria chica and the fact that, like Echo Park more broadly, the Nayarit was an inclusive space in which people could be themselves.

In some cities, like New York and Barcelona, people are said to live in restaurants because they prefer to socialize there rather than in their small apartments. Restaurants become integral parts of their social worlds. Los Angeles in the 1950s was not such a city, but Nayarit was such a restaurant. "There were other Mexican restaurants, but the Nayarit had something special," recalled Jaime Jarrín. "Indisputably, the Nayarit was the number one place." The excellent food, lively atmosphere, and late hours alone would

Figure 14. The Nayarit's float in the Hollywood Christmas Parade, mid-1960s. Photograph provided by María Perea Molina.

have made the Nayarit many people's go-to spot. But its appeal ran deeper than that: it was an urban anchor that gave solace and strength to the Latinx community in and around it. Unlike a school, a swimming pool, or even a beach, the Nayarit afforded Mexicans and Latinx immigrants an uncontested public space. They were in a city with a history of segregation and in a nation that largely saw Mexicans as one-dimensional laborers. But at the Nayarit, Mexican customers were served by people who looked like them, spoke their language, shared their customs, and accepted them. While Mexicans were the restaurant's core clientele, other groups that did not easily fit into the dominant culture found refuge there too. These varied groups had something in common: they were making constant calculations as to where they could go in order to merely feel at ease. At the Nayarit, under the care of Doña Natalia, María, and other immigrant employees, they could let their guard down and enjoy themselves and one another. They became insiders.

CHAPTER THREE

The Emotional Life of Immigration

In 1953, Pedro Cueva decided to immigrate from Acaponeta, Nayarit, to Los Angeles. He was eighteen years old, gay, and tired of being harassed by boys his age and people on the town square. His family loved and supported him, but he was ready for a change. Pedro had trained to be a pianist but otherwise had few marketable skills, and prospects for young men in his situation were limited. As a matter of statistics, the likeliest path for Pedro—assuming he was fortunate enough to secure a visa—would have been to a job in the fields or performing manual labor.[1] But he was lucky. His tía Natalia owned a restaurant and had a track record of helping family members get settled in the city. She could provide him with a job as a waiter at the Nayarit, the proof of employment letter required to obtain a visa, and a place to live, in her own home, with María, in Echo Park.

Pedro disliked restaurant work, however, and candidly told his aunt he really wanted to find a job as a musician. As the Nayarit became more successful and Doña Natalia was able to obtain an entertainment license, she hired Pedro as the restaurant's resident piano player. Over the years, she worked hard to help her nephew establish himself: not just in a job that earned him a wage, but one that honored his talent; not just with a roof over his head, but with a social network; not just with the bare necessities of life, but with pleasure and community. And while the United States was certainly not free of homophobia, Pedro was able to establish a more open life in the accepting neighborhood of Echo Park than Acaponeta would have allowed.

Although Doña Natalia and Pedro called each other aunt and nephew, he was in fact a more distant relation: his mother's brother had married Doña Natalia's half sister, Gregoria "Goya" Barraza de Díaz, who lived in Acaponeta. Anthropologists and sociologists call such relationships—in which people think of one another as a family based on their affective ties—"fictive kinship." Like familial relationships, fictive kinships come with a sense of duty, responsibility, and mutual obligation, which is one reason that, as the anthropologist Robert Alvarez has shown, such relationships have been integral supports for Mexican immigrants to the United States.[2] In Mexico, fictive kinship includes *compadrazgo*, the relationships formalized between parents, godparents, and children during religious ceremonies like baptism and first communion. Compadrazgo does not translate precisely into English, but *compadre* and *comadre*, which parents and godparents of a child call one another, literally mean "co-father" and "co-mother." The fictive kinship that Doña Natalia nurtured at the Nayarit was not rooted in religious ceremony but in a shared sense of place, a collective affinity for their patria chica and a shared experience in the community created by and around the Nayarit. Taken in the aggregate, it created compadrazgo. Like a godparent at a Catholic confirmation ceremony, she sponsored people on their journeys. Doña Natalia was a single woman, and a divorcée at that, but as she provided aid, employment, and housing to dozens of family and fictive kin, she assumed the status usually reserved for a family's patriarch.

Through my interviews, I identified sixty-eight people whom Doña Natalia helped through the immigration and/or settlement process between 1951, when she opened the Nayarit in Echo Park, and 1968, when her health began to deteriorate. These people—about half of them women and half of them men—were a mix of kin and fictive kin and lifelong friends and their children, as well as people she met when they took jobs at her restaurant. She helped them successfully integrate into the United States and move up the proverbial ladder.[3] In the decades to come, sociological literature would confirm that the same strategies she used were, in fact, best practices. As an urban anchor, the Nayarit gave los de afuera both work and a way to expand their social networks.[4] She regularly invited newcomers to stay in her home for their first weeks, months, or even years in the United States, allowing them to plug into her own community, share in her middle-class comforts, and benefit from the care and support of family.[5]

Kinship networks kept Doña Natalia connected to Nayarit, but at the restaurant, she was oriented to a future in the United States. At the same time, she was concerned with far more than the bottom line. She made business decisions in tandem with her commitment to caring for others, and the new immigrants she supported both deepened and benefited from her place-making efforts. With a shared affinity for their patria chica and a shared experience in the community created by and around the Nayarit, immigrant workers felt a sense of obligation to help one another in the settlement process, too, whether by offering a couch to sleep on or introducing people to their own families, friends, and possible employers.

Many of the employees at the Nayarit were gay; others were women—sometimes young and single and sometimes, like Doña Natalia herself, older and divorced. Even as she maintained careful control over her business, gay and female employees were able to achieve a level of independence and self-realization that had they stayed in Nayarit might not have been possible. They benefited from their mutual care and from the welcoming atmosphere of Echo Park itself.

Pedro had been living with Doña Natalia and María in the United States for seven years when, under Doña Natalia's sponsorship, his mother, María del Rosario ("Chayo") Díaz Cueva, who was divorced, and his sisters, twenty-year-old Eduwiges ("Vicky") and fifteen-year-old Luisa, followed him to Los Angeles. Then the family got a place of their own. Their stories—like those of other employees whose lives unfolded in and out of the Nayarit—remind us that immigrant spaces were host to intertwined forms of emotion, mutual obligation, and kinship. Natalia Barraza was one of countless immigrants who after arriving and setting up a life for themselves labored to help others make similar journeys and transitions. Such people—not satisfied with personal survival and success in this new country—comprise an essential feature of the immigrant experience, though they are not always acknowledged in our perceptions of how immigration works. That lack of acknowledgment may have been how Doña Natalia preferred it. She thought that helping others was just what you did, and she did it well.

THE JOURNEY TO *EL OTRO LADO*, THE OTHER SIDE

In a study of Chinese immigrant workers at the turn of the twentieth century, the scholar Heather Lee writes that "restaurants were . . . sites of a complex network of chain migration, labor, and familial obligation."[6] Lee has found several cases of Chinese business owners who went into food service for the express purpose of helping others migrate. Restaurant owners were regarded as merchants and thus could sponsor immigrants, a loophole Chinese business owners used to circumvent the 1882 Chinese Exclusion Act. Many Chinese restaurants had several owners, so that each could use that position to help others immigrate. Doña Natalia was not using the Nayarit as a front for an immigration ring—she needed her business to earn income—but her restaurant, too, facilitated immigration.[7] Many of the family members and fictive kin whom she employed had no restaurant experience and needed a great deal of training. But her dedication to them increased their allegiance to her, to one another, and to the restaurant itself.

Strengthened by these rich, affective ties, the Nayarit became an urban anchor for immigrants.

But before immigrants could partake of Doña Natalia's placemaking practices, they needed to find a way to immigrate to the United States, preferably legally. Whether immigrants were documented shaped the possibilities available to them before, during, and after immigration.

Doña Natalia understood the necessity of having one's papers in order. During her lifetime, she saw the policies on immigrant documentation become increasingly stringent. With the passage of the Alien Registration Act of 1940, immigrants, both documented and undocumented, were required to go to their local post office to register with the US Immigration and Naturalization Service (INS). Then, no matter their legal status, they received an Alien Registration Receipt Card (Form AR-3) confirming proof of registration. This is how Doña Natalia received the initial paperwork to become a permanent US resident (she never became a citizen). After World War II, the INS began to issue different kinds of Alien Registration Receipt Cards to reflect immigrant admission status: the I-94C was for visitors; the I-100a was for temporary foreign laborers; and the coveted Form I-151, commonly referred to as a "green card" because of its color, gave immigrants the ability to work and live in the United States permanently. As the Cold War began, the passage of the Internal Security Act of 1950 made laws against the undocumented more punitive. Those who had both proof of legal immigration and an AR-3 card could exchange it for a Form I-151,[8] but those who were undocumented were subject to prosecution for violating US immigration laws. The act also ordered that all immigrants who were or had been Communist Party members be excluded from entry or deported. In some cases, communism was used to justify stripping naturalized citizens of their citizenship. Having one's legal paperwork in order was more important than ever.

By 1965, documented immigration from Mexico to the United States had become extraordinarily difficult without a family connection. The Bracero

Program, which for two decades had provided 450,000 guest worker visas each year, officially ended. Resident visas were harder to obtain, too: under the national quota system established in 1924, 50,000 resident visas had been set aside for Mexican immigrants each year, but the 1965 Immigration Act established an annual ceiling of 120,000 from the entire Western Hemisphere. (It imposed a 170,000-person limit on the Eastern Hemisphere.) The 1965 Immigration Act also continued several changes first established by the 1952 McCarran-Walter Act, including giving preference to the family members of citizens (particularly parents, spouses, children, and siblings of US citizens), as well as to immigrants with professional, technical, and other labor market skills deemed valuable to US employers. And yet, because of global wage inequities and US reliance on cheap labor, many Mexicans continued to immigrate anyway. In the wake of the new laws, there was a sharp rise in immigration *sin papeles* (without papers).[9]

Under the Bracero Program, documented Mexican immigrants had already been treated as disposable workers within a system of racial capitalism, their labor extracted with no regard for their humanity. To apply for guest worker visas under the program, men often traveled hundreds of miles from their hometowns to cities that had recruitment centers, where they underwent intrusive health exams. Those who were selected were contracted to perform grueling stoop labor, bent over or squatting to reach crops. Conditions were typically far worse than their contracts had promised, with temporary and ramshackle housing, inedible food, woefully unsanitary bathroom facilities, and inadequate health care, even in cases of dire accidents. With little local oversight, braceros were at the mercy of their employers. They knew that if they complained they could simply be replaced and be forced to return to Mexico. To leave the job would nullify their visas, rendering them undocumented and, hence, deportable.

Although the program ended, US employers' demand for Mexican laborers did not. Indeed, many American employers hired undocumented labor not in spite of those workers' legal status but because of it: it ensured a cheap and even more vulnerable, more easily exploitable workforce. Undocumented workers' complaints about being shortchanged on a paycheck, overcharged at the company store, or living in subpar conditions in work camps could lead to the employer or foreman simply calling the Border Patrol to take them all away—conveniently before payday. No matter where they were employed, or by whom, no matter if they ran their own businesses, no matter how long they had lived in the United States, and no matter if their own spouses, children, or grandchildren were US citizens, the undocumented—then as now—lived with the specter of deportation.[10] Even those who were documented themselves but lived with undocumented family members might limit their interactions with any kind of government entity (colleges and universities, financial aid offices, social services, hospitals and public health services) to avoid putting their family at risk. Although Mexicans had some privileges relative to African Americans, in that they were legally classified as white and could walk the color line in some ways, "illegality" was an axis that nullified that ability.

Tangibly and intangibly, being documented meant lower costs and fewer risks than being undocumented. Obtaining a visa cost much less, and was infinitely safer, than traveling with a "coyote," or smuggler. Once documented immigrants were settled, they had more opportunities for higher-paying jobs; in fact, having legal status was even more important than level of education in determining a migrant's potential income. Being documented also made it possible for immigrants to leave their jobs without leaving the country, transitioning instead to new positions in the United States. Documented immigrants were likelier to take advantage of opportunities that would help them get ahead, like English-language courses, and even if they were not citizens, they could get a driver's license and move freely across the city or even the country in search of employment or leisure. Those with green cards were eligible for workers' compensation. And because documented immigrants could legally return home to visit their families, they did not live with the same emotional burdens as undocumented immigrants, who might be separated from their loved ones for months or years.[11]

In a study of documented and undocumented immigrants from El Salvador, the sociologist Leisy Abrego found that documented immigrants displayed a "level of entitlement not evident in the narrative of undocumented immigrants," which she attributed to their being "unburdened by the repressive features of illegality."[12] Having a sponsor like Doña Natalia relieved immigrants of the burdens of illegality. Without such support, immigrating legally from Mexico was nearly impossible. Those who tried would register their intent to apply for an immigrant visa to the United States and then be put on a waiting list, on which they might languish for five, ten, or even fifteen years.[13] But Doña Natalia was prepared to help her family and fictive kin navigate the process legally and relatively quickly.

The first step in Doña Natalia's sponsorship came in the form of helping people *arreglar sus papeles* (fix their papers) and amass the documentation required to register for an immigration visa. As a business owner, Doña Natalia provided an affidavit stating that a would-be immigrant had a job waiting in the United States and thus would not likely become a public charge. She often covered the fees associated with applying for visas and green cards.[14] Most of the immigrants Doña Natalia sponsored were from small towns with limited employment opportunities, and though they were not destitute, global wage inequalities made it virtually impossible for them to advance within their own country. Acaponeta and Tecuala were small municipalities, with populations of 21,000 and 31,000, respectively, and most men worked in agriculture.[15] But with Doña Natalia smoothing the way, they would be able to journey to the United States without accumulating excessive debts. And as legal immigrants, they would be able to work in the United States without fear of being apprehended by the INS. That meant taking not only "back-of-house" jobs as cooks and dishwashers but also working in the "front of the house," where they could interact with customers, make more money in tips, and gain valuable cultural capital.

Even for immigrants with a sponsor, the visa application process was taxing. There were only fourteen US Foreign Service offices in Mexico that issued visas. Mexicans applying for visas relocated to cities where there were offices and then waited nearby until their visa was issued, which could take weeks. The immigrants Doña Natalia sponsored generally went to the Tijuana office on the US–Mexico border; there were offices closer to Acaponeta, but Tijuana positioned them to receive their visas and immediately cross the border for the 120-mile journey north to Los Angeles.[16] Doña Natalia supported the immigrants she sponsored during this phase of the immigration process as well. When Lola Barragan, the daughter of one of Doña Natalia's childhood friends, immigrated to the United States with her husband and children, they waited in Tijuana for weeks. Virginia "Vicky" Lizárraga Tamayo, a small child at the time, remembers receiving care packages from Doña Natalia, containing necessities like food and clothes, as well as a doll for her. Doña Natalia understood not just the survival needs of immigrants but their emotional needs as well.[17]

Quite unusually for a Mexican immigrant of this time, Doña Natalia had an attorney, which allowed her to offer the immigrants she sponsored some access to a legal safety net as well. Since she did not know how to read and write and routinely relied on others to help her, having access to trustworthy legal advice must have been invaluable for her business. It is not clear whether she paid a retainer, but her relationships with her attorneys—first Carlos Teran and then Phillip Barnett—were steady and long-lasting. Teran and Barnett were not immigration specialists, but they were able to smooth the settlement process for the immigrants Doña Natalia helped. For example, when her niece Vicky Cueva Tavares received a moving violation ticket in the early 1960s, Doña Natalia asked Phillip Barnett to accompany Vicky to court.[18] Doña Natalia's insistence that an attorney accompany her niece to traffic court may have signaled her awareness that no encounter with the law could be considered "routine." Even Mexican Americans who understood the legal system or had mastery of the language had little reason to trust that the legal system would treat them fairly. Mexican Americans had been systematically excluded from serving on juries until the 1954 case *Hernandez v. State of Texas* overturned this practice. But in the years that followed, juridical discrimination, like police brutality, continued apace.[19]

Like her real estate agent and landlord, the attorneys served Doña Natalia as cultural brokers. Carlos Teran had deep ties to what the *Los Angeles Times* in 1959 called the "Mexican colony" in East Los Angeles. Originally from El Paso, Teran grew up in Los Angeles, attending Garfield High School in East Los Angeles and then UCLA. After college he enlisted in the US Army, where he was awarded a Bronze Star, and he later earned a law degree from USC. He was active in the civic life of the Mexican American community and served as president of many civic organizations in East Los Angeles. Teran acted as Doña Natalia's attorney until 1958, when he became the first judge of the newly created District Three Municipal Court in East Los Angeles; a year later, then-governor Edmund G. "Pat" Brown appointed him to the Superior Court bench, making Teran the first Mexican American to serve as a California Superior Court judge.[20] Teran invited both Doña Natalia and María to his personal and professional events and often brought his colleagues to eat with him at the Nayarit. This expanded the women's network and showed them that with the proper education, resources, and help from others, members of their own community could achieve new levels of success.

Doña Natalia's second attorney, Phillip Barnett, was a white man who had a solo practice in Echo Park. Barnett did not have the same ties to the ethnic Mexican community that Teran did, but he and Doña Natalia shared a neighborhood in which communicating across different cultures was part of daily life, and, even though she could not speak English, she was ready to cross ethnic and racial lines for the sake of her business. Barnett had a broad practice that included family law, probate, and personal injury, and he did a number of appeals. Some of his cases were reported on in the *Los Angeles Times*, suggesting that he was an attorney of some reputation, which by extension may have lent some prestige to Doña Natalia.[21] But what mattered most to Doña Natalia and the immigrants she sponsored was that he helped them secure their visas and green cards. With their papers in order and attorneys to serve as a safety net should anything go sideways once they were settled in Los Angeles, the immigrants Doña Natalia sponsored were ready to begin their journey in a new land on a road that Doña Natalia had helped pave.

Although Doña Natalia worked to make sure that the immigrants she sponsored had a firm foothold in the United States, she did not spurn undocumented workers. Rodolfo Lora, who worked at the Nayarit as a dishwasher in the 1960s, told me that, fifty years later, he was still grateful for the opportunity Doña Natalia had given him. I interviewed him in Novillero, just outside of Acaponeta, Nayarit. "It's thanks to her that I could retire here," he said, explaining that rather than pay him under the table, she put him on the payroll, which made him eligible for Social Security, which he was still receiving.[22] (Undocumented immigrants were not excluded from applying for and receiving Social Security cards until 1972, when Congress created the Supplemental Security Income [SSI] program.)[23] After the Nayarit closed, Rodolfo went on to work for a manufacturer for many years before retiring to Mexico.

Ramón Barragan, who worked as a cook at the Nayarit, remembered a time when a young man, unrelated and unknown to Doña Natalia, showed up at the restaurant in need of a job. "She sighed and turned to me and said, 'Another *mojadito!*'" (a pejorative word for "undocumented" but said using the affectionate diminutive form). When I asked whether Doña Natalia was prejudiced against undocumented workers, Ramón quickly clarified: "No, she understood their plight. But she also knew it almost always meant training them from the ground up, which she did in this case, which meant more work for her, and some of them just did not catch on well to the restaurant business."[24] Doña Natalia trained not only this young man, but her own family members and fictive kin frequently and without complaint. Perhaps she minded her outlay of social capital less if it was part of a larger system of social remittance and placemaking. Running a business was not transactional for her: it was a way to provide support and live in accordance with emotional ties that the business itself strengthened.

THE EMOTIONAL LIFE OF LABOR

When the Nayarit opened in 1951, it employed eight workers. Over the years, that number grew to between ten and fifteen employees at any given time. The day kitchen staff was responsible for receiving food deliveries (boxed and canned goods, fresh produce and meats) in the morning, organizing them in the dry storage area and the walk-in cooler, taking stock, and then prepping foods to be used throughout the day. The head cook oversaw the back of the house and also served as the expediter, receiving the tickets and telling his assistants (one or two, depending on how busy the shift was) what to cook and in what order. The back of the house also included one or two dishwashers. The front-of-the-house staff consisted of the hostess, who doubled as the cashier (this was often María in the evenings), and around five servers. On busy shifts, such as Friday and Saturday nights, there was an extra hand to bus the tables and, after the restaurant received its liquor license in the year 1968, a bartender.

Over the course of Doña Natalia's life, she employed an estimated one hundred workers at the Nayarit. Though many people, including customers and María herself, described how strict and no-nonsense Doña Natalia was about her business, they also characterized her as fair and respectful to her employees. A small, core group of workers stayed at the Nayarit for years. Others left after a year or two, mostly for personal reasons—getting married, finding a job in another industry, or moving out of the area. Some came to work for a few months at a time so that they could save money, return home, and buy a car or start a small business in Nayarit. Many were drawn not just by the promise of work or good money but also by intangible things like adventure and the desire to enjoy life and leisure in a big city like Los Angeles. All this meant, of course, that some employees left the Nayarit, but no one I interviewed did so to work at another restaurant. Nor did anyone mention any employees who did. Workers at the Nayarit recognized that this was a good gig. Doña Natalia rarely fired anyone, as she knew that her workers' visas depended on having a job.

The stable employment she offered on arrival stood in stark contrast to the precarious, nonunionized jobs into which many Mexicans (along with African Americans) tended to be shunted: hired when needed, let go when jobs were completed or business flagged, and, in the case of agricultural work, perpetually moving to follow the crops. A typical migrant labor route in California, for example, covered five hundred miles in just half a year, from picking vegetables in the Imperial Valley on the US-Mexico border in January to harvesting peas farther northwest in March, heading north for apricot season in June, and circling south again in the hot late summer to work in the vineyards of San Bernardino County. Other routes were even longer, extending from the Imperial Valley to the San Joaquin Valley, near Sacramento, with its grapes, cotton, apricots, peaches, and prunes, or even as far as Colorado to work in the beet fields.[25] This kind of migrant work prevented Mexicans from settling down and kept them from connecting with a wider community.[26] Agricultural laborers often lived on the farms they worked, meaning that there was little separation between their home and work lives. If they managed to carve out some leisure time, labor camp management monitored extracurricular activities, such as drinking and gambling, in order to avoid any possible interference with productivity.[27] Traveling into town to pursue leisure on their own terms was a challenge, and those who managed it were often unwelcome. It was not unusual for businesses and restaurants in places like Salinas, California, to practice segregation, announced by signs that read, "No Mexicans allowed."[28] And although the Bracero Program brought only unaccompanied men to work in the fields, entire families, including young children, often worked the fields together.[29] Alicia Schmidt Camacho compares the agricultural camps to a carceral regime, in which "the state and employers retained control over workers' representation and also over their mobility."[30] Isolated and dehumanized, migrant workers and their families were, in essence, locked away from the rest of the United States.

The Nayarit, however, employed people at a vibrant crossroads where on any given night the dining room was host to a mix of cultures and languages. Doña Natalia wanted the workers she sponsored to learn English, and she ensured they had time during the day to go to classes. While only a few of her protégés became fluent, learning even a smattering of English helped them communicate with non-Spanish-speaking customers and, during their leisure time, to explore other parts of the city. Though one waitress, Lupe Reyes, said that she never learned to speak English, she was nonetheless able to communicate with her customers. "I didn't speak English, but I spoke food," she told me.[31] When language barriers arose, María was available to translate.

Restaurant work could be tiring and the hours long, but workers took pleasure in having friends and family come to dine or catching up with their regulars. On special occasions, customers sometimes brought in a bottle of wine or a cake from a bakery, like Hansen's Cakes on the Westside, and invited their servers to a glass or gifted the leftover cake to the staff. (To this day, when my family celebrates a special occasion out, we order cakes from Hansen's and gift the remaining cake to the restaurant workers.)

The restaurant also fostered connections among its employees. Like many restaurants, the Nayarit provided workers with a staff meal before the dinner rush. This communal meal rarely included the more expensive dishes like *steak picado*, specialty meat, fish, or shrimp and sometimes included ingredients that would not keep until the next day so as to prevent them from going to waste. Still, it was well-prepared regional cuisine, such as dishes in which the meat was combined with other ingredients to stretch out the portions, including *caldos* (hearty stews), *carne en sus jugos* (beef cooked in a meat broth, with beans added), or *machaca*, in which leftover meat is shredded and cooked with garlic, onions, peppers, and sometimes eggs. Doña Natalia also encouraged servers to taste all the dishes, to deepen their knowledge and be ready to guide customers, especially American customers, through the menu. Eating was both a source of pleasure and an essential part of the job.

Since most of the immigrants Doña Natalia sponsored had no restaurant experience, she and María invested many extra hours providing extensive on-the-job training and supervision. Doña Natalia had to train her workers to live up to her high culinary and service standards, but first and foremost she had to keep them safe. Restaurants are dangerous places, and one small mistake can result in a trip to the emergency room: there are knives, slicers, grinders, hot pans, and boiling water. It's easy to slip and fall on a slick floor or collide with a coworker when hurrying through a narrow space or around a blind corner, especially when off-balance from carrying a heavy tray. Many workers started off bussing tables, washing dishes, and making tortillas and then worked their way up to positions as servers, cooks, or cashiers. When Pedro's mother, Chayo Díaz, Doña Natalia's sister's sister-in-law, followed her son to Los Angeles, she had no previous restaurant experience. Doña Natalia trained her to be a cook. Bringing a novice up to Doña Natalia's standards must have required a significant investment and considerable risk. Had Doña Natalia's goal been merely to find cheap and efficient labor to build her business, she could have done so in much easier ways. But helping her friends and family immigrate was not a simple business decision. She was

Figure 15. María del Rosario ("Chayo") Díaz Cueva, Natalia Barraza, and Luisa Cota (Doña Natalia's cousin) on a visit to Acaponeta, Nayarit, for the wedding of Luis Díaz, Doña Natalia's nephew, to Livier Díaz in 1951. Photograph provided by María Perea Molina.

committed to those she sponsored. That commitment extended to the rest of her staff, too. Blanca Arrevillaga was a single mother, newly arrived in the United States, when she sought work at the Nayarit in 1967. Perhaps Doña Natalia sympathized with her plight. "I didn't speak English," Blanca told me. "I thought I spoke English, but when I arrived from Mexico and heard the different accents and idioms, I didn't know what people were saying! Nonetheless, and with no waitress training, Doña Natalia gave me a chance."[32]

Although immigrants retained ties to family members in Mexico, most of the people Doña Natalia sponsored were not under pressure to send remittances to their home country. Remittances can constitute one of the major expenses of immigrant life, and many immigrants make great sacrifices while in the United States so that they can send the largest remittances possible. As Abrego writes, "Remittances are more than mere economic markers; they represent a sense of obligation between family members and often the expression of deep emotional bonds between relatives across borders."[33] They can also change the landscape back home,[34] when, for example, immigrants invest in public spaces, such as helping finance a new statue in the plaza, or in themselves and their families, by building or expanding homes and businesses. The immigrants Doña Natalia sponsored, however, tended to come from families with some means, such as a home or a small business, in Mexico. For her part, Doña Natalia sent some money back to Acaponeta for municipal projects, including refurbishing the bells of the church located on the main plaza. But the emotional bonds and sense of obligation that drive remittances were, for her, reason to build a robust community in Los Angeles. Her placemaking worked because she gave her fellow nationals jobs, settlement support, necessary skills, training, and a network of rich affective ties, enabling them to thrive in their new world.

QUEER PLACEMAKING

Of the ten to fifteen workers the Nayarit employed at any time, four or five were gay men.[35] There are many possible reasons for this high proportion of gay employees. As a divorced woman who migrated on her own to Los Angeles, opened a business, and adopted two children, Doña Natalia knew what it meant to transgress tradition. Perhaps she felt an affinity with gay men, who, like her, made their own lives outside of social norms. It may also be that as a single woman (for all intents and purposes), she felt safer working with men around and knew that gay men were unlikely to harass her or the women on her staff. Another important factor was the location of the Nayarit in Echo Park, with its visible gay community; out gay men gravitated to the area and made up a larger part of the available labor pool than in other parts of L.A. Echo Park offered gay Mexican men the opportunity to speak Spanish and be around fellow nationals without the constraints that they might have experienced in ethnic enclaves.[36]

Like many migrants before and after, being gay shaped these men's decision to immigrate in the first place, as well as the journey that followed.[37] Once Pedro was settled in Los Angeles, he persuaded his friend Ildefonso "Poncho" García, who was also gay, to immigrate as well. Acaponeta had a population of fewer than eight thousand; the closest big city, Guadalajara, was over two hundred miles away. Los Angeles, Pedro emphasized to Poncho, would provide him with freedom to go out without being shamed for his sexuality. Poncho came, but as he told me, "Pedro no hallaba como llevar me a la casa" (Pedro could not find a way to take me to his house). Pedro shared a home with his mother and two sisters, and although Poncho was known to the whole family, it was, Poncho told me, a "delicate situation." Pedro and Poncho were both out and accepted by their community, and they were not lovers, but tacit understandings about Catholic Mexican immigrant decorum limited the ways in which they could move through the world. Pedro's family, as Poncho described it, "no captaban la amistad que teníamos" (did not understand the friendship we had), referring to their bonds not just as friends but also as gay men who had similar experiences and challenges.

Poncho ended up rooming with Carlos Porras, who allowed Poncho to stay rent-free in his room in a boardinghouse. While this arrangement might have been a little cramped, it surely had its advantages; the boardinghouse has a long history as a space free from supervision and familial control.[38] But the proprietor was not unaware of Poncho's presence, and after a month, Poncho had to move. By this time, Pedro had managed to explain Poncho's situation to his family satisfactorily enough for Poncho to stay with them, and he slept on the couch.

Poncho did not have an easy time settling into a job. He first worked at a restaurant owned by a woman named Cristina, whom he described as a *paisana* from Tecuala, the neighboring town to Acaponeta and also its rival. Poncho had never worked at a restaurant before, and, naturally, he made mistakes. Cristina yelled at him one day; as Poncho remembers it, she called him dumb, and then to add insult to injury, she denigrated his hometown, saying that he was "so typical for someone from Acaponeta." Poncho became upset and left. His next job was at the Nayarit; he already knew Doña Natalia through Pedro. When Doña Natalia hired Poncho, she told him, "Aquí vas a trabajar derechito" (Here, you will work right [straight]). It is not clear if she was referring to his past work history or his gay identity. She had already chided Poncho on one occasion when he had visited the Nayarit wearing shorts and a T-shirt while taking a break from doing his laundry at the laundromat down the street. Doña Natalia disapproved of his appearance, asking him, "¿Cuándo en tu vida te vestiste así?" (When in your life did you dress like that?). Whether she was criticizing what she saw as his excessively American informality or suggesting that his outfit revealed something about his sexuality, Poncho was unsure, but he did not seem insulted or intimidated by Doña Natalia's words years later, laughing as he told me this story.

After Poncho moved out of Pedro's home, he found a place in Silver Lake. Doña Natalia provided him with a reference and paid his deposit. She also sent him to the International School of Bartending, located down the street from the restaurant and run by another countryman, Tomás Lau, from Tecuala, Nayarit. When Poncho's mother fell ill back home in Acaponeta, he went to spend a month with her. Doña Natalia held his job for him and paid his rent while he was gone. When I interviewed Poncho decades later, he was still living in the same apartment. "To this day," he said fondly, "my gas bill is still in [Doña Natalia's] name."

As a gay man, he said, it was easier to live and work in Silver Lake and Echo Park than it would have been in an ethnic enclave; the neighborhood, he said, was more "bohemian." He felt safe walking home from work at night and enjoyed going out there.[39] None of my straight interviewees ever referred to Echo Park as "bohemian," perhaps signaling that Echo Park had a sensibility that not everyone was attuned to—or needed. While some gay workers took advantage of Echo Park's central location to seek out other gay communities nearby, Carlos Porras rarely left the neighborhood to socialize. "All he needed was Sunset Boulevard," Ramón Pack recalled.[40]

The lives of the immigrants who worked at the Nayarit were, of course, filled with decisions about where to live and where to work, whom to trust and befriend, and when to accept help from others and how to offer others help in turn. The glimpses of daily life that people shared with me are a reminder of how much historians don't know, because we still have not fully studied gay immigrant communities or brought their experiences into mainstream narratives of immigration. But as the lives unfolding in and around the Nayarit reveal, when we discuss fictive kin or social networks among immigrants, we must heed the important role that gay people played in them.

We seldom see gay men (or women) portrayed in historical accounts of ethnic Mexican communities; it is similarly rare to find ethnic Mexicans in historical accounts of gay communities.[41] In part, that is because the gay immigrant community did not leave much of an archival trace. For substantial accounts about doubly marginalized people, like gay Mexican immigrants, we must turn not to official archives but to more organic, contemporary accounts, often conducted by anthropologists and sociologists.[42] But the erasure of sexuality in historical accounts also has to do with an artificial divide that treats gay and immigrant communities as separate entities. According to Lillian Faderman and Stuart Timmons, by the late 1960s, Silver Lake and Echo Park contained "perhaps the greatest concentration of gay population and gay businesses in the nation."[43] Yet Silver Lake, with its majority white and more affluent population was (and continues to be) imagined as a gay space, while Echo Park was imagined as a space for immigrants and people of color.[44] Historians who see sexuality and race as separate areas of inquiry—whether because of archival limitations, personal blind spots, or the conservative views of the subjects about whom they write—can end up reproducing such falsely tidy divisions.[45] Yet there is much to be gained by accurately reflecting the complexity of immigrant sexuality, which shaped people's lives both before and after they left their countries of origin, including their experiences of settlement and their roles as placemakers.[46] Attention to immigrant sexuality also reveals how deviancy has been used to define normalcy—in this case, who can be considered "good immigrants," worthy of acceptance or inclusion, and who is positioned outside the boundaries of social membership.[47]

Many of the gay men who worked at the Nayarit in the 1950s and 1960s have since passed away. But I have pieced together some of these missing voices from interviews with surviving gay Nayarit workers and customers. Some of the gay men Doña Natalia hired, like Pedro, were members of her own family, and she welcomed them, just as she welcomed all the immigrants she sponsored, to live with her and María until they established themselves in Los Angeles. Salvador "Chavo" Barrajas, who started working at the Nayarit as a waiter and would go on to open his own restaurant, for example, first lived with Doña Natalia and María, though he was not related, and then rented the small apartment over their carport.[48]

Yet there were limits to Doña Natalia's acceptance of these men's sexuality. She discouraged gay men from being out at work and asked them not to behave or dress in such a way that customers might readily read as gay. Perhaps her outlook was influenced by a conservative approach to sexuality rooted in her Mexican culture or her Catholic upbringing. Perhaps she wanted to protect her business and the community that depended on it, knowing she might lose customers or attract the attention of the police should the restaurant become known as a gay meeting spot. She was, after all, a Mexican immigrant and a woman and needed to guard against that kind of risk. Whatever her reasoning, her attitude toward gay employees, as María summed it up, was "puede ser pero no ver" (you can be it but not look it).[49] Although Doña Natalia never actually spoke these words to her workers, she got her point across. At the same time, she made clear that whatever people did outside of the restaurant was their business (unless, of course, she was their chaperone). If anyone ever tried to share gossip with her about one of her workers, gay or straight, Doña Natalia refused to hear it.

Her attitude was not exceptional in Mexican culture. Decades later, for example, when an interviewer asked the renowned Mexican singer-songwriter Juan Gabriel if he was gay, Gabriel sighed with exasperation and said, "Mijo, dicen que lo que se ve no se pregunta" (Son, they say one does not question what is apparent). That maxim, like "puede ser pero no ver," is in keeping with what the sociologist Hector Carrillo describes as "sexual silence," a Mexican cultural approach that leaves enough flexibility for things not to be said explicitly while at the same time allowing information to be shared. Ironically, this tacit acceptance of sexuality can speak quite loudly.[50]

The code of how to be and look was nuanced. For their part, the workers acquiesced to Doña Natalia's wishes. Carlos Porras and Juan "Juanito" Torres worked at the Nayarit for most of the years it was open. María describes them both as acting "differently" around Doña Natalia: in her presence they were "not effeminate." At the same time, Carlos and Juanito did not act so constrained around María. Perhaps this was because María was not their chief employer. They may have recognized a different sensibility in her, whether because of her age or because of her outlook as a Mexican American. Whatever the case, workers at the restaurant were likelier to cut loose a bit when Doña Natalia was not around. One waiter, Enrique, nicknamed "La Tonga," would walk around on tiptoe, pretending to wear high heels. Guillermo Burges, a longtime busboy whom everyone called "La Pelona" (meaning, roughly, "Baldy") was known as a joker and sometimes used his toupee to bus the restaurant tables. Several of my interviewees laughed as they recalled his spot-on impersonation of Doña Natalia, in which he rushed through the restaurant carrying her purse as a prop and checking officiously to see that things were in order.

Figure 16. Doña Natalia and some of her fictive kin. Back row, left to right: Eloisa Wongpec, Salvador ("Chavo") Barrajas, Natalia Barraza, Irene Wongpec, Carlos Porras; front row: Lilia Wongpec holding María's son David on her lap. Permission to reprint photograph provided by Irene Wongpec. Photograph provided by Irene Wongpec.

The rule "puede ser pero no ver" did not preclude Doña Natalia and her workers from forging close relationships. Carlos Porras, in particular, was vital to Doña Natalia's daily life. Carlos worked as a waiter at the restaurant, but he also chauffeured Doña Natalia, accompanying her on many outings, errands, and trips. Carlos would even drive Doña Natalia to the US–Mexico border at Mexicali to pick up visiting family members arriving by train. (Flights to and from the nearest big city in Nayarit did not begin until the mid-1960s and even then were prohibitively expensive.) The round trip from Los Angeles could easily take a full day, so the pair spent many hours together. Doña Natalia is said to have "adored" Carlos, and so did the other workers, who warmly recalled his elegant demeanor when I interviewed them. It was Carlos who introduced Ramón Pack and Evelia Díaz Barraza, who later married; many Nayarit workers told me that he was "the glue that kept everyone together."

Though there were limits to how out the workers could be at the restaurant, there seems to have been a general understanding and acceptance of their sexual identities. For example, people from Acaponeta tend to use the article *the* before a person's name when talking about them. In Spanish, *el* is the masculine form of "the," and *la* is the feminine form. Thus, you would refer to María in a conversation as "La María." But both gay and straight workers at the Nayarit consistently used the article *la* when referring to gay men by their nicknames, even decades after the restaurant had closed. Juanito Torres, for example, remained "La Tonina."

One Mexican immigrant whom Doña Natalia had not sponsored but hired to work as a busboy was married and had children. At work, however, he was openly gay, at least when Doña Natalia was not around.[51] Being at work was where he could be more himself, and being at home was where he hid his identity. Other workers told me that they felt little need to be secretive about how they spent their time away from the job, and this included gay men who engaged in activities typically considered "women's work." Poncho, the waiter, enjoyed styling women's hair and often did the hair of other Nayarit workers on his days off. La Pelona deep cleaned the homes of other workers on his days off, and his colleagues described him as truly enjoying cleaning houses.

While the Nayarit did not have a reputation as an affirmatively gay-friendly restaurant, it offered a safe place where gay customers could come without fearing harassment by the police or other customers.[52] That may not seem like much, but at the time, the L.A. chief of police, William Parker (1950–66), crusaded against homosexuality, ordering raids on gay bars and hiring actors to lure unsuspecting men into sexual acts for which they would then be arrested.[53] At the Nayarit, no one took issue when employees' gay friends patronized the restaurant for a meal or used it as a meeting place before going out for the night. Gay men became regulars and knew many workers—not just the gay men—well. María remembers a customer named Alfonso (whom she called "Alfie") doting on her young son and my brother David gifting him trinkets and asking after him when he was not at the restaurant. Felipe Portillo, another gay man, often came to the Nayarit with his mother, Lupe—an example of how urban anchors can be immigrant spaces, family spaces, and gay spaces at once.[54]

The Nayarit facilitated long-lasting friendships among gay men, as well as between straight women and gay men. Refugio "Cuca" Arriaga, a single mother who worked as a waitress at the restaurant, and César Ortega, a gay man and longtime waiter, maintained a decades-long friendship. Similarly, María was very close to Chavo Barrajas before he passed away in the late 1980s and remains close friends with Poncho. Carlos Porras befriended Socorro "Coco" Rubio, a regular customer who lived in Echo Park. Coco's daughter, Rosa Blanca Arrevillaga Sánchez, called him her uncle Charlie. "It was years," she laughed, "before I figured out he wasn't actually my uncle!"[55] Juventina "Conchita" Alcaraz, who was a waitress at the restaurant, helped her cousin, Guadalupe Osuna, immigrate to Los Angeles and settle in Echo Park. She was a regular at the restaurant, and her son, Steven Osuna, remembered Echo Park as the site of some of her (and therefore his) first and most important interactions with gay men. Working as a housekeeper in Echo Park and Silver Lake, Guadalupe Osuna had many gay men as clients, and her son credited those working relationships with making them both accepting of gay men.[56]

At the same time, there were limits to the kinds of friendships that developed. None of my interviewees gave examples of primary friendships developing between gay men and straight men, but they socialized together in groups, and there were moments of solidarity. Héctor Molina, who would become María's husband, recalled a night in the late 1960s when he and

Figure 17. Socorro ("Coco") Rubio and Carlos Porras, 1964. Permission to reprint photograph provided by Rosa Blanca Arrevillaga Sánchez. Photograph provided by Rosa Blanca Arrevillaga Sánchez.

Pedro went out drinking at a straight bar. As they were leaving, a group of men assumed they were a couple and began to harass them. Whether to stand up for Pedro or to protect his own honor as a straight man, Héctor got into a fight with them.

The spatial metaphor of "the closet" took hold in the Cold War period and spoke to the repressiveness of the era's politics regarding gay men.[57] But the image suggests a more static relationship to space than many gay men, including those who worked and ate at the Nayarit, actually had. Gay men moved in and out of a range of spaces, downplaying their identity in some spaces and not others, depending on the context. Men who socialized in openly gay establishments also lived as Mexican immigrants, and the Nayarit allowed them to work and socialize in an ethnic Mexican space with some degree of openness about their sexuality. They constructed situational identities in relationship to who was around them, what their needs were, and where they found themselves. In other words, place is a part of what makes identity fluid.

THE WOMEN OF THE NAYARIT

Doña Natalia sponsored numerous women immigrants who, like Doña Natalia herself, had their own visions and forged their own, independent paths. Some came to work, some to serve their families, and some simply to enjoy themselves within the confines of work or outside it. Moving to a new place nearly always happens for multiple reasons, both economic and emotional. Immigrant and US-born women alike sought autonomy and adventure by migrating from one country to another or from a rural area or small town to a city where they could get away from the prying eyes of the church or the expectations of family and achieve some degree of anonymity.[58] The rationales and motivations of Mexican immigrant women during this period can be hard to discern from the institutional records, which document their lives from the perspective of immigration agents, social workers, or teachers who took for granted that assimilation should be the women's goal. Scholars of Mexican American history who have tried to get at women's interior lives, however, have taught us much about how racism and misogyny complicate standard immigration stories.[59] Young Mexican and Mexican American women faced immense difficulties, including educators who underestimated them, social workers who wished them to abandon their culture, and police who criminalized them. At home, these women also experienced tensions with their parents, nearly all of whom lamented in one way or another how much their children changed in this new land and worried about their daughters adopting American ways and abandoning their culture, and perhaps their morals.[60]

The women whom Doña Natalia sponsored certainly had to navigate such tensions, but she was a willing and capable guide. She supported women of all ages and marital statuses in their immigration efforts. At the time, the majority of Mexican immigrants were men, partly because the available jobs favored men (e.g., laborer or farmworker) but also because of the gendered expectation that migration was a role for the head of household. Men who had come to the United States to work in the Bracero Program typically tended to help other men migrate. As these migration networks matured, they expanded to include others: women, children, and the elderly. But as the sociologist Pierrette Hondagneu-Sotelo has shown, it was not until the 1970s that young single women began to immigrate in larger numbers and establish their own networks.[61] Doña Natalia's support and sponsorship of women immigrants in the 1950s and 1960s was unusual.

When young women migrated under Doña Natalia's sponsorship, they did so within a framework of social and cultural mores that was maintained across borders. The arrangement often began with a discussion between Doña Natalia and the would-be immigrant's parents, who were either Doña Natalia's relatives or fictive kin. Their approval hinged on the assurance that Doña Natalia would serve not just as sponsor to their daughter but also her chaperone—

something of great importance to Mexican parents.[62] Doña Natalia's chaperon-age did not entail watching their daughters around the clock, but she promised that their days would be highly structured and that they would be accounted for whether they were at school, the restaurant, or her home. If the sponsored immigrant wished to go on a date, Doña Natalia made sure another relative or even an employee accompanied her, even if her charge was of legal age. As Marlon Brando discovered, to his probable chagrin, Doña Natalia was not shy about putting a stop to propositions she deemed beyond the pale. Even as an adult, María, too, was subject to Doña Natalia's strict rules. María recalled that in her early twenties, when she was preparing to go to the movies, she was given a firm curfew. If María protested that the allotted time was not even enough to see the full film, Doña Natalia would simply say, "Then don't go."

I cannot overstate the importance of Doña Natalia giving her word to a parent, especially a father, that she would watch over his daughter. For example, Doña Natalia facilitated the immigration of two sisters, Evelia and Nelly Casillas. When Nelly's sister-in-law María de Los Ángeles Casillas went to the Bay Area to live with her brother and study English, her father demanded that she come back to Mexico early. She wanted to stay, but since a brother was essentially a peer, he could not be trusted to provide the same level of supervision as a matronly aunt who gave you her word that she would look after your daughter.

When one of Doña Natalia's friends in Nayarit worried that her daughter, Sara "Sarita" Gutiérrez Loera, was getting too serious about a relationship with her hometown boyfriend, Doña Natalia agreed to help. Unbeknownst to Sarita, her mother and Doña Natalia arranged the paperwork for Sarita to immigrate to Los Angeles. Sarita worked at the Nayarit and lived in Doña Natalia's home, but the mother's effort to control Sarita's love life proved fruitless: Sarita found a new suitor in Los Angeles and ran away to live with him. When Doña Natalia found out where they were, she sent María to tell him he needed to do the "proper" thing and marry Sarita. He did.[63]

When Doña Natalia helped her niece Evelia Díaz Barraza come to Los Angeles in 1956, at the age of sixteen, Evelia was motivated not by prudence or economic necessity—her father was a businessman in Acaponeta and owned some property—but by a sense of adventure. Evelia participated in an exchange program at Belmont High School. Belmont's student body reflected the diversity of Echo Park, where it was located, with white, Mexican, Asian, and a few Black students. Because Evelia immigrated at a young age and was educated in the United States, she was able to master English better than many others Doña Natalia sponsored, most of whom studied the language as adults while working. That made Evelia an invaluable resource to Doña Natalia, who eventually entrusted her with writing much of her correspondence.

Evelia had an effervescent personality, which she retains to this day, laughing easily, dressing in bright, beautiful dresses, and ready to break out in song at a family gathering. (She was chosen as ambassador of the Echo Park parade in 2014.) An article in "Rueda Ferris" (Ferris Wheel), the aptly named gossip section of *El Eco*, describes her attendance at a party held in Acaponeta in 1964: "The Limbo Rock danced by the beautiful Evelia Díaz Barraza caused such a sensation at the party thrown by Marissa Suarez de Espinosa that she [Evelia] was forced to repeat it."[64] Chubby Checker's popular song "Limbo Rock" had come out two years earlier, but since Acaponeta lacked access to television signals until 1967, it was Evelia who transported the song and its accompanying dance home. The date of the story suggests that she was likely in town for *Semana Santa*, the holy week leading up to Easter. The sexual revolution of the 1960s in the United States had not spread to Acaponeta, but Evelia claimed a physical freedom that challenges our assumptions about the restraint young Catholic women in Mexico were expected to embody.

Evelia sometimes chafed at working for Doña Natalia. "Era dura," Evelia remembered—she was strict. Even after Evelia graduated from high school, Doña Natalia required that she have a chaperone on dates. "Conchita" Alcaraz, a fellow Nayarita and cashier at the restaurant, was often pressed into service in this role. At one point, Evelia became so frustrated at the constraints around when and where she could go, for how long, and with whom that she moved back to Acaponeta. But she eventually returned to Los Angeles to work at the restaurant, until she married Ramón Pack in 1966.[65] By then, Evelia was in her midtwenties, but Ramón asked Doña Natalia's permission before he proposed. Asking Doña Natalia rather than Evelia's father—Doña Natalia's brother-in-law in Acaponeta—for Evelia's hand in marriage highlights how Doña Natalia's role as a sponsor, chaperone, and business owner lent her status often reserved for men.[66]

Evelia Pack's sister, Nelly Díaz Barraza Casillas, remained in Acaponeta but visited Evelia in Los Angeles for pleasure. By 1953, these trips seem to have been putting some strain on her relationship with her boyfriend, Juan Casillas. That February, the gossip column in *El Eco* joked that Juan was making devotionals to his patron saint—"cuarenta rosarios y diez novenas" (forty rosaries and ten novenas, a nine-day period of prayer)—so that his adored girlfriend, Nelly, would not leave for "gringolandia."[67] Two months later, the column reported that Nelly, visiting Evelia in L.A., had sent a postcard with "recuerdos gringos" (gringo memories) to her "palomilla," or moth, presumably suggesting that Juan was drawn to her like a moth to a flame. Soon after, Nelly returned home and married Juan.

Unlike her sister, Evelia, Nelly told me, she preferred living in her small town in Mexico to the United States. I interviewed her when she was on a visit to Los Angeles to see Evelia. She "felt more comfortable" in Acaponeta, she told me; it was, she declared with a smile, "what I knew."[68] The year she and Juan married, he moved to Los Angeles without her and worked at the Nayarit for six months. Even though Doña Natalia was Nelly's aunt, not his, no one seems to have questioned that he would be the one to make the trip. Nelly did not wish to return permanently to the United States, but after Juan passed away, she began to come back during the summers, to work in the neighborhood market Evelia owned and operated.

Another adventurous immigrant, Irene Wongpec, grew up in Tecuala and could not wait to leave her small hometown (population 8,975) to "see the world."[69] Irene's family and Doña Natalia were not related, but they were close enough that Irene called Doña Natalia "tía." Irene attended high school in Mazatlán, a Mexican beach town one hundred miles north of Acaponeta on the Pacific coast, and after graduating, made arrangements to remain at the school with the nuns who ran it. Seeing that Irene was bright and ambitious, Doña Natalia asked Irene's father if he would allow her to come to Los Angeles to study English. He agreed. Irene went to school full-time during the week and worked Friday and Saturday nights at the Nayarit, first as a bus girl and then as a cashier. Irene described her time there: "I loved it! . . . The dresses! We dressed up, even to bus tables. We'd put on aprons and go into the kitchen to separate the meat for the machaca." Even relatively menial tasks, in her reflections, were suffused with some of the glamour of the place.[70]

Irene, like Evelia, immigrated when she was young enough to master English. The head start that Doña Natalia provided her, Irene said, helped her build a successful career in Los Angeles, where she was a booster for the community of immigrants from Nayarit and a bridge between Mexican immigrant and Mexican American communities. For fourteen years Irene directed the historic East Los Angeles parade, attended by an estimated five hundred thousand, which commemorates Mexican Independence Day. The work helped her make long-lasting connections with political and cultural institutions, such as city hall and the Mexican consulate based in Los Angeles, and she remained heavily involved in local Latinx politics and cultural events after retiring. In 2012, she worked with Amigos de Siqueiros to restore David Siqueiros's controversial mural, *América Tropical*, on Olvera Street, which had been whitewashed soon after its unveiling in 1932. *La Opinión* chose Irene as one of its 2014 "Mujeres Destacadas," an honor that celebrates "extraordinary women for their outstanding contributions[;] . . . the unsung heroes of the Latino community who have dedicated themselves to making this a better world." Irene was being honored for her placemaking.[71]

While Vicky Cueva Tavares, Pedro's sister, worked for a short time at the Nayarit when she first immigrated to L.A. in the 1960s, she also branched out from the restaurant, although she stayed connected to the community it fostered. Vicky did not want to work at the restaurant full-time, so Doña Natalia helped her secure a job with a friend who owned a garment factory. Vicky enjoyed sewing and excelled in it and, having been promoted to making the high-end items, earned a good paycheck.[72] But she continued to work at the Nayarit on Friday and Saturday nights, largely because of the lively atmosphere. She enjoyed seeing diners dressed up on weekend nights and soaking up the energy as late-night customers, arriving from a club or dance, brought the atmosphere of new hot spots with them into the dining room. Single men and women flirted, couples canoodled, and the staff got to see and hear everything. Vicky liked picking up the extra income that weekend work afforded her, too. Since her family had migrated together—her mother and brother continued to work at the restaurant, and they lived with her younger sister—she did not feel pressured to send remittances home and was able to spend some of her earnings on herself. She eventually purchased a Ford Mustang, which she loved to drive.

As Doña Natalia's niece, Vicky enjoyed certain advantages at the Nayarit, such as ducking out with María for occasional errands. If they had time, Vicky and María might sneak in for a dance or two at Montezuma's dance club on Sunset Boulevard. "Allá fuimos a escondidas" (We went there on the sly), Vicky told me, laughing, still tickled by their rebellion several decades later. By this time, the Nayarit boasted a modest dance floor, along with a bar and live music. Vicky recalled a time when she and María both got their hair done in upswept buns, one with the bun to the right of her face and the other with the bun to the left of her face. That evening, they entered the Nayarit from opposite sides of the dance floor and floated across it until they met in the middle. Their hairstyles came together in symmetry, Vicky told me warmly.[73]

Such deep, affective relations among workers at the Nayarit sped up the process of settlement, made the restaurant an enjoyable place to work and to visit, and made life deeper, richer, and more meaningful. Workers bonded not just through their shared sense of themselves as los de afuera—from Nayarit, in particular, Acaponeta—but also through their shared experiences at the restaurant and in the neighborhood. Echo Park's diversity allowed workers from small towns in Mexico the opportunity to have encounters with customers from different racial and ethnic groups, enabling customers and workers to see one another beyond mere professional roles or social types.

I do not mean to suggest that workers who were serving their customers were necessarily engaging in equitable, two-way friendships, but these relationships mattered, too. Anyone who has ever been a regular at a restaurant where a server brings your "usual" before you even have a chance to order it knows what it is to feel recognized and cared for while dining out. Given how geographically, socially, and culturally isolated Los Angeles's midcentury neighborhoods were from one another, there were few spaces in which folks from different backgrounds could meet, interact, and connect. And some real friendships were formed. Evelia Pack considered a "tall English man" named Lindsey, a regular at the restaurant, a good friend. Doña Natalia's niece Lilly met her future husband, Stewart, who worked for the phone company, when he was a customer at the Nayarit.

As a restaurant owner, Doña Natalia provided the place where such interactions could happen. As a sponsor in the immigration process, she opened up doors for women and gay men to immigrate to a new city, often without their families. And as an employer, she hired with a commitment to the value of affective ties: her end goal was not to make a profit but to help others settle successfully. Even though she actively upheld norms of sexuality and gender, she nurtured independent women, accepted her gay relatives and employees, and helped create a space where, however tacitly, they could live more authentic lives.

I thought about all this when during the course of research for this book I met Poncho for dinner at a new downtown restaurant. We were lamenting the demise of El Conquistador, one of several urban anchors founded by Doña Natalia's former employees. Salvador "Chavo" Barrajas, who had worked as a waiter at the Nayarit, opened El Conquistador in 1973, in the historically gay neighborhood of Silver Lake. It became a haven for Latinx immigrants, gay men, and many others; now it was the latest casualty of gentrification. What would happen, Poncho and I wondered, to people like Ricardo de la Torre, El Conquistador's openly gay host? He was beloved for, among other things, his colorful and creative wardrobe; one memorable Easter outfit included full-dress tails paired with bunny ears and a poofy tail. Would he and his coworkers be able to find jobs? At some point in the conversation, Poncho mentioned that there would soon be a job opening for a host at a Mexican restaurant in East Los Angeles. "Ricardo could work there!" I suggested.

"No," Poncho replied in Spanish, "that would never work." When I asked why, he struggled to find the words and finally outlined the shape of a small box with his hands. "Lo encajaría," he said. "It would confine him." Poncho was referring to the fact that though Ricardo spoke Spanish and was a Mexican immigrant, he would feel trapped in a space where he could not be fully himself. It occurred to me that Poncho knew what that kind of entrapment felt like, as well as how important it was to avoid: it was what had pulled him to Los Angeles, with Pedro's encouragement, many years before and why the supportive community Doña Natalia had nurtured at the Nayarit continued to be part of his life, decades after the restaurant had closed.

CHAPTER FOUR

Venturing Forth

Doña Natalia encouraged María and the many people she sponsored to step out of their usual routines at the Nayarit and explore different parts of Los Angeles, giving them time off work at least once a month for that express purpose. She would lend her female relatives and fictive kin her own nice accessories, like wraps, hats, and jewelry, so that they could dress up and enjoy dining at a fancy Westside restaurant, see a famous singer perform at the Million Dollar Theater, or go dancing at the Palladium. María would lead the expeditions while Doña Natalia held down the fort at the restaurant. Vicky Cueva Tavares, Pedro's sister, who worked at the Nayarit on weekends, fondly recalled those evenings out, with her cousin acting as cultural broker. "I didn't know anything when I got [to Los Angeles]," she told me. "I just used to do whatever María did when we went out. They would ask her, 'What would you like to drink?' and she'd coolly answer, 'A Tom Collins.' So I would also order a Tom Collins."[1]

When I asked María if these trips to chic locations were ways for Doña Natalia to elicit respect, to demonstrate that she was now a woman of some means, María seemed taken aback. "No," she responded, "when we went out to nice restaurants or a dance, we had to be back at the restaurant before the late-night rush. We'd get back, change out of our nice dresses and into our uniforms, and get straight to work." These field trips, she explained, were not a means of embodying bourgeois aspirations but of building knowledge. A similar dynamic played out in reverse when María and Doña Natalia would return to Acaponeta as los de afuera. María explained, "When we went to Mexico and stayed with her family, she still preferred to sleep on a cot like she did growing up. My mother also had us visit poor areas and stay in modest places when we visited Mexico. She just wanted us to learn. She said it was important to know both [worlds]." María's answer suggests how highly Doña Natalia valued her culture and her family's connection to Nayarit, as well as her certainty that differences in wealth or status did not correlate to individual or cultural worth. In the decades after World War II, the divide between the haves and have-nots in Mexico was increasing, and the kinds of opportunities available to Doña Natalia in the United States were simply not an option for her relatives and fictive kin in Nayarit. She did not judge them for that. What mattered to her was being able to move about confidently and feel at home, in both the place she came from and the place she adopted.

Gracefulness, fortitude, loyalty, diplomacy, and a host of other qualities can help with that. But to amass cultural capital in the United States, one usually needed money and formal education.[2] Those weren't readily available to most ethnic Mexicans, but exploration was. Doña Natalia's life had been enriched by her sense of exploration, and she must have wanted the same for her family and fictive kin. She may also have regretted that even with all her success as an entrepreneur, she was still dependent on cultural brokers like her real estate agent and attorneys, as well as her daughter, María. She knew how valuable it was to be able to go outside the confines of one's neighborhood with comfort and ease, to move through the city with the assurance of an insider. Whatever her motivations, she ran her restaurant in such a way that its immigrant workers could amass a kind of cultural capital for themselves—insider knowledge that they could use not just at work but also in the city at large. She encouraged her workers to be both placemakers and place-takers.[3]

While on the job, the waiters, waitresses, and hostesses at the Nayarit came in contact with customers from all walks of life, ordinary people and the rich and famous. Such cosmopolitan interactions, along with Doña Natalia's encouragement, helped Nayarit employees feel more of a sense of comfort in and ownership of Los Angeles. On their evenings out, they learned to navigate both the familiar local community and the posh areas of town, crossing geographic and cultural boundaries into places where they were not likely to resemble the average clientele. In the process they connected themselves to what the historian Anthony Macías has termed the "multicultural urban civility" of mid-twentieth-century Los Angeles.[4] Some of them went on to found businesses of their own, building on the community that had grown up in and around the Nayarit, expanding it, and rooting it even more firmly in Echo Park and Silver Lake. America as a whole may not have felt like home, but the dozens of Nayarit workers who spoke with me said that Echo Park eventually did and that over time, segregated geography and all, so did Los Angeles.

The Nayarit workers joined a tradition of people who in various ways and across time ventured forth into a wider and often unaccepting world, asserting their dignity in a society that did not view them as fit to be citizens. Decades of innovative scholarship has explored how youths of color, African Americans of all ages, and the US-born children of immigrants claimed their right to belong in America. The workers at the Nayarit started from a quite different place. They were mostly in their twenties and thirties and primarily Spanish speakers, and almost all of them had immigrated to the United States quite recently, as adults. Nonetheless, like the second-generation youths, they developed a feeling of comfort and familiarity with the urban landscape that led to a sense of ownership.

It is easy to overlook such place-taking among recent immigrants; the popular picture of the immigrant experience is built on the stereotype of people who kept their heads down, worked hard, and sacrificed their own lives for the betterment of their children. Certainly, many new immigrants did those things, but when these are the only stories the culture tells, they reinforce stereotypes of Mexicans as quiet laborers and service workers, on the margins of society, neither taking nor deserving space and attention, let alone civil rights. (Many ethnic Mexicans I know can tell you about being mistaken for a store employee when shopping or being confused for a hired gardener when tending their yards.) But even the most self-effacing immigrant engages in some amount of place-taking, whether acknowledged or not. The Nayarit workers were unusual in that they had more structured opportunities for place-taking.

PLACE-TAKING ON THE JOB

Many immigrant workers had limited access to cultural capital, either because they worked in spaces that lacked it—farms, brickyards, construction sites—or because they were so isolated as domestic workers in the private homes and gardens of wealthy Angelenos that they couldn't share whatever privilege they might access. Restaurant work was different. It put immigrants in touch with people they otherwise might not meet, in places they otherwise might not go. Staff in both the front and the back of the house could gain cultural capital through their employment and share some of that cultural capital with coworkers and friends. Héctor Molina, who eventually left his job at the Ambassador Hotel and tended bar at the Nayarit—and, over the years, at many other well-heeled establishments downtown and on the Westside—took real pleasure in being tipped *and* in tipping. He knew how to tip in a way that was discreet, and he enjoyed using his smooth moves to help his friends and family. He always got us the best tables when we went out to restaurants or the nicest rooms when we checked into hotels.

The Nayarit would occasionally cater events for patrons, including the singer Bobby Vinton, dubbed "the Polish Prince" and known for hits like

"Blue Velvet" and "My Melody of Love." He hired the Nayarit to cater the reception at his family's lavish home after their infant daughter's christening. Doña Natalia provided the meal, then members of Vinton's family set out about six or eight cakes for dessert. María was struck that someone would serve more than one cake at a celebration. At the next family birthday that was celebrated at the Nayarit, she copied the idea and served a few different cakes. (Her sister-in-law thought this was excessive, so she took one of the cakes off the table and put it in her car to take home to her own family. She told María that no one would even miss the extra cake.)

María also acquired new ideas from the monthly excursions that her mother encouraged. One of the restaurants she visited with other Nayarit workers had a dessert cart, which the waiter would wheel around to tempt customers. María had never seen that before and immediately bought a dessert cart for the Nayarit that she and the waitstaff wheeled around, tempting customers with *flan* (a silky Mexican custard with a clear caramel sauce), *arroz con leche* (rice pudding garnished with plump raisins and the cinnamon sticks used to cook it), and *capirotada* (bread pudding bursting with nuts and dried fruits). On another occasion, she and other Nayarit workers visited the Warehouse in Marina del Rey, a popular steak house decorated in a rustic nautical and Malaysian-Hawaiian style, complete with real wharf posts incorporated into the architecture. The Warehouse had hung Christmas trees from the ceiling for the holidays; María made these part of the Nayarit's holiday decor as well, decorating them with silver tinsel and glittering ornaments.[5] Such changes reflected a cultural coalescence enabled by María's place-taking activities. Her expeditions show how mass culture can, in the words of the historian Lizabeth Cohen, "build bridges between isolated ethnic neighborhoods" and the larger urban landscape without requiring ethnic groups to abandon their culture.[6]

Sometimes customers, many of whom were restaurant workers themselves, took an active role in connecting Nayarit workers to new places. In

1967, Héctor Molina—a regular at the restaurant who would go on to date María, marry her, and become my father—set the waitress Blanca Arrevillaga up on a blind date with his friend Raúl. Héctor worked at the Cocoanut Grove nightclub at the Ambassador Hotel and arranged for Blanca and Raúl to see the Supremes play there. Héctor was a working-class Mexican immigrant with an eighth-grade education and accented English, but employment outside of ethnically bound spaces gave him access to cultural capital that he could share with his immigrant compatriots. Blanca and Raúl married one year later.[7]

The working-class Mexican immigrants employed at the Nayarit learned to go out into wider (and whiter) Los Angeles, asserting their right to the city via placemaking. When Poncho, a waiter, learned that a newly hired dishwasher had a birthday coming up, he initiated a night out on the Westside. As Poncho recalled it, "There were two dishwashers at the restaurant, brothers, Honario and the other who we called 'El Güero,' from Zacatecas. They were newly arrived to L.A. and had never been anywhere. We wanted to show them a good time, so Cuca and Lupe [waitresses at the Nayarit] and I took them for a nice dinner and to hear music at Casa Escobar."

Some employees moonlighted at other restaurants. Pedro Cueva, the restaurant's resident piano player, sometimes played at the Ramona Gardens on Sunset Boulevard near Chinatown; Nayarit employees and customers would go to see him there. The Ramona Gardens was not a major venue in Los Angeles, but the owner would promote Pedro's appearances with a sign outside the restaurant: "Tonight! Pedro Cueva and his diamond hands."[8] Poncho remembered the thrill of sipping on a cocktail and telling other customers that he was a friend of the musician. He said he felt like a VIP. Other workers from the Nayarit and other restaurants on Sunset Boulevard took second jobs in food service at Dodger Stadium, working the approximately eighty-one home games over the six-month season. Some worked the fast-food stands; others staffed more exclusive areas they would never have had

Figure 18. Nayarit workers out on the town at Casa Escobar in Santa Monica, ca. 1968. Left to right: Honario (last name unknown), dishwasher; Refugio ("Cuca") Arriaga, waitress; Guadalupe ("Lupe") Reyes, waitress; Ildefonso ("Poncho") García; "El Güero" (real name unknown), dishwasher and Honario's brother. Photograph provided by Ildefonso ("Poncho") Garcia.

access to without their jobs: the private members-only Stadium Club, which housed its own bar and restaurant, and by extension the Club level, which housed the press box and where one was more likely to bump into former Dodgers and celebrities. Once workers had gained access to these exclusive spaces, they extended the entrée to many of their friends, giving them complimentary tickets or letting a friend slip in the door when the manager was on a break. My brother, David Porras, remembered going to the Stadium Club with friends as a young boy in the 1970s thanks to one of María's connections, a Mexican bartender who worked there. They drank complimentary Shirley Temples packed with extra maraschino cherries and marveled at the nine-foot three-inch taxidermied polar bear, which Walter O'Malley had killed on a hunting trip in northern Norway, that towered over the room on a specially built pedestal.[9] (David still knows who can get us into the Stadium Club without passes.) Access to these kinds of spaces gave ethnic Mexican workers and their friends real and imaginative mobility; they could enjoy and share the perks of their jobs.

That sense of shared pleasure was typical of late nights at the Nayarit, as restaurant workers poured into the dining room to relax after their own shifts had ended. Carlos Estrada Lira was watching the Nayarit dining room fill up in the mid-1960s when he had an idea. Why not have some sort of regular night out that workers could enjoy together, from the beginning of the night on instead of waiting for their shifts to end?[10] Most restaurants were closed on Monday nights, so that seemed a good candidate for the event. Lira, who had immigrated to Los Angeles in 1947 from the state of Coahuila in northern Mexico, was the editor of *El Águila*, an independent Spanish-language weekly headquartered in East Los Angeles, where he now lived.[11] Lira contacted different restaurants and clubs on Los Angeles's Eastside and asked them to take turns opening on Monday nights for events that were dubbed "La Noche de Esclavos" (NDE), or the Night of the Slaves. One announcement for an NDE evening read, "Se les desea a los amantes de sanas diversiones y a los simpatizadores de las Noches de la Libertad de los Esclavos divertirse el próximo lunes" (We hope that lovers of healthy diversions and sympathizers of the Night of the Liberation of the Slaves will have fun next Monday).[12] The event's name and description highlighted, with prickly political humor, the hard, often invisible toil of restaurant workers.

Anyone who has worked in a restaurant knows that the demanding schedule means you must often miss holidays, family events, and time with friends. Lira built NDE around workers' needs and schedules, placing restaurant workers at the center rather than pushing them to the margins. It should come as no surprise that the event found a ready audience. *El Águila* was not well archived, but a lone surviving issue from 1969 reveals that the NDE was well organized and had been successful for long enough that it was described as a "tradition."[13] *El Águila* published a calendar at the beginning of each month announcing which restaurants would host the NDE that month. Lira likely also advertised the NDE when wearing his other hats, such as when he guest deejayed for Tejano Tonny Treviño's "La Hora Alegre" radio show, which was broadcast out of El Mercado de Los Ángeles ("El Mercadito"), a three-story shopping center and community landmark in Boyle Heights that opened in 1968 and continues to serve as an urban anchor.[14] Under Lira's leadership, the NDE remade sites of labor into sites of leisure, providing a place where workers could move freely.

Each week, a woman representing one of the businesses that took part in the event was crowned the evening's "queen." Such competitions were quite common in the context of social clubs such as immigrant hometown associations both in the United States and Mexico; the queen served as an ambassador for the organization, representing it at community events and dances and the like. At the NDE, the competition had the additional asset of providing the restaurants with relatively low-cost advertising. The contestants and the restaurants they represented were prominently featured in *El Águila*; the June 1969 issue, for example, put them on the front page, above the fold. Carmen Rubio represented El Río Club el Kikiriki Place, Judith Ramírez represented El Trópico Club, Susie Saavedra represented the Verdugo Inn, Elba Valenzuela represented the Belmar Café, and Chabelita Sánchez represented Tily's Place. (The Nayarit did not host as it was open seven days a week.) It is not clear if all these women worked at the restaurants they represented or if they were connected to the restaurant in other ways, perhaps as customers or family members of employees. Their photos were not the typical staged, professional images that one might associate with beauty contestants. Most were amateur snapshots or simple headshots, and the full-body photos included showed the women dressed in everyday clothes, not bathing suits or formal evening wear. Angelita Salas, who represented Tonny's Place, used her green card photo, the stamp mark visible if one looked closely. Perhaps she and her fellow contestants had neither the time nor the money to worry about more professional photographs. Or perhaps they were not too concerned with how outsiders might perceive them. African American women used beauty pageant contests strategically, to challenge negative stereotypes by cultivating a composed and refined appearance that dovetailed with the long-standing practice of embracing a "politics of respectability."[15] But the contest at the NDEs, advertised in a Spanish-language community paper, was by and for their community as they carved out their own sense of place, celebrating themselves and one another.

In the post–World War II era, ethnic Mexicans came together in more formal and explicitly political ways, too, organizing to end segregation and gain equal rights. The ideologies, memberships, and tactics of such organizations differed greatly. For example, the League of United Latin American Citizens (LULAC), founded in 1929 and active to this day, was strongly middle class; its members embraced an assimilationist approach, demanded civil rights as Americans, and emphasized their European rather than Indigenous roots. But El Congreso de Pueblos de Habla Española, or El Congreso (the Congress of Spanish-Speaking Peoples, or the Congress), which was active in California and especially Los Angeles in the 1930s and 1940s, organized across citizenship lines, fighting for Mexicans and Mexican Americans alike. The Community Service Organization (CSO), a Mexican American group that challenged structural racism, fought for equality in housing, education, and employment. Other ethnic Mexicans organized for rights as workers, joining unions that were not racially segregated, such as the United Cannery, Agricultural, Packing and Allied Workers of America (UCAPAWA).[16]

Doña Natalia, María, and the Nayarit's workers were not affiliated with these groups or with any other organized social movements.[17] This was not because of pressure from the top. Doña Natalia neither encouraged nor discouraged political behavior: as with her workers' personal lives, she believed that what her workers did on their own time was their business. It's possible that Nayarit workers did not seek out organizational alliances because their social network already met many of their needs. Or it may have been that, like many working-class immigrants, they found it challenging to add advocacy and organizing to their existing obligations, including long hours on the job. Or they may have felt it was pointless, given that they were not citizens and could not vote. This lack of formal engagement was fairly typical of immigrants of their generation. Of the 629,000 Mexican Americans in Los Angeles in 1960, only about 2 percent were registered to vote.[18]

There may also have been an intimidation factor, driven by Cold War politics' growing obsession with the threat of enemies residing within the country. By the early 1950s, when Doña Natalia was expanding the Nayarit and sponsoring immigrants, organizations and individuals who offered left-wing or Communist political critiques of the government were vilified as un-American, subversive, and dangerous. Anti-Communist campaigns were often thinly veiled efforts to intimidate unionized workers, and they had a considerable chilling effect. El Congreso, which had welcomed activist immigrants into its ranks, had been suppressed. And after the passage of the Internal Security Act of 1950 and the Immigration and Nationality Act of 1952 (McCarran-Walter Act), immigrants who were suspected Communists or Communist sympathizers could be deported or have their naturalized citizenship stripped away. Whatever the case, the Nayarit workers I interviewed told me they did not talk much about American politics in their daily lives. Nor did they participate in the Chicanx movement. Yet they still felt connected to the nation's history and politics, thanks to events that unfolded in and near the restaurant itself.

The newly formed Mexican American Bar Association, for example, considered El Farolito, in East Los Angeles, their official meeting place, but they held regular meetings at the Nayarit, too. These meetings brought in

Figure 19. Los Angeles City Councilman Edward Roybal (sitting center, right) at a dinner event with a Mexican American women's organization, Las Madrinas del Niño, location unknown, ca. 1950. Shades of L.A. Photo Collection, Los Angeles Public Library.

customers from different class and geographic backgrounds and provided restaurant staff with opportunities to seek counsel. Los Angeles City Council member Edward Roybal regularly held meetings and banquets at the Nayarit, where he would spend time talking to the workers. Roybal served on the city council from 1949 to 1962; in 1962, he was elected to the US House of Representatives, where he served for the next thirty years; he is remembered, in part, for building a broad-based multiracial constituency.[19]

In 1967, Doña Natalia decided to open a bar at the restaurant. Neither she nor María knew how to run one, so in January 1968, María enrolled in a six-week course at the International School of Bartending on Sunset Boulevard. (Doña Natalia later sent Poncho to the same school.) María learned how to make 112 different cocktails at the school's mock bar and was paired with another student in the course, James Earl Ray. They shared a workstation and took turns playing customer and bartender, as one called out cocktail orders and the other made them. "I went to class, did the bartending exercises, and left. I never really got to know him," she recalled.[20] Soon after their training ended, Ray left Los Angeles and traveled to Memphis, where on April 4, 1968, he assassinated Martin Luther King Jr.[21] Tomás Lau, owner of the bartending school, provided the FBI with a photograph of himself and Ray taken at the end of the course, when Ray received his bartending certificate. They used it to help identify Ray.[22]

Two months later, on June 5, 1968, presidential candidate Robert ("Bobby") Kennedy was assassinated in Los Angeles. His death roiled ethnic Mexican communities, who held the Kennedy family in high esteem. John F. Kennedy and his wife, Jackie, had won the hearts of many Mexicans during their 1962 visit to Mexico City, where they attended Mass at the Basílica of Our Lady of Guadalupe. The basilica is famous for its image of Our Lady of Guadalupe, which devout Mexicans believe is a miraculous image of the Virgin Mary who appeared to an Indigenous peasant on that site in the 1500s; it is the second most visited Catholic shrine in the world after St. Peter's in Rome. Two thousand people attended the Mass and another 250,000 listened outside over a loudspeaker. When it ended, Jackie Kennedy placed a bouquet of red roses before the holy relic.[23] The visit received scant attention in the US press and appears in very few of the copious books on the Kennedys, but the Mexican papers gave it weeks of coverage. I myself grew up hearing from many sources that the First Lady had crawled on her knees from the square outside the basilica to the framed picture of Our Lady of Guadalupe at the altar, a distance of more than three hundred yards, following the custom of those who make the pilgrimage to the shrine. There are no written sources to corroborate this story, but proud Mexicans cited it as proof of the Kennedys' devotion to Catholicism and of their respect for the Mexican people. By the mid-1960s, Bobby Kennedy, then serving in Congress, had won his own place in the hearts of ethnic Mexicans for his support of César Chávez and the farmworkers' movement. Bobby Kennedy led a Senate inquiry into farmworker conditions, supported the boycotts and strikes that took place in California from 1965 to 1968, and sat by Chávez's side when Chávez ended his twenty-five-day hunger strike in 1968.

Workers at the Nayarit felt the horror of Bobby Kennedy's assassination especially keenly because three of their regular customers, Héctor Molina, Bobby Salcedo, and Victor Arrevillaga, worked as bartenders at the Ambassador Hotel and were on the job when Kennedy was assassinated there. Although Héctor, Bobby, and Victor did not actually meet Bobby Kennedy, another Mexican immigrant from Nayarit, Juan Romero, did. Romero, a seventeen-year-old busboy at the Ambassador, first encountered Kennedy when making a room-service delivery. "He shook my hand as hard as anyone has ever shaken it," he recalled. "I walked out of there 20 feet tall, thinking, 'I'm not just a busboy, I'm a human being.'" Later, after Kennedy had won the California primary and delivered his victory speech, he tried to avoid the throngs of supporters by going through the hotel's kitchen. A crowd had gathered there, too, and Romero was among them; Kennedy reached out to shake Romero's hand again, and then Sirhan Sirhan opened fire. Kennedy, hit three times, fell to the floor in front of Romero, who knelt to help him, reaching his hand under Kennedy's head to support it. As Ethel Kennedy squeezed him aside to kneel next to her husband, Romero's final contact was to press his own rosary beads into Kennedy's hand.[24]

The police and the FBI had kept everyone who was at the hotel at the time of the shooting overnight for questioning. No one was released until morning. In the days that followed, Héctor, Bobby, and Victor all came to the Nayarit and told their stories of that night again and again. Knowing that a countryman, Romero, had tried to offer Kennedy comfort in his last moments touched the entire community. Romero's involvement was reported in *El Eco* soon after the assassination and has been retold over the decades many times within ethnic Mexican communities in both the United States and Mexico.[25] Even for immigrants who did not—and, in the case of most Nayarit workers, could not vote—the nation's history and politics seemed to be unfolding within their very workplaces.

THE BRAVERY OF PLACE-TAKING

Though Los Angeles was known as the city of dreams, where Hollywood magic made anything seem possible, the nightmares of segregation, discrimination, and racial violence, including at the hands of the police, were lived reality for immigrants and people of color. The city's geographic boundaries were especially stark for African Americans. The African American community had grown dramatically during World War II, as Blacks moved to the area to work in the defense industry; when they sought housing outside of Black neighborhoods, they faced hostility. In the 1940s, when a public housing project was proposed for the then mostly white suburb of Compton, just south of Watts, residents and their political representatives fought the project with the slogan, "Keep the Negroes North of 130th Street." A 1947 Los Angeles Urban League study cited by the historian Josh Sides identified twenty-six different techniques used by white home owners to "scare off" prospective Black home owners, ranging from vandalism to death threats.[26] By the early 1950s, most Black Angelenos lived in Watts and rarely ventured beyond its borders except for work. They wanted to protect themselves from suspicion, harassment, or worse, and given the incidents of racial profiling and racist violence that Sides has documented, their fears were well founded.

Traversing Los Angeles's sprawling racialized landscape entailed some risk and tended to cast one's "otherness" into sharp relief. As Zora Neale Hurston wrote, "I do not always feel colored. . . . I feel most colored when I am thrown against a sharp white background."[27] Mexican Angelenos, most of whom lived in East Los Angeles, had similar experiences. Mexican women often commuted to the Westside to work as housekeepers or nannies. Some Mexican men took the same routes, to work as gardeners, while others traveled outside the city limits to work on citrus, avocado, poultry, or dairy farms.[28] But at the end of the day, most Mexicans got back on the bus or into their cars and returned to East Los Angeles. As one study put it, residential segregation in Los Angeles was an indicator not just of the geographic distance between ethnic Mexicans and their white neighbors but the social distance between them as well.[29]

When ethnic Mexicans ventured to predominantly white—and often middle-class or upper-class—locations outside of Echo Park, they were often seen as being out of place.[30] Ethnic Mexicans knew, both firsthand and through communal memory, that this was dangerous. From the start of American settlement in California, Mexicans were seen, first and foremost, as laborers; those who broke out of that mold, those who carried themselves differently, paid the price. After the American takeover in 1848, Californios, the Mexican elite, were dispossessed of their lands by both legal and extra-legal measures justified by a racial hierarchy in which whites were on top. During the gold rush, Mexican miners who tried to get their piece of the American dream found themselves shut out by measures such as the Foreign Miners Tax, which targeted nonwhites, and many of the would-be prospectors returned to Mexico. As Mexican immigration began to increase in the early twentieth century, driven by the push-pull of the Mexican Revolution and the increasing labor demands of large-scale agriculture in the US Southwest, white America insisted repeatedly that Mexican immigrants were welcome as laborers but only as laborers. Although large-scale employers successfully lobbied to exempt Mexican laborers from the 1924 Immigration Act's quota system, they fiercely resisted when those laborers attempted to organize. During a large strike in the Imperial Valley in 1934, union workers who protested their conditions were tear-gassed and arrested for vagrancy or trespassing. The historian Zaragosa Vargas has described extensive collusion among growers, border agents, and the INS during the 1930s that led to deportations.[31] Speaking out or claiming rights and space could get ethnic Mexicans removed not just from their workplace, but from the nation. William Deverell put it eloquently: "Much like darkroom alchemists, who fix and immobilize an image in time, place, and space, Anglos tried diligently to do the same to the Mexicans in their midst, to fix them in space and around a particular set of characteristics or traits tied ubiquitously to a social and ethnic category known as 'the Mexican.'"[32] This alchemy regularly affected Mexicans who ventured out of their designated sphere, and it took many forms, including racist mobs, the refusal to serve Mexicans at a restaurant, or the assumption that an ethnic Mexican at a place of business must be the help rather than a customer or guest.

Even cultural representations of ethnic Mexicans were confining. The movie stars who frequented the Nayarit loomed large in real life, but on screen they were often reduced to ethnic stereotypes. Rita Moreno frequently played exoticized Mexican spitfires, and Anthony Quinn was regularly cast as an ethnic villain (although marrying Cecil B. DeMille's daughter Katherine helped boost his career opportunities). Such recurrent stage images naturalized hierarchies outside the theaters, making it difficult for people to be seen out of character offscreen.[33]

Of course, many people of color, especially young people, challenged such boundaries, flouting norms in order to seek out opportunities, collaborations, or simply a good time outside their neighborhoods.[34] George Lipsitz teaches us that such boundary crossing can lead people to discover "similarities [in] the experience and culture of other groups" and thus to forge "families of resemblance."[35] When people interact in shared spaces, they can discover that they are bonded by "shared historical and cultural experiences."[36] Families of resemblance can be forged around any number of commonalities—a sports team, a cuisine, a song. Lipsitz gives the example of the Black saxophonist Chuck Higgins's 1952 single "Pachuko Hop," which was inspired by Chicanx aesthetics, slang, and dance moves he witnessed when playing in East Los Angeles halls.[37]

The shared spaces that enabled boundary crossing and the creation of "families of resemblance" represented a major threat to the status quo, in part because they were fraught with the specter of miscegenation. California had had anti-miscegenation laws on the books for decades, until they were overturned by the 1948 California Supreme Court case *Perez v. Sharp*. It would take almost twenty years more for the US Supreme Court to overturn laws banning interracial marriages throughout the United States, in *Loving v. Virginia* (1967).[38] Of course, while the laws changed, people's hearts and minds did not necessarily follow suit; there was still much moral panic over mingling in mixed racial and ethnic spaces lest it lead to interracial relationships. For example, in the late 1950s, Los Angeles began banning the rock 'n' roll concerts to which teens of all races were flocking. When organizers sought to hold dances outside the city limits, at the El Monte American Legion Stadium, El Monte officials initially denied the request. An official stated the rationale baldly: "We can't have these niggers dancing with these white kids." The matter was resolved only when representatives of the musician's union, the National Association for the Advancement of Colored People (NAACP), and the Jewish organization B'nai B'rith confronted city hall officials.[39]

In such a context, Doña Natalia's decree that her relatives and employees visit different parts of town—that they become place-takers—was a prompt to be daring, even to subvert the status quo. Though Nayarit workers may not have been trying to challenge social norms outright, venturing into the historically white neighborhoods of segregated Los Angeles must have required real bravery. The Nayarit's gay employees helped lead the way.

Like New York and San Francisco, midcentury Los Angeles had a vibrant gay subculture, though it was always vulnerable to attack by those in power. During World War II, thanks to the port in San Pedro and scores of manufacturing jobs, especially in aviation, the Los Angeles population boomed. Gays and lesbians were of course part of the migration of military members and job seekers, and many stayed on after the war because of the freedom and anonymity they found in the sprawling city. According to Lillian Faderman and Stuart Timmons, "Historically, more lesbian and gay institutions started in Los Angeles than anywhere else."[40] Wealthier gays and lesbians tended to live and play in the Hollywood Hills and West Hollywood; working- and middle-class gays and lesbians were more likely to live in Silver Lake or Echo Park. Some of the best-known bars and restaurants where they congregated were within a couple of miles of Echo Park, in Silver Lake, near MacArthur Park, and—for working-class gay bars—downtown Los Angeles.

Gay workers at the Nayarit, like other members of Los Angeles's gay community, socialized both close to home, within their neighborhood and ethnic networks, and farther afield, in gay neighborhoods and establishments where they could seek anonymity. Such outings were especially precarious for gay immigrants, who faced the risk not just of being entrapped by the police but also subsequently having to navigate the legal system with scant resources and limited English. Faderman and Timmons tell the story of Rudy Ruano, a Guatemalan immigrant who was charged with propositioning an officer in the late 1950s. Ruano, who could not afford an attorney, explained to the public defender that he could not possibly have propositioned the officer as he was accused: he could hardly speak English. The charge was downgraded to lewd conduct. Still, Ruano endured a terrifying two days in jail, and the arrest interfered with his plans to apply for US citizenship.[41]

Being arrested for homosexual behavior could permanently alter a person's life, and for immigrants, it could ruin the chance of getting a green card or a visa. Section 647 (a) of the California Penal Code prohibited soliciting or engaging in lewd or dissolute conduct. Section (d) prohibited loitering in or around a public toilet for the purpose of soliciting or engaging in lewd or dissolute conduct—and what constituted "lewd or dissolute" conduct was almost entirely up to the discretion of the arresting officer. While these were misdemeanors, anyone convicted of such violations was required to register as a sex offender, which stayed on a person's record for the rest of their life. Convictions for oral or anal sex were punishable by up to fifteen years in prison or a life sentence, respectively.[42] None of my interviewees described having this kind of experience—perhaps because they never had or perhaps because it's not the kind of information someone readily shares. Yet they doubtless were aware of the stakes. And as a historian, I recognized their bravery as place-takers, facing risks to live out their identities.

The gay and straight employees at the Nayarit gathered in and out of work, visited each other's homes, and talked on the phone. Carlos Porras often went out with Socorro "Coco" Rubio, a Nayarit customer, and Evelia Díaz Barraza Pack, both before and after she was married, to popular spots like the Hollywood Palladium. Carlos was part of what Evelia's husband, Ramón Pack, remembered as "the trio" of gay men, along with Pedro and Poncho, but Ramón socialized with them, too. "When we went out as a group," Ramón said, his gay companions "acted like men." Ramón's remark can certainly be understood as inflected with homophobia. But it was also a recognition that being read as gay in public was risky (as it still can be today). Poncho, too, remembered feeling the need to act "more macho" when he went out with groups of straight men from the Nayarit. Even contemporaneous gay rights groups like the Mattachine Society advocated that gay men publicly comport themselves in a conventional rather than flamboyant manner.[43] Certain nightclubs and bars with a primarily straight clientele allowed gay customers, Faderman and Timmons write, as long as they "behaved with discretion: no touching, no flamboyant clothes, no effeminate gestures."[44] Doña Natalia was not the only one who insisted on the rule "puede ser pero no ver."

When gay male employees went out together, they sometimes ventured far from Echo Park, often in groups comprising both employees and

Figure 20. Men out on the town, ca. 1960. Left to right: Luis Jiménez, a cook's helper at the Nayarit; two unidentified men; Ramón Barragan; Ricardo de la Garza, a waiter at the Nayarit. Both Barragan and de la Garza would go on to found urban anchors of their own. Photograph provided by Rosa Blanca Arrevillaga Sánchez.

customers. Poncho described going to the beach in Santa Monica, known as a gay pickup spot, with his coworkers Pedro Cueva and César Ortega and with regular customers such as Alfie and Jorge (last names unknown) and the Portillo brothers. The famous gay Mexican American novelist, John Rechy, described the scene:

> All the representatives of that world are here: the queens in extravagant bathing suits[;] . . . the masculine-acting, -looking homosexuals with tapered bodies and brown skins exhibiting themselves lying on the sand, trunks rolled down as far as possible . . . ; the older men who sit usually self-consciously covered as much as the beach-weather allows[;] . . . the

male-hustlers, usually not in trunks, usually shirtless, barefooted, levis-ed, the rest of their clothes wrapped beside them, awaiting whatever Opportunity may come at any moment.[45]

Others went downtown. The first gay bars in Los Angeles opened downtown on Skid Row, where—among the many boardinghouses, single-room hotels, factories, rail yards, and other marginal spaces—they could operate at least partly under the radar.[46] Some of these bars and clubs, like the 326, were known to be friendly to "'queens' who dressed effeminately," though the police arrested those who cross-dressed. Undeterred, Enrique (known at the Nayarit as La Tonga) dressed in drag and frequented gay bars on his nights off. Poncho recalled him going to bars frequented by "los morenos," as ethnic Mexicans commonly referred to African Americans.[47] Working (and in some cases, living) at a geographic crossroads gave these men a launching pad from which, within the constraints of the time, they could explore those additional agendas and claim space for their authentic lives.

CREATING NEW URBAN ANCHORS

Between 1959 and 1973, the spirit of placemaking and place-taking that Doña Natalia had nurtured helped at least six former Nayarit employees open businesses of their own, all of which went on to become urban anchors. Five were Mexican restaurants, all on Sunset Boulevard, some within walking distance of each other; the sixth was a small, bustling market. The owners and employees of these businesses, and of the Nayarit, supported one another and patronized one another's businesses, establishing an extended community in Echo Park and Silver Lake where ethnic Mexicans could feel safe in a home away from home. Yet they did not have a monolithic customer base: they welcomed everyone from neighborhood residents and white leftists to downtown white-collar employees on a lunch break and hungry people from across the city.

The first of these restaurants, Taxco (renamed La Villa Taxco when it expanded), was founded in 1959 by Virginia ("Vicky") Lizárraga Tamayo and her husband, Ernesto ("Ernie"), at the western edge of Silver Lake, where Sunset and Hollywood Boulevards meet. Ernie was single and did not cook. He dined at the Nayarit nightly and laughed and conversed with the other regulars and with the workers. "He was twenty-five, tall, and handsome, and I was only seventeen. He didn't even notice me!" laughs Vicky, remembering meeting him at the Nayarit where she worked for a stint as a cashier. A couple of years later, they met again at Los Cocos, the restaurant of another Nayarita, Andrea Ramos, and the relationship blossomed from there. They married in January 1959 and opened Taxco a few months later. Vicky's uncle, Ramón Barragan, had lived with Doña Natalia when he was seventeen and trained as a cook at the Nayarit. When Taxco opened, Ramón was still working nights at the Nayarit. In the morning, he would go to Vicky and Ernie's restaurant and help train the kitchen staff and prepare for the day. Favorites at the twelve-table restaurant included *carne asada* (grilled citrus-marinated flank steak), steak picado (steak sautéed with onions, garlic, tomatoes, and a little heat from a serrano chili), and *arroz con pollo*. Like the Nayarit, Taxco stayed open until 4:00 a.m., hoping to catch the late-night crowd after the bars and clubs had closed. Around 1966, they bought the building across the street, which they remodeled into a 280-person-capacity restaurant, complete with a banquet room, at which point they decided that they had had enough of such late hours and began to close at 2:00 a.m. On the first night of the new closing time, the manager turned away a customer seeking *menudo* (a tripe and hominy soup considered a hangover cure) after a night of drinking. Incensed, the man yelled, "¡Nomás se hicieron ricos y se hicieron huevones!" (As soon as they got rich, they got lazy!). The Tamayos grew their first small restaurant into a chain of twelve restaurants (La Villa Taxco and Casa Vallarta) that spanned Los Angeles, Orange, and San Diego Counties; they sold the business to a restaurant corporation in 1986. Fifteen years after they sold the chain, people were still writing to the *Los Angeles Times* food section asking the paper to republish past columns that featured the restaurant's enchilada sauce recipe, with its secret ingredient, Mexican chocolate.[48]

In 1961, drawing on the expertise he had attained at the Nayarit and Taxco, Ramón Barragan and his then-wife, Grace, established a small restaurant of their own, three blocks east of the Nayarit and six blocks west of Dodger Stadium: the eponymous Barragan's. Doña Natalia provided some seed money, and Ramón and Grace borrowed against their home in order to purchase the restaurant and property. This ultimately protected them from the rent hikes and redevelopment that threatened leased restaurants, especially when the neighborhood gentrified in later years, but it was a bold move. When the restaurant opened, the couple had four children (they would later have two more daughters). The family lived in Echo Park, exactly one mile from the restaurant, and they did not own a car. This meant that errands for the restaurant had to be carried out on foot. They bought food for the kitchen at the Pioneer Market, which was across the street. In the morning, they would walk to a shop a few blocks down Sunset to buy donuts for the breakfast rush before opening their restaurant at 6:00 a.m. Ramón worked the back of the house as the cook, and Grace worked the front, waiting on customers.

Barragan's benefited from Grace's acumen as a cultural broker. Along with Carlos Porras and María, Grace was one of the few Mexican Americans in this social network, and she had experience working at an American restaurant, Larry's, on Sunset Boulevard in Echo Park. When Barragan's began, its business card stated, in English, that they offered both Mexican and American fare, and the menu included tacos, enchiladas, machaca, and costillas, along with beef stew and corned beef and cabbage. Grace told me that their American-friendly menu was a conscious choice to carve out a niche distinct from the Nayarit, since Doña Natalia was a "little" displeased with the competition. While this may seem at odds with Doña Natalia's gift of seed money to the Barragans, she may have felt simultaneously competitive and obligated, or desirous, to help Ramón, the son of a close friend from her hometown. In any case, demand for the Mexican food at Barragan's quickly grew. "Our little pot of beans was this big," Grace told me, spreading her hands a few inches apart, "and people liked it, and so it grew and grew and we eventually had to give up the beef stew." Within a few years, Barragan's reputation for excellent Mexican food was unquestioned. Years later, a 1983 *Los Angeles Times* reviewer described their food, collectively, as "shockingly good," compared to the homogenized, Americanized Mexican food she expected, showing once again how distinct regional Mexican fare still was even decades after Doña Natalia opened the Nayarit.[49]

Barragan's became an urban anchor, even earning an official certificate of recognition from the Mayor's Office. It served movie stars and Dodger players and, once, Prince Philip of Spain, but like the Nayarit, it retained a solid customer base of working-class Mexicans. When it first opened, Barragan's could serve a maximum of twenty-five customers, but it later expanded into a seven-thousand-square-foot establishment that could accommodate three hundred customers. Ramón went on to open two additional locations, in Burbank and Glendale.

Around 1967, when the Tamayos relocated Taxco across the street to their larger establishment, two former waiters from the Nayarit, Ricardo de la Garza and his business partner and boyfriend, Salvador "Chavo" Barrajas, opened El Chavo at the site of the former Taxco. "Chavito," as he was affectionately called, was well liked, and employees and regulars from the Nayarit became frequent patrons. A 1974 *Los Angeles Times* review lauded the restaurant for its mole, machaca, and flan and for an overall menu of "well-prepared dishes that are not found in many Mexican restaurants."[50] After Chavo and Ricardo split up, Chavo opened a new restaurant, a few blocks east on Sunset Boulevard, in 1973. El Conquistador, located on the border of Echo Park and Silver Lake, served traditional Mexican fare such as tacos and

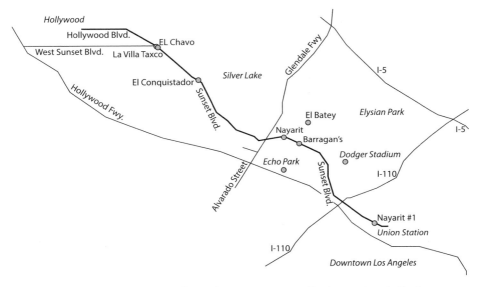

Map 2. Immigrant entrepreneurs as place-takers: restaurants and businesses founded by former Nayarit workers.

enchilada plates and, like El Chavo, lethal margaritas. Chavo and his new partner and co-owner, Jesús "Jesse" Pinto, hired mostly Mexican immigrants, many of whom—like the beloved waiter and host Ricardo de la Torre—were gay men. El Conquistador became an unofficial headquarters for the Mexican and gay communities alike. The restaurant always felt festive, with its boisterous atmosphere, eclectic artwork covering all the brightly painted walls, Christmas lights strung from the high ceiling from which hung a two-tiered chandelier, and flower-patterned stained-glass windows, about which *Los Angeles Magazine* noted, "During lunchtime and happy hour, they become spotlights—blurry ones when tequila is involved." One newspaper columnist called its bold aesthetic, which included paintings of gay icons like Liza Minnelli and Marilyn Monroe, along with bright and showy seasonal decor, "caliente kitsch."[51]

During the 1950s and 1960s, police commonly raided bars where gays congregated, abusing and arresting the gay clientele. The openly gay environment at El Conquistador signaled the growing strength of the gay liberation movement. The restaurant was just two blocks from the Black Cat, a Silver Lake bar where in 1966, as patrons gathered to ring in the New Year, police arrested and beat fourteen men. Two men who were arrested for kissing each other were later convicted under state law and required to register as sex offenders. In February 1967, hundreds of protesters gathered outside the bar to decry the police and the ensuing legal actions, sparking new efforts to fight for gay rights. Two years later, in 1969, when police raided the Stonewall Inn, a gay bar in New York City's Greenwich Village, patrons and communities fought back physically, launching protests that lasted for several nights. The Black Cat, like Stonewall, is now considered one of the homes of the gay liberation movement. It is an official historical-cultural monument in Los Angeles.[52]

Chavo and Jesse wanted to establish El Conquistador as a similarly central gay urban anchor, so they created a welcoming, festive environment.[53] The restaurant would become a central site for gay and gay-friendly groups to congregate during the Sunset Junction Street Fair, becoming thronged with even more customers than usual during the fair, which cordoned off five city blocks for two days every August from 1980 through 2010. The festival, organized by the Sunset Junction Neighborhood Alliance, grew to attract tens of thousands of people before permit issues and a backlog of debts brought it to an end.[54]

Just off of Sunset Boulevard, on Echo Park Avenue, another Nayarit alumna, Evelia Pack, joined her husband, Ramón, and his family in launching a mom-and-pop neighborhood market in 1967, El Batey. The name, which refers to a one-stop grocery store where one can also obtain household goods, nodded to the pride Ramón Pack took in his Cuban roots. Their connections from the Nayarit followed them. According to Ramón, El Batey's first customer was Ramón Barragan, who generously tried to place an order for hundred-pound sacks of rice and beans for his restaurant, which was just a few blocks away. But El Batey, Ramón Pack recounted with a laugh, only sold five-pound bags.

Evelia, Doña Natalia's niece, had been a young cashier at the Nayarit when she caught Brando's eye. Now she worked as the cashier at her own market, but as at the Nayarit, she did far more than make change: her warmth suffused the space and made El Batey a place people wanted to be. Seven days a week for almost fifty years, Evelia perched on a stool behind the cash register as a placemaker, greeting customers with a smile and connecting regulars with one another. Evelia extended credit to her Latinx customers, many of whom lived in the apartments upstairs in the building. Sometimes she even cooked for them at her home in Echo Park, inviting them over for a meal or bringing the food to share at the store. At other times, she was a guest at their tables. A *Los Angeles Times* article on Evelia and her store called her the neighborhood's "spiritual anchor" and noted, "She's history. She's community. She's block mother."[55] Evelia and her family continued to run the market for decades.

In many ways, the stories of the Nayarit, La Villa Taxco, Barragan's, El Chavo, El Conquistador, and El Batey resonate with well-documented histories of "Black capitalism," in which Black entrepreneurs opened businesses where the Black community would be welcomed rather than discriminated against. Abiding by the slogan, "Don't Spend Your Money Where You Can't Work," Black-owned businesses and their customers boycotted racist businesses and pressured white-owned businesses to hire Black employees. Such strategies have been in use for generations, as African Americans have sought to leverage economic self-empowerment to boost community and political power.[56] As a Mexican immigrant, Doña Natalia did not have access to these same types of strategies, but her placemaking and place-taking created the conditions through which such institutions could be created in decades to come (though gentrification would upend these urban anchors decades later).[57] The businesses that Doña Natalia helped usher into being, whether with seed money or with training, advice, and knowledge, economically empowered this community of Mexican immigrants in Echo Park.

These were also welcoming places that, for a few decades, helped define the character of Echo Park and Silver Lake. Doña Natalia had encouraged her family, friends, and employees to venture out across Los Angeles and claim the city as their own. Now, the businesses they founded attracted loyal customers from within the neighborhood and across the city. When I was a child, I knew that on any given day my family and I would run into people I knew up and down Sunset Boulevard. We might stop at El Conquistador, order a combo plate that came with a simple but nourishing cup of *sopita* (a vegetable and noodle soup), and catch up with Chavo and Jesse. As kids, and later as adults, we would sometimes walk to Dodger Stadium on game day so that we could visit friends and fictive kin along the way, stopping at Barragan's. I would place my order, and Lupita Ramos, a former Nayarit waitress, or Armando, Ramón Barragan's son, would ask after my mom or aunts, and I would ask about their families. That sense of being in an extended home wasn't just something my family experienced; it was part of the spirit of the place. Customers gathered at these restaurants with friends and family for quick bites and lavish, celebratory meals, and the restaurants hosted countless wedding receptions, birthday parties, anniversaries, and baptismal celebrations. After a festive night out, hungover revelers knew they could come by for much-needed bowls of restorative menudo. These restaurants were places where customers' memories of family, food, and place fused, sometimes centered in Echo Park and sometimes stretching back to their hometowns in Mexico. Going out to eat affirmed that you were never alone. You were always connected. You were rooted. You had a place.

CHAPTER FIVE

Maintaining Ties

Even as Doña Natalia and her family, friends, employees, and colleagues built their communities in Los Angeles, they stayed connected to life in Nayarit. Many immigrants returned to Nayarit for special events and visits, often toting an extra suitcase or two filled with luxury items like clothing, makeup, perfume, and See's Candies—referred to as *los chocolates de la abuelita* because of the white-haired woman pictured on the box. They distributed these gifts not just to their own friends and family but also to others, on behalf of fellow immigrant coworkers and friends in Los Angeles. Those same suitcases would then be filled with gifts from relatives in Nayarit to send back to Los Angeles: beaded jewelry, artwork, and healing balms made with peyote by the Indigenous Huichol; baptismal gowns; wedding favors; dried shrimp; dried fruit candies; beans, cheeses, and tamales; cake (cake in the United States was considered too sweet); medicine (no one trusted the doctors in the United States); and tequila (no one trusted Jose Cuervo). When Doña Natalia traveled to her home country, which she did regularly, she would bring extra gifts to be raffled off for donations to the Catholic church in Acaponeta. People also wrote letters and kept up with the news by reading *El Eco*, the Nayarit paper, which reported on goings-on in both Nayarit and Los Angeles. In the late 1960s, other Nayaritas in Los Angeles formed a hometown association that connected them with one another and raised funds to support civic projects in Nayarit. These immigrants' placemaking efforts unfolded in and out of restaurants on Sunset Boulevard, but they also extended from Echo Park and Silver Lake to Acaponeta and the neighboring town of Tecuala.

The idea that immigrants' lives are often shaped by ties to their home countries, even when they have lived in their new country for years, decades, or generations, is not new. Immigration scholars long have explored, to excellent effect, the important roles immigrants have played in establishing and maintaining transnational connections while adapting to their new homes. Immigrants cultivated social networks that—as at the Nayarit restaurant—could facilitate immigration and sometimes transformed the culture and political economy in their country of origin.[1] Scholars who have examined this phenomenon at the local scale call it, variously, the "glocal," "transnational urbanism,"[2] or "translocal," which is the term I prefer because it emphasizes the granular texture of these interactions.[3] After all, Doña Natalia and the other immigrants whose stories I have been following understood their identities not so much as a matter of nationality, but as shaped by patria chica. They saw themselves as part of a specific, contingent community of Nayaritas in Los Angeles. When they needed help, they did not turn to the US or Mexican government or to the Mexican consul (though he, too, was a Nayarita). They looked instead to each other, to the networks embedded in and created by their own placemaking, which was both local and translocal.

EL ECO: A TRANSLOCAL PLACEMAKER

Los Angeles's flagship Spanish-language daily, *La Opinión*, had one of the largest circulations of any Spanish-language paper in the country. It was founded in 1926 by Ignacio E. Lozano, a Texan who had already started another important Spanish-language paper, *La Prensa*, in San Antonio.[4] By the 1950s, Nicolas Avila, a Nayarita, was the paper's editor, and though *La Opinión*'s readers hailed from all across Mexico, he freely expressed his attachment to his home state. In his weekly column, "Panoramas Angelinos," Avila wrote fondly of Nayarit, addressing Nayaritas directly in his column and referring to himself as a "patriotic servant," though some readers wrote in to criticize his partiality. Avila responded that anyone who loves his own patria chica knows how to respect others' homelands and pointed out that he did so, too: he praised all of Mexico. Where the rest of *La Opinión* was concerned, though, there was scant attention to the daily lives of Nayaritas, whether in Mexico or abroad. *La Opinión* covered some major community events in Los Angeles, but its social column, "Sociales," which appeared on Sundays, focused primarily on the lives of middle- and upper-class ethnic Mexicans.

The immigrant community of Nayaritas in Los Angeles certainly read *La Opinión*, but *El Eco* was far more important to them, and by all accounts, they read it with more frequency, loyalty, and interest. *El Eco* was not only vital in keeping immigrants abreast of what was happening in their hometowns; it was also a central vehicle in reinforcing and reinvigorating the ties that knit Nayarit and L.A. together and shaped their mutual sense of identity. Founded in 1917 and based in Acaponeta, *El Eco de Nayarit* is the fourth-oldest newspaper in Mexico.[5] Whereas other newspapers of the time functioned as mouthpieces for the government, *El Eco* prided itself on its independence. According to the small boxed text in each edition, "El Eco de Nayarit, para orgullo de Acaponeta es el único periódico de la República que no vive del favor Oficial" (*El Eco de Nayarit*, for the pride of Acaponeta, is the only newspaper of the Republic that does not live by Official favor).[6] This was particularly important for readers who were not members of the elite class and who felt that they were not a priority in Mexico's vision for its future.

In theory, the postwar shift to industrial capitalism, commonly called the "Mexican miracle," led to more opportunities and new jobs. But in practice, these jobs often offered low salaries, and the government repeatedly responded to organized labor's efforts to improve wages and workers' rights with intimidation, even mobilizing federal troops to put down striking workers and arresting union leaders. The working class increasingly felt that the government was corrupt and that bribery and rigged elections were part of a larger strategy to produce and protect millionaires. Frustration grew through the late 1950s and 1960s, which were marked by rapid population growth, urbanization, rising illiteracy rates, and a widening gap between the haves and the have-nots.[7] Nayaritas were hit particularly hard by the postwar economic changes, in part, because their state was slow to implement the types of agrarian reforms that would have ensured they could earn a living wage.[8]

El Eco published biweekly, on Sundays and Thursdays, and was the main news vehicle for Nayaritas until the first municipal television towers were installed in Acaponeta in 1967. Even then, access to television news was limited to those who could afford to buy a set and install a home antenna.[9] Under the leadership of Martín Sáizar, who by the late 1960s had edited *El Eco* for some forty years, the paper reported on both national and local stories; it also offered some international news, mostly relating to the United States, and included a social column in every issue. "Rueda Ferris" (Ferris Wheel), the gossip column, covered all the ups and downs of life: births, deaths, baptisms, birthdays, courtships, weddings, parties, and accounts of family and friends visiting one another in Mexico and the United States. Few of these stories featured the goings-on of the elite, a handful of wealthy business owners and local politicians; most columns were dedicated to ordinary residents. Sáizar used his platform to fundraise on their behalf. His efforts helped finance a bridge connecting Novillero Beach (near Acaponeta) to the mainland and to assist the Indigenous Huichol people in the region. Today, his legacy is commemorated in the name of the local baseball stadium: the Estadio Béisbol Acaponeta Martín M. Sáizar.[10]

Beginning in August 1964, the forty-seventh anniversary of the paper's founding, *El Eco* published an annual anniversary edition, with extra pages of advertisements printed in color that had been purchased by both Acaponeta business owners and los de afuera who wanted to promote their new lives and their accomplishments. Doña Natalia's ads for the Nayarit ran in these issues. So did more personalized messages from people like Carmen Morales Díaz, who worked as the head housekeeper and nanny for the writer and producer Dominick Dunne, his wife, Ellen ("Lenny"), and their three children.[11] Morales took out a full-page ad congratulating Sáizar on his successful newspaper. Morales did not mention her profession in *El Eco*, but she made sure to list her hometown as Beverly Hills at the bottom of the ad, presumably to convey an air of success.[12]

"Rueda Ferris" and the anniversary ads helped readers who were still in Acaponeta keep their finger on the pulse of the cultural life of los de afuera in Los Angeles, from dance clubs and restaurants to Dodgers games and concerts. Thus, although *acaponetenses* may not have had television sets, they knew a fair amount about life north of the border. For example, when Doña Natalia hosted a going-away party at her home in Echo Park for Chayo's brother, Luis Díaz, who was moving to New York, someone sent a photo of some of the guests to *El Eco*. The newspaper ran a brief mention of the event in the "Rueda Ferris" column, and when the photo was returned, my mother or grandmother pasted a piece of the column to the back of the photo. It records not just the event, but how the news about it traveled from one place to the other and back again.

Like Facebook (often referred to as "El Face" in Spanish), *El Eco* functioned to help keep the community together, even as it was spread over thousands of miles. It also helped Nayaritas in Los Angeles keep in touch with their hometown and with the broader news of the state, in addition to offering glimpses into the texture of everyday life back home—something *La Opinión* could not or did not do.

Figure 21. A going-away party hosted by Doña Natalia Barraza at her home in Echo Park for Luis Díaz, brother of Chayo Díaz Cueva. Left to right: Carlota Silva, Evelia Díaz Barraza, Concepcion ("Concha") Alcaraz (cashier at the Nayarit), Vicky Cueva, María Perea (listed on back as María Barraza).

Unlike *La Opinión*, *El Eco* was not available on newsstands in the United States, but it was ubiquitous in Los Angeles's Nayarita communities. Some people had subscriptions and would receive a bundle of recently published editions by mail once a month. Others read copies sent by their family members in Mexico.[13] Every Nayarita family in Los Angeles that I knew when I was growing up there subscribed to *El Eco* but not necessarily to *La Opinión*. I have a vivid memory of my tía Chayo on the porch of her home in Echo Park in the late afternoon reading *El Eco*. People often passed by and said hello—she was a fixture in the neighborhood, friendly

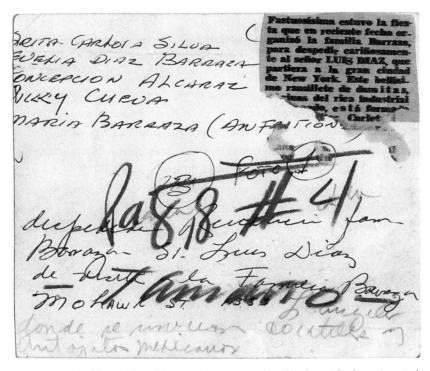

Figure 22. A brief description of the event that appeared in *El Eco*'s social column is pasted onto the back of the photo. Photograph provided by María Perea Molina.

and chatty—but I knew that when *El Eco* came she was not to be disturbed. She read it straightaway, and later the whole family would talk about the news, comparing notes and impressions. Decades later, while doing research for this project, I found that many of my respondents had kept old issues of *El Eco*, which they saw as important records of community life. Rosemary Castillo, a second-generation Nayarita, offered to lend me all of her family's anniversary editions. Guillermo "Willy" Casillas said his family possessed a similarly comprehensive archive. "We kept all of our issues of *El Eco*," he told me.[14]

At the same time, *El Eco*'s coverage of los de afuera helped with the more complex, and less recognized, process of what I call "cultural priming," whereby Nayaritas still living in Mexico could imagine what it would be like to live in the United States. Historians of the Great Migration have chronicled how African Americans more readily relocated from the South after hearing from loved ones who had resettled in the North or West, giving them a glimpse of how life might look there.[15] *El Eco* had a similar effect. While American newspapers, radio shows, movies, and job recruitment materials suggested that Mexican immigrants might fill the role of laborer, *El Eco* showed them much more: where they might live and play, how they might spend time and with whom. When Nayaritas traveled to el Norte, whether to visit, to work temporarily, or to settle, they had a sense of place before they went.

Martín Sáizar, *El Eco*'s managing director and owner, developed this translocal connection through extensive in-person contact. Beginning in 1964, Sáizar took annual extended trips to California to connect with los de afuera, advertise the newspaper, and collect payments for new and renewed subscriptions. While Sáizar's trips were meant to boost *El Eco*'s bottom line, they were not merely transactional. Each year, he wrote a multipart series for the paper describing the many ways in which he connected with los de afuera, bringing la patria chica to them and fortifying translocal ties in the process. Nayaritas put him up in their homes, hosted parties to gather fellow nationals, and drove him around town. Guillermo "Willy" Casillas, a child at the time, would accompany his father, who was originally from Acaponeta, when he showed Sáizar around. "It was a big deal when Señor Sáizar came to town," Casillas recalled.[16]

The strength and density of his ties with Los Angeles's Nayarita community made Martín Sáizar more of an insider than Nicolas Avila, editor of the local and far more prestigious *La Opinión*. After Sáizar announced his retirement in 1967, a group of Nayaritas threw a retirement banquet in his honor. The Friday before the banquet, Sáizar visited Avila at the offices of *La Opinión* and filled him in on the latest news from Los Angeles's Nayarita community. Excited at the prospect that celebrating Sáizar's retirement would also serve to "unirnos a los Nayaritas dispersos" (to unite us scattered Nayaritas), Avila was astonished to learn of the size and activity of that community. "¡Oh sorpresa!" (Oh surprise!), he exclaimed. "I've discovered there are many more of us than I thought."[17] Even as the editor of the largest Spanish-language paper in the United States and loyal to his patria chica, he was not aware of the numbers of his fellow Nayaritas living in Los Angeles.

After Martín Sáizar stepped down, his son Antonio Sáizar became *El Eco*'s director. (Sáizar stayed on as managing editor during the transition.) Though Antonio Sáizar had worked at the paper since 1951, he apparently had not accompanied his father on earlier California trips. Yet he clearly benefited from the legwork his father had done. During his first trip as editor, the same network of Nayaritas who had helped his father ushered him around Los Angeles. Antonio Sáizar wrote about his experiences in a two-part article, "Travel Notes," which shows that he moved around with striking ease.[18] He went to the typical tourist spots, including Hollywood and Chinatown, but he also visited Cypress Park, a mostly Mexican working-class neighborhood in northeastern Los Angeles, and traveled to the San Fernando Valley, stopping in Canoga Park, likely visiting los de afuera who had settled there. And he spent time at many of the places that Doña Natalia and her former employees had built into community landmarks. "I woke up this morning in the mood for an outing so I went to Ramoncito Pack's store to pick up folks," he wrote of Ramón and Evelia Pack's El Batey. "We went over to Doña Natalia's house to see how she was. We then went nearby to a park where we could watch the baseball team from Nayarit play."[19] In the evening, they ate on Olvera Street, then took in some late-night mariachi music at La Fonda. (Nati Cano, leader of Mariachi Los Camperos, had opened La Fonda earlier that same year, motivated in part by having been denied entrance to a restaurant in Lubbock, Texas, because he was Mexican. La

Fonda became a landmark, and stayed open for nearly four decades.)[20] On a different evening, Antonio Sáizar reported, "The whole group of us went to dinner at Restaurant Nayarit . . . [where] the talk continued, we received the attention of Evita Díaz López, Alfonso García, the always genteel Mary Perea, and that is how once again who knows how many hours flew by." The restaurant afforded Sáizar a place to easily encounter people he knew: Evita was a waitress from Nayarit; Alfonso was Poncho, the waiter whom Pedro had convinced to come to the United States; and "Mary" was how Sáizar Americanized María's name. The sense of familiarity Sáizar described gave readers in Nayarit a sense of Los Angeles as lively and fun, a place where they, too, could find a sense of welcome familiarity.

El Eco was such an important part of the life of the community of Nayaritas abroad that when Martín Sáizar announced his retirement, almost one hundred people gathered at the banquet held in his honor.[21] Even more were turned away at the door, because the venue—El Zarape restaurant, in Inglewood—could not accommodate the crowd. It was the largest formal gathering of Nayaritas to date in the city. Most had emigrated from Acaponeta or the neighboring town of Tecuala, including Tomás Lau, who owned the bartending school that both María and Poncho had attended, as well as Pedro Cueva, Doña Natalia's piano-playing nephew. A few honored guests, like the deputy chief of the Acaponeta telegraph office, had traveled from Mexico for the occasion to meet and mingle with los de afuera.[22] Arriving guests were greeted by the enthusiastic music of a mariachi band. (With eleven members or more, mariachi bands are costly to hire; their presence signals the importance of an event.) As Sáizar and the Mexican consul, Raúl González Galarza, entered the room, accompanied by their wives, the mariachis played "El Corrido de Nayarit," the state's unofficial anthem, whose opening line asserts, "Yo tengo el orgullo de ser Nayarita" (I am proud to be a Nayarita). As the music coursed through the room, the assembled crowd sang along, some of them crying with emotion.

The evening was a testament to the spirit of patria chica. People greeted each other with laughter and hugs. Guests from Acaponeta and Tecuala competed with one another through hoots, cheers, and applause to see which town was best represented. The food was authentic Nayarit cuisine—something the kitchen staff at El Zarape, which catered to an Americanized clientele, ironically lacked the knowledge and skills to prepare; three women originally from Acaponeta took over for the evening.[23] An impressive flower arrangement featured a placard reading, "For a better Nayarit," underscoring the connections between Los Angeles Nayaritas and their counterparts in Mexico. Jesús Robles, the brother of El Zarape's owner, Rigoberto Robles López, made a toast extolling the crowd's shared bonds:

> Dear friends, dear fellow countrymen, let us drink to the friendship that brings us together, the camaraderie that we profess, and the joy of being together. May it never fade but on the contrary, grow every day, becoming stronger and never dying.[24]

There were speeches throughout the evening, from high-profile guests like Consul González and Nicolas Avila, editor of *La Opinión*, as well as from community members such as one Isabel Sandoval de Shisler.[25] Jesús Robles wrote a piece about the evening for *El Eco*, describing these speeches as "sincere," "eloquent," "deep and sentimental," and "unifying." Sáizar was nearly overcome. When it was his turn to speak, he clenched his fists to keep his emotions steady. After he thanked those who had gathered, the mariachis began to play "Las Golondrinas" (The Swallows), a traditional Mexican song of farewell, in which the migrating swallows represent a longing for home. "The 90-plus people gathered here sang it like it had never been sung," wrote Robles, noting that tears rolled down Sáizar's cheeks.[26]

A week after Robles's story ran, *La Opinión* covered the event, too; in fact, its account was reprinted in *El Eco*.[27] Though separated by thirteen hundred miles and an international border, readers in Nayarit and Los Angeles were reading the same coverage of the same event, making it easier for them to understand themselves as part of a translocal community. The coverage also let them know about a key purpose of the evening: in addition to celebrating Sáizar, it was intended to serve as a springboard to launch a new hometown association (HTA), or *club de oriundos*, for Nayaritas in Los Angeles.

HOMETOWN ASSOCIATIONS

Working-class Mexican immigrants in Los Angeles generally steered clear of the state except when it was inescapable—if, for example, they needed to obtain or renew visas. Knowing they could not depend on the US government to look out for their welfare—it was ready, after all, to deport those it deemed "public charges"—Mexican immigrants in the first few decades of the twentieth century formed mutual aid societies to help themselves. Members pooled resources to pay for medical expenses, funerals, and other basic and emergency needs in their new homeland. The societies also provided members with a sense of connection in an often dauntingly unfamiliar land. By the 1940s, when the second generation of ethnic Mexicans in the United States had come of age, the societies dwindled, though some found their footing in other organizations such as unions and nascent civil rights organizations. But by the 1960s, as immigration surged and Mexicans became the largest single foreign-born group in the United States, many immigrants came together to form HTAs.[28] HTAs built on and formalized the looser networks that places like the Nayarit had nurtured and provided concrete ways for immigrants to help their communities in Mexico and in their new homes.

Ana Minian, in her powerful book, *Undocumented Lives*, notes that because of Mexico's precarious economic situation, the Mexican government viewed Mexican migrants who sought work in the United States as a burdensome surplus population and was relieved to be rid of them. Once in the United States, these migrants were not only left to fend for themselves but also had to use their own capital and energy to take on what ought to have been government responsibilities. By the 1960s, HTAs sprang up to fill the void, forming what Minian calls an "extra-territorial welfare state" that funneled money home. Some of this money went to pave roads or construct and maintain schools, but since many immigrants wanted a more tangible connection to their culture, many of their donations funded the churches and plazas that were at the heart of civic life. It would take decades for the Mexican government to acknowledge the tremendous opportunities for economic and social change these funds presented for local development projects. The government then created policies that shifted remittances for public works from private and individual matters to transactions organized and amplified in public programs.[29] At the time that the Nayaritas in Los Angeles founded their HTA, the state considered them community members operating on their own.

The HTA the banquet helped launch was named Club Social Nayarita en Los Angeles and came to be known simply as Club Nayarit. Its organizers aimed to help their compatriots living in the state of Nayarit, their patria chica. For Nayaritas in Los Angeles, Club Nayarit was intended as a source of support and solidarity. One news story called it a place to gather "coras que andamos por estas tierras de California" (Coras who go about these lands of California). Describing the members as "Coras," an Indigenous people of Nayarit, was a celebration of native heritage (akin to the Nayarit's Christmas parade float) and a reflection of the HTA's highly local sense of identity.[30]

From its inception, Club Nayarit had support from key leaders in the community, including Nicolas Avila and Mexican consul González. The initial meetings were announced in both *La Opinión* and *El Eco*, since, though it was published in Nayarit, it had so many readers in Los Angeles. The first meeting took place at the Casa del Mexicano, which the Mexican consulate had established in 1931 as a safe haven amid the discrimination directed at Mexicans during the Depression.[31] Consul González presided over Club

Nayarit's first meeting in 1967, although all agreed this would be a onetime thing, as the club was to be an organization for all, "without social or regional distinctions." Newspaper coverage stated that three hundred people signed up that day, and though it is not clear whether all of them were present, the meeting was declared a success. Attendees agreed that every member would pay "modest" dues, which suggests that they took into account that their membership included people of different classes.[32] They also agreed to host events, like dances, in order to raise funds to improve education and public projects in Nayarit. In its first official disbursement of aid, reminiscent of the mutual aid organizations of the early part of the twentieth century, the club paid to have the body of a deceased campesino shipped to Nayarit from Los Angeles and gave his widow $1,000.

Attendees at this first meeting also elected a president: José Inés Jiménez. Inés hailed from Tepic, the capital of Nayarit, and was part of the "old guard" of Mexican immigrants who had arrived during and, like Doña Natalia, after the Mexican Revolution. In 1921, Inés had opened a furniture store in East Los Angeles that he named Nayarit Furniture. Described as "un apasionado mexicano" (a passionate Mexican),[33] Inés already had amassed extensive civic and charitable experience through his work with the Mexican Civic Patriotic Committee, the Mexican Chamber of Commerce, and El Comité de Beneficencia Mexicana (the Mexican Charity Committee), the last two of which were formed during the Depression by ethnic Mexicans in response to scapegoating.[34] Inés was also director of the Mexican Independence Day Parade, a high-profile event that since 1927 had been held annually in East Los Angeles and was a more or less mandatory occasion for any politician wanting to reach out to the Latinx community.[35] Inés, in short, had been a placemaker for fifty years, with an extensive network and an ongoing commitment to his immediate community, conationals, and patria chica. *La Opinión* described him as "el más connotado de nuestros Nayaritas" (the most notable of us Nayaritas).[36]

In September 1968, on the occasion of its first anniversary, the Club Nayarit held its first dance. *El Eco* promoted the dance in its widely read anniversary issue, running a one-page story complete with a half-page group photo of fifty-two of the club's members.[37] (In contrast, the L.A.-based *La Opinión* had no announcement of the dance.) Though the majority of Mexicans at the time lived in East L.A., Club Nayarit's members seemed ready to traverse the city, irrespective of its segregated racial landscape. They had started the club in South L.A., and now, they hosted their dance at St. Peter's Catholic Church Hall, an ornate and elegant building that was the spiritual home of L.A.'s Italian community. The hall was on Broadway, at the edge of downtown, near Chinatown, just a couple of miles east of Echo Park, on the other side of the hill from Dodger Stadium. The dance was a major fundraiser for the club's ongoing projects in Nayarit. In their first year, the club had raised money for the poor in three municipalities (Acaponeta, Tecuala, and Huajicori), as well as the General Hospital in Tepic, capital of Nayarit.[38] But it was also a celebration in its own right, and an important vehicle for placemaking. The Luis Bustos Orchestra, which had recently placed fourth in a competition of 350 bands held at the Hollywood Palladium, played, as did a mariachi.[39] KMEX TV's writer-producer Alejandro ("Alex") Nervo crowned the club's queen, Ana Lilia Sandoval (who did not appear to be of any special social standing), and the ceremony was broadcast on KMEX.

Club Nayarit made a point of inviting special guests who could advertise the dance. The guests included Jaime Jarrín, the Spanish-language radio broadcaster for the Los Angeles Dodgers (and a regular at the Nayarit restaurant); representatives from Radio KALI and Radio KWKW, AM stations that broadcast in Spanish; and three newspaper reporters, including one from *La Opinión*.[40] Press coverage does not mention whether *La Opinión*'s editor, Avila, attended, but Antonio Sáizar, the new editor of *El Eco*, traveled from Acaponeta for the occasion.

The dance also served as a venue to announce Club Nayarit's new president, Estanislao "Tani" López Robles. (Inès remained active in the club, serving as treasurer.) Robles had left Nayarit for Los Angeles in the mid-1950s and did not visit for ten years, but he remained connected to his homeland in other ways.[41] He had hosted Martín Sáizar on his earlier visits and was a noted sponsor of *El Eco*'s first special anniversary issue, demonstrating his connection to Acaponeta. Along with his brother Rigoberto López, who hosted the dinner that had launched the organization at his restaurant, El Zarape, Robles had supported the founding of the club.[42] He worked at Western Aviation Company and lived in Inglewood with his wife, Victoria León de Robles, and their children.[43] Robles was well established in Los Angeles but dedicated to Nayarit.

The following June, Club Nayarit held another dance, again at Saint Peter's Hall and again with music by Luis Bustos and his orchestra. Both KWKW and KALI broadcasted the event. Earlier that day, Vicky Cueva, the daughter of María del Rosario "Chayo" Díaz Cueva, married José "Pepe" Tavares. Doña Natalia hosted their wedding reception at her home in Echo Park, and when it was over, Vicky, José, and many of their guests, some of whom had come from Nayarit to attend the wedding, dropped by the dance.[44] Their attendance may seem to blur the lines between the privacy of a wedding and the public nature of the dance, but for members of this trans-local community, it made perfect sense. Nayaritas wanted to be together.

The guest list for the June 1969 dance suggests that this was an important moment for Nayaritas in establishing themselves in L.A. In addition to welcoming the editor of *El Eco*, Antonio Sáizar, Club Nayarit invited all the presidents of the other Mexican hometown associations in Los Angeles, demonstrating that while regional identities were important, they could all unite.[45] To strengthen connections with the mainstream Los Angeles political establishment, the club also invited the mayor of Los Angeles, Sam Yorty. For the president of the club, Tani Robles, Yorty was a known ally. Robles had already volunteered on Yorty's reelection campaign, attracted possibly by Yorty's track record (albeit slim) in appointing Latinx to key positions or perhaps because of the potential impact of his Office of Latin American Affairs. Yorty was not able to attend, but he sent his regrets and a congratulations telegram to be read at the banquet. In the mayor's place, organizers asked commissioner of public works for the City of Los Angeles, Aleríco "Al" Ortega to be their guest of honor. Latinx did not tend to be represented in public office, but Ortega, who was bilingual and bicultural, moved across social worlds with ease. He oversaw seven thousand workers in a department with a budget of $231 million. His position reflects the growth of the Mexican American middle class, but as his acceptance speech at the dance made clear, he understood himself to be connecting not just with other residents in Los Angeles, but translocally. Ortega thanked Robles for all of his hard work and said he wished that Nayarit would send more people like Robles to help make Los Angeles a more progressive city.[46] It is difficult to conceive of a high-ranking elected official today wishing aloud that there were more Mexican immigrants to help make America great again.

Club Nayarit's attempts to strengthen government ties with Mexican immigrants seems to have worked, even if their gains were limited. The Monday after the dance, Club Nayarit officers, as well as Antonio Sáizar, took a tour of City Hall at Ortega's invitation. During the course of the day, they also met with the assistant to the head of Mayor Yorty's Office of Latin American Affairs, Angel Alvarado.[47] The visit culminated with a reception held in a stately room on one of the highest floors in City Hall with a breathtaking panoramic view of the city. Yorty credited both the ethnic Mexican and the African American vote for helping him win reelection, but he did not live up to his campaign promises for either group. In particular, he fell short where civil rights and federal funding distribution for ethnic Mexicans were concerned, perhaps because of the pervasive tendency to reinscribe ethnic Mexicans, including Mexican Americans, as noncitizen immigrants and therefore not really deserving of a seat at the US table. In this, Yorty was fairly typical of mainstream politicians of the time; even his Office of Latin American Affairs framed Mexicans as immigrants or trade partners, not as long-term residents or citizens. In the imagination of elected officials, Latinx Americans were perpetual outsiders.[48] All the more reason, then, for the HTA to work to give Nayaritas a more permanent foothold in the urban landscape of L.A., helping them stake a claim to belonging and to connect with and support one another.

+ + + +

Doña Natalia died in 1969, after a steady but quick decline from kidney failure. Many years later, María's voice was still somber as she described her mother's funeral Mass at the historic Nuestra Señora Reina de los Ángeles Church. Tani López, president of the Nayarit Club, newly formed at the time, spoke at her funeral.[49] There were so many mourners, María said, that they could not all fit in the church. The radio station Radio Express played "Las Golondrinas" in her honor. *El Eco* wrote about her funeral and the many lives she had touched in Mexico and California. By the time of her death, she had established the Nayarit, sponsored dozens of her conationals, and helped other Mexican restaurants get their start by providing seed money or by helping their owners and workers learn the business. She had spent most of her adult life laying the groundwork for Nayaritas in Los Angeles, who, in turn, did the same for others. The church bells in Acaponeta, hanging in a tower Doña Natalia's donations had helped construct, rang out to commemorate her passing.

Epilogue

Losing Places

If you walk down Sunset Boulevard today, you can still see the old sign for the Nayarit, though the neon has gone dark; it sits above the marquee for a music venue, the Echo. The yuccas that used to grow out front are gone, the walls covered in flyers. María sold the restaurant's lease in 1976, and the new owners kept the old name. It stayed in operation until the building was sold to a music promoter who, in 2001, opened the Echo.

Since the early 2000s, Echo Park has been rapidly gentrifying, and many of the residents who made it such a desirable place to live have been pushed out. Barragan's closed the Echo Park location in 2013. El Conquistador, which for decades had been a haven for gay and Mexican customers, closed its doors the same year. Evelia Pack and her family continued to run El Batey market until 2014, when skyrocketing rents forced them to close the business. In his article, "Los Angeles Is Eating Itself," Ben Ehrenreich lamented the loss that gentrification wrought, even as he acknowledged he was part of the neighborhood change.

> Pioneer Market, which had anchored the neighborhood for more than 50 years, closed in the summer of 2004. That was unthinkable until it occurred. One after the other, both pupuserías—La Fe and La Paz—closed. So did El

Carmelo, where the white-haired Cuban men argued at a back table from early morning until late afternoon. For a little while I would see them arguing on bus benches, with no place else to gather. The Mexican bars turned white. The one gay bar turned straight. At some point the stray dogs disappeared—I didn't notice until after they were gone—and I found myself missing the roosters that I had cursed every weekend morning. Sure, there were fewer shootings, but a different kind of violence reigned, the less obvious sort that breaks up families without a bullet, just a rent hike or a notice from the sheriff in stark officialese. A neighborhood, it turns out, is a fragile thing.[1]

It was not just businesses that were feeling the impact. Apartment rents went up 36.7 percent from 2000 to 2017, and home values increased 144.6 percent from 2000 to 2018. Demographic data show the median home value in Echo Park ($680,100) is higher than the regional median ($514,150), and a look on Redfin in 2021 shows how shockingly difficult it is to purchase a home in Echo Park today; even a two-bedroom, one-bath sells for over a million dollars.[2]

The relentless wealthification of Echo Park shows the ways in which specific policies (e.g., the granting of home and business loans and liquor and entertainment licenses) allow communities that have been denied investment for decades to be displaced by communities that are seen as more "worthy."[3] We have seen the enormous human toll: children of immigrants unable to afford a home in the neighborhood where they grew up despite their college degree; elderly residents who can no longer afford their rents forced to move many miles from the neighborhood they had lived in for decades, far from the community ties that had sustained them. Scholarship and journalism have added to our understanding of the market forces at work in gentrification, including the decimation of affordable housing as real estate developer groups take over properties, the lack of rent control, and the minimal set-asides for low-income housing in new developments. Such work has also provided a more nuanced portrait of the individuals who move into these neighborhoods, who sometimes closely resemble those being displaced in terms of race and ethnicity (a shift sometimes called *gente-ficación*). In addition, we have learned of the myriad ways that longtime residents have pushed back, both as individuals (e.g., by suing to remain in their homes) and collectively (e.g., by forming tenants' unions). Yet while we all may be better informed and even sympathetic to those who have been displaced, this has not moved us as a society to make structural change.

Along with pushing out businesses and people, gentrification erases history and culture. When I envisioned this project, I wanted to bring attention to those who were being erased, those who helped shape the urban landscape of Echo Park and places like it. When I first spoke publicly about this project, in a 2014 talk, many Latinx people who had never been to this lecture series before were in the audience and stayed afterward to talk to me about what was going on in their neighborhoods. Some were from Echo Park, others from Boyle Heights or Highland Park, all Latinx neighborhoods in Los Angeles undergoing gentrification. "You need to tell *our* story," they urged. That is what this book has tried to do.

Even before gentrification reached its current, frenzied pace, other forces were smoothing over the texture of life in Echo Park. The neighborhood had already sustained major losses. In the 1980s and 1990s, the AIDS epidemic ravaged gay communities. And as residents age and die or are forced to move far away, their stories, if not set down, will be lost altogether. If we fail to acknowledge and value these placemakers and their roles, we risk viewing gentrification as a type of urban renaissance in which "urban pioneers" revitalize a cultural wasteland filled with crime and blight.

Even honoring placemakers won't result in a meaningful difference in the absence of real structural change: we may sympathize with those affected by gentrification, but very few of us work to pass the legislation needed to make housing more affordable. Lamenting the loss of neighborhood character while ignoring the work needed to preserve neighborhoods and the people who live in them reminds me of the chilling words of Rebecca Solnit: "Gentrification is just the fin above the water. Below is the rest of the shark: a new American economy in which most of us will be poorer, a few will be far richer, and everything will be faster, more homogenous and more controlled or controllable."[4] Without structural change in housing policies, our sympathy does not matter: the shark will take its toll.

As I write this, early in 2021, the COVID-19 epidemic has again exposed how vulnerable communities of color are, immigrant owned and operated restaurants included. Restaurants were already economically vulnerable, threatened by rising rents and the atomization of our hypercapitalist era. As the chef, author, and radio show host Evan Kleinman wrote in the *Los Angeles Times* in late 2019, food trends have reshaped what it means to dine out. Long-standing relationships between restaurants and their customers, foundational to the establishment of urban anchors, are being replaced by something more transactional and exoticizing. Customers are increasingly on the prowl for the next hot place or cool experience. It is becoming more and more difficult for restaurants to cultivate a dependable clientele. At the same time, restaurants are increasingly reliant on high-stakes investors, such as hedge fund managers and venture capitalists, for large infusions of cash, which can make them more responsive to investors' demands than to their customers' needs. "That means," Kleinman argues, "that customers often need to conform to what's being offered, rather than restaurants being able to respond to customers. In the best of worlds, eating establishments both help define their neighborhoods and are defined by their neighborhoods."[5] But changes in the restaurant industry, gentrification, and now COVID-19 are eating away at those relationships.

When COVID-19 cases began to increase in March 2020 and many states went under stay-at-home orders, restaurants were hit hard. Daily headlines told of urban anchors holding on by a thread or closing altogether. Alongside these articles were others proclaiming how much we mourned our exile from restaurants. It was not only the food that people missed, which they were more often than not able to procure through takeout and delivery services; it was the place and all that it afforded them: a sense of community, the feeling of being *seen* by restaurant staff and fellow customers and regulars that made them feel connected. As one writer lamented, "I want a nice dimly lighted place where I can soak in the atmosphere, a perch where I can people-watch, gossip or sit alone and read a newspaper."[6]

COVID-19 also put a spotlight on how restaurants are made possible by immigrant labor. Before the pandemic, many restaurants managed to stay afloat by hiring immigrants, both documented and undocumented, thereby keeping their labor costs down. Immigrants, especially the undocumented, often do the jobs others reject because they cannot afford to say no. They work long hours, take shifts others may not want, clean up dirty jobs, and work without adequate protections. In Los Angeles, the undocumented are estimated to make up 40 percent or more of the restaurant workforce.[7] Right-wing talking points notwithstanding, many of these immigrants pay taxes. In California in 2019, the estimated 10 percent of the workforce who are undocumented paid more than $2.5 billion in taxes,[8] much of it in the form of withholding from the paychecks of employees using either a fake Social Security number or a real Individual Taxpayer Identification number, as well as state sales taxes.[9] Now those same workers are disproportionately bearing the brunt of COVID. Latinx are more likely than the rest of the population to report a pay cut or lost job due to COVID, in large part because Latinx, compared to the general population, tend to be younger, to have less education, and are more likely to work in the service industry—cohorts hit especially hard by the pandemic.[10]

And the pandemic has complicated the prospects for new immigrants looking to engage in placemaking of their own. Julio and Micaela Jaimes, proprietors of Aquí es Taxco, immigrated from Taxco, Guerrero, Mexico, to

Los Angeles in 1999 and began serving customers in a South Los Angeles parking lot in 2008. They catered to Mexican and Central American immigrants, selling foods such as *birria* and *barbacoa* that gave customers a "precise taste of home."[11] In 2019, they opened a brick-and-mortar restaurant but struggled financially from rising rents and narrow margins. When COVID-19 hit, they closed the restaurant and, in March 2020, returned to the parking lot where they had started.[12] It's not clear what will happen to their enterprise in the years to come.

During the pandemic, my family and I started ordering food from a taco place near us; I could tell, from the tomato broth poured over the crisp potato tacos, that the food must have been prepared by a Nayarita. When I asked the chef where he was from, he didn't expect me to know it, but we ended up having a long conversation about all the places and tastes we had in common. We bonded over his mother's tamales—*rajas con queso* (chili and cheese), *pollo* (chicken), and *dulce* (sweet)—that tasted just like my aunt Vicky's in Echo Park, that taste just like we could get in Acaponeta during the holidays. Stuck as we were in pandemic-wracked Los Angeles, those tamales were all the more special. I am third generation, but I remain tethered to Nayarit, as Doña Natalia and María were before me.

The community that grew up around the Nayarit remains tethered to one another, too. Pedro died in the early 1990s, and a couple of years later, we gathered in my tía Chayo's living room on the anniversary of his death, to say the rosary. I looked around and realized that everyone there—some family and some not—had worked at the Nayarit: María, Vicky, Chayo, Evelia, Poncho, Irene, Coco, Carlos, some now with children of their own in tow. All were there out of respect for Pedro—whom they had loved for his charisma, his musical talents, his humor, his friendship—and for one another. This was their community. And they remembered.

I think about this community when I eat from the dishes, given to me by my mother, that Doña Natalia collected. They're from the Franciscan Ceramics plant in Atwater, hand-painted with apples and leaves around the edges. The plant has since closed, but it's a popular pattern: as a kid watching *I Love Lucy* (my first English lessons growing up in a Spanish-speaking household), I noticed that the Ricardos owned the Franciscan Ivy pattern. Those dishes say a lot about my reserved grandmother. She wanted elegant tableware, and she got it for herself, piece by piece. I like to imagine her setting her place and enjoying the sheen and the color of those dishes, not just as a sign of aspiration, but also as a way of embracing the place where she lived and asserting her belonging.

INTRODUCTION. PLACEMAKING IN A NEW HOMELAND

1. *Los de afuera* (literally, "those on the outside") refers to Mexicans who are living outside of Mexico. The phrase was regularly used by Nayaritas to refer to those who had immigrated to the United States.

2. *El Eco*, August 26, 1965, 21, Hemeroteca Nacional de México, Instituto de Investigaciones Bibliográficas, Universidad Nacional Autónoma de México. On Los Angeles boosterism, see Mike Davis, *City of Quartz: Excavating the Future in Los Angeles* (London: Verso Press, 1990), ch. 1, "Sunshine or Noir?"; Kevin Starr, *Americans and the California Dream, 1850-1915* (New York: Oxford University Press, 1973); Kevin Starr, *Inventing the Dream: California through the Progressive Era* (New York: Oxford University Press, 1985).

3. On Mexican immigrants and *patria chica* during the 1960s, see Stephen J. Pitti, *The Devil in Silicon Valley: Northern California, Race, and Mexican Americans* (Princeton, NJ: Princeton University Press, 2003), 133-36.

4. In this book I use the term "ethnic Mexican" to refer to both Mexican Americans (people of Mexican heritage born in the United States) and Mexican immigrants (people born in Mexico who immigrated to the United States). I will distinguish between the two groups when it is important to the narrative, as well as when my source material clearly makes a distinction. However, the dominant culture usually made no distinction between US- and Mexico-born Mexicans.

They were simply seen as "Mexican." The term "Chicanx," popularized during the social movements of the 1960s, connotes a political consciousness around race. "Latinx" is an umbrella term that refers to those from Latin America. I use the ending "x" as a gender-neutral and nonbinary alternative to "Latino" or "Latina." I also use the term "immigrant" to refer to people who move from their homeland and settle in another nation. Others prefer the term "migrant" because it does not make distinctions among those that move across borders (such as refugees, asylum seekers, or undocumented immigrants) and because it puts the emphasis on the movement, not the settlement. However, because the people I look at in this book tended to settle in Los Angeles, rather than engage in circular migration, I believe the term "immigrant" is more appropriate here.

5. For more on gentrification, see the epilogue.

6. There are no overarching histories of Echo Park written. *Bohemian Los Angeles* tells the important history of gay men and women, as well as progressives, and their political work in the area. *Ghosts of Echo Park* is a pictorial history of Echo Park meant to provide a counternarrative to the much-maligned neighborhood. Ron Emler, *Ghosts of Echo Park: A Pictorial History* (Los Angeles: Echo Park Publications, 1999); Daniel Hurewitz, *Bohemian Los Angeles and the Making of Modern Politics* (Berkeley: University of California Press, 2007).

7. Henri Lefebvre, *The Survival of Capitalism: Reproduction of the Relations of Production* (New York: St. Martin's Press, 1976), 31. On the social production of space, see also Edward W. Soja, *Thirdspace: Journeys to Los Angeles and Other Real-and-Imagined Places* (Cambridge, MA: Blackwell, 1996); Dolores Hayden, *The Power of Place: Urban Landscapes as Public History* (Cambridge, MA: MIT Press, 1995); Henri Lefebvre, *The Production of Space* (Oxford: Blackwell, 1991).

8. George Lipsitz, *How Racism Takes Place* (Philadelphia, PA: Temple University Press, 2011), 5. On place as an analytic concept, see also Tim Cresswell, *Place: An Introduction*, 2nd ed. (Chichester: Wiley Blackwell, 2015).

9. Geographers use the term "placemaking" to describe, as Susan Price puts it, "the way we collectively shape our public realm to maximize its value; the planning, design, management, and programming of public spaces, rooted in community-based participation." Scholars with an interest in both race and place have pointed out that the types of public spaces geographers tend to have in mind—including city festivals, parks and parklets, or farmers markets—have

not always been welcoming for marginalized and racialized people, but as Patricia Price points out, the fields "have not yet engaged with each other in a substantive fashion." Susan Mayhew, *A Dictionary of Geography* (Oxford: Oxford University Press, 2015); Patricia L. Price, "At the Crossroads: Critical Race Theory and Critical Geographies of Race," *Progress in Human Geography* 34, no. 2 (2010): 147–74, 149. For important work bridging geography and critical race theory, see Katherine McKittrick and Clyde Adrian Woods, eds., *Black Geographies and the Politics of Place* (Toronto: Between the Lines, 2007); Laura Pulido, *Environmentalism and Economic Justice: Two Chicano Struggles in the Southwest* (Tucson: University of Arizona Press, 1996); Clyde Woods, *Development Arrested: The Blues and Plantation Power in the Mississippi Delta*, Haymarket Series (London: Verso, 1998); Laura R. Barraclough, *Charros: How Mexican Cowboys Are Remapping Race and American Identity* (Oakland: University of California Press, 2019); Genevieve Carpio, *Collisions at the Crossroads: How Place and Mobility Make Race* (Oakland: University of California Press, 2019); Wendy Cheng, *The Changs Next Door to the Diazes: Remapping Race in Suburban California* (Minneapolis: University of Minnesota Press, 2013); Juan D. De Lara, *Inland Shift: Race, Space, and Capital in Southern California* (Oakland: University of California Press, 2018); Laura Pulido, Laura R. Barraclough, and Wendy Cheng, *A People's Guide to Los Angeles* (Berkeley: University of California Press, 2012).

10. A rich example is Lanita Jacobs-Huey, *From the Kitchen to the Parlor: Language and Becoming in African American Women's Hair Care* (Oxford: Oxford University Press, 2006).

11. In this effort I am indebted to George Lipsitz's work showing how Blacks challenged the ways racist practices shaped institutions and places through what he termed a "Black spatial imaginary." By using discursive practices—art, literature, music—to make visible the political visions that their experiences of segregation and congregation helped produce, Black Americans provided modes of confronting and destabilizing entrenched hierarchies and help us imagine what democracy might look like. Lipsitz, *How Racism Takes Place*.

12. Anchor institutions, which frequently consist of public-private partnerships, are often major employers in their area and bring in leadership from outside. In these cases, anchor institutions can actually prove harmful to the surrounding community, especially if community partnerships are not

cultivated and allowed to take a major role in development. Some scholarship focuses on anchor institutions created by the community for the community; however, these analyses still focus on large institutions with civic backing, such as cultural centers. See, e.g., Nancy Cantor, Peter Englot, and Marilyn Higgins, "Making the Work of Anchor Institutions Stick: Building Coalitions and Collective Expertise," *Journal of Higher Education Outreach and Engagement* 17, no. 3 (2013): 17–46; Meagan M. Ehlenz, "Gown, Town, and Neighborhood Change: An Examination of Urban Neighborhoods with University Revitalization Efforts," *Journal of Planning Education and Research* 39, no. 3 (2019): 285–99; Kelly L. Patterson and Robert Mark Silverman, *Schools and Urban Revitalization: Rethinking Institutions and Community Development* (New York: Routledge, 2013).

13. Michel de Certeau's *The Practice of Everyday Life* (Berkeley: University of California Press, 1984) has long informed my thinking on the importance of everyday life.

14. On restaurants as sites of contestation in terms of race, labor, production, and consumption, see Sarumathi Jayaraman and Eric Schlosser, *Behind the Kitchen Door* (Ithaca, NY: ILR Press, 2013); Donna R. Gabaccia and Jeffrey M. Pilcher, "'Chili Queens' and Checkered Tablecloths: Public Dining Cultures of Italians in New York City and Mexicans in San Antonio, Texas, 1870s–1940s," *Radical History Review* 110 (2011): 109–26. On the importance of other types of businesses as sites of empowerment and contestation in the fight for equal rights, see Victoria W. Wolcott, *Race, Riots, and Roller Coasters: The Struggle over Segregated Recreation in America*, (Philadelphia: University of Pennsylvania Press, 2012); Robert E. Weems, *Desegregating the Dollar: African American Consumerism in the Twentieth Century* (New York: New York University Press, 1998); Suzanne E. Smith, *To Serve the Living: Funeral Directors and the African American Way of Death* (Cambridge, MA: Belknap Press of Harvard University Press, 2010).

15. On the challenging and incremental process of desegregation, see William H. Chafe, *Civilities and Civil Rights: Greensboro, North Carolina, and the Black Struggle for Freedom* (New York: Oxford University Press, 1980).

16. James C. Scott, *Domination and the Arts of Resistance: Hidden Transcripts* (New Haven, CT: Yale University Press, 1990), 183.

17. Josh Kun, *To Live and Dine in L.A.: Menus and the Making of the Modern City* (Santa Monica, CA: Angel City Press, 2015), 31.

18. The literature on the politics of race and food grows richer every year. See Matt Garcia, E. Melanie DuPuis, and Don Mitchell, *Food across Borders* (New Brunswick, NJ: Rutgers University Press, 2017); Mark Padoongpatt, *Flavors of Empire: Food and the Making of Thai America* (Oakland: University of California Press, 2017); Sarumathi Jayaraman and Eric Schlosser, *Behind the Kitchen Door* (Ithaca, NY: ILR Press, 2013); Rachel B. Slocum and Arun Saldanha, *Geographies of Race and Food: Fields, Bodies, Markets* (Burlington, VT: Ashgate, 2013); Sarah J. Portnoy, *Food, Health, and Culture in Latino Los Angeles* (Lanham, MD: Rowman & Littlefield, 2017); Psyche A. Williams-Forson, *Building Houses out of Chicken Legs: Black Women, Food, and Power* (Chapel Hill: University of North Carolina Press, 2006); Monica Perales, "The Food Historian's Dilemma: Reconsidering the Role of Authenticity in Food Scholarship," *Journal of American History* 103, no. 3 (2016): 690–93; Madeline Y. Hsu, "On the Possibilities of Food Writing as a Bridge between the Popular and the Political," *Journal of American History* 103, no. 3 (2016): 682–85; Matt Garcia, "Setting the Table: Historians, Popular Writers, and Food History," *Journal of American History* 103, no. 3 (2016): 656–78; Kyla Wazana Tompkins, *Racial Indigestion: Eating Bodies in the Nineteenth Century* (New York: New York University Press, 2012); Robert Ji-Song Ku, Martin F. Manalansan, and Anita Mannur, eds., *Eating Asian America: A Food Studies Reader* (New York: New York University Press, 2013).

19. For restaurant reviews by Jonathan Gold, see Jonathan Gold, *Counter Intelligence: Where to Eat in the Real Los Angeles* (New York: LA Weekly Books, 2000). For a sense of the impact Jonathan Gold's work made socially and culturally and the cultural shift he spearheaded, see Laura Gabbert, dir., *City of Gold* (2015; New York: MPI Media Group, 2016), DVD. Other L.A.-based advocates bringing attention to these issues today include journalist and author Gustavo Arellano; chef, author, and TV show host Roy Choi; chef, author, radio host, and restaurateur Evan Kleiman; and food writer Bill Esparza. Gustavo Arellano, *Taco USA: How Mexican Food Conquered America* (New York: Scribner, 2012).

20. Cited in Gustavo Arellano, "Anthony Bourdain Was the Eternal Compadre of Overlooked Latinos," *Los Angeles Times*, June 8, 2018, www.latimes.com /opinion/op-ed/la-oe-arellano-anthony-bourdain-20180608-story.html.

21. Molly O'Neill, "New Mainstream: Hot Dogs, Apple Pie and Salsa," *New York Times*, March 11, 1992, C1.

22. Jeffrey M. Pilcher, *Planet Taco: A Global History of Mexican Food* (Oxford; New York: Oxford University Press, 2012); Arellano, *Taco USA*; Kun, *To Live and Dine in L.A.*, 71–73.

23. Yong Chen, *Chop Suey, USA: The Story of Chinese Food in America* (New York: Columbia University Press, 2014); Haiming Liu, *From Canton Restaurant to Panda Express: A History of Chinese Food in the United States* (New Brunswick, NJ: Rutgers University Press, 2015).

24. Matthew F. Bokovoy, *The San Diego World's Fairs and Southwestern Memory, 1880–1940* (Albuquerque: University of New Mexico Press, 2005); Phoebe Kropp, *California Vieja: Culture and Memory in a Modern American Place* (Berkeley: University of California Press, 2006); William Deverell, *Whitewashed Adobe: The Rise of Los Angeles and the Remaking of Its Mexican Past* (Berkeley: University of California Press, 2004); Carey McWilliams, *Southern California: An Island on the Land* (Salt Lake City, UT: Peregrine Smith Books, 1946); Starr, *Americans and the California Dream, 1850–1915*.

25. Following the lead of the historian Ernesto Chávez, I use the term "US war with Mexico" rather than the "Mexican War" or "Mexican-American War." Ernesto Chávez, *The U.S. War with Mexico: A Brief History with Documents* (New York: Bedford/St. Martins, 2007), ix.

26. Deverell, *Whitewashed Adobe*.

27. On Los Angeles as a "white spot," see Eric Avila, *Popular Culture in the Age of White Flight: Fear and Fantasy in Suburban Los Angeles* (Berkeley: University of California Press, 2004), esp. ch. 2, "The Nation's 'White Spot.'"

28. On Los Angeles's entrenched history of segregation, see, e.g., Davis, *City of Quartz*; Raphael Sonenshein, *Politics in Black and White: Race and Power in Los Angeles* (Princeton, NJ: Princeton University Press, 1993); Dana Cuff, *The Provisional City: Los Angeles Stories of Architecture and Urbanism* (Cambridge, MA: MIT Press, 2000); Becky M. Nicolaides, *My Blue Heaven: Life and Politics in the Working-Class Suburbs of Los Angeles, 1920–1965* (Chicago: University of Chicago Press, 2002); Josh Sides, *L.A. City Limits: African Americans in Los Angeles from the Great Depression to the Present* (Berkeley: University of California Press, 2003); Avila, *Popular Culture in the Age of White Flight*; Greg Hise, "Border City: Race and Social Distance in Los Angeles," *American Quarterly* 56, no. 3 (2004): 545–58.

29. My first book, *Fit to Be Citizens?*, focused on this differential racialization. In it, I demonstrated that if we want to understand how racial categories (e.g.,

"Mexican") are constructed, we must see how they are understood and treated in relation to other racial and ethnic groups. Natalia Molina, *Fit to Be Citizens? Public Health and Race in Los Angeles, 1879-1939* (Berkeley: University of California Press, 2006).

30. Douglas Flamming, *Bound for Freedom: Black Los Angeles in Jim Crow America* (Berkeley: University of California Press, 2005), page 2.

31. Richard Rothstein, *The Color of Law: A Forgotten History of How Our Government Segregated America* (New York: Liveright, 2017); Douglas Massey and Nancy Denton, *American Apartheid: Segregation and the Making of the Underclass* (Cambridge, MA: Harvard University Press, 1993).

32. Genevieve Carpio, "Unexpected Allies: David C. Marcus and His Impact on the Advancement of Civil Rights in the Mexican-American Legal Landscape of Southern California," in *Beyond Alliances: The Jewish Role in Reshaping the Racial Landscape of Southern California*, ed. Bruce Zuckerman and George Sanchez (West Lafayette, IN: Purdue University Press, 2012), 1–32; David G. García, *Strategies of Segregation: Race, Residence, and the Struggle for Educational Equality* (Oakland: University of California Press, 2018); Martha Menchaca, *The Mexican Outsiders: A Community History of Marginalization and Discrimination in California* (Austin: University of Texas Press, 1995); Charles Wollenberg, *All Deliberate Speed: Segregation and Exclusion in California Schools, 1855-1975* (Berkeley: University of California Press, 1976).

33. On *Mendez*, see Philippa Strum, *Mendez v. Westminster: School Desegregation and Mexican-American Rights* (Lawrence: University Press of Kansas, 2010); Vicki L. Ruiz, "'We Always Tell Our Children They Are American': *Mendez v. Westminster* and the California Road to *Brown*," *College Board Review*, no. 200.

34. Philip J. Ethington, Anne Marie Kooistra, and Edward DeYoung, "Los Angeles County Union Census Tract Data Series, 1940-1990, Version 1.01," created with the support of the John Randolph Haynes and Dora Haynes Foundation (University of Southern California, Los Angeles, 2000), 18.

35. Earl Lewis, *In Their Own Interests: Race, Class, and Power in Twentieth-Century Norfolk, Virginia* (Berkeley: University of California Press, 1991), 90.

36. Historically, faced with institutional racism, African Americans provided for their own communities through various institutions, including churches, settlement houses, and clubhouses. See Evelyn Brooks Higginbotham,

Righteous Discontent: The Women's Movement in the Black Baptist Church, 1880–1920 (Cambridge, MA: Harvard University Press, 1993). For histories of Black Los Angeles in the first half of the twentieth century, see Flamming, *Bound for Freedom*; R. J. Smith, *The Great Black Way: L.A. In the 1940s and the Lost African-American Renaissance* (New York: Public Affairs, 2006).

37. Anthony F. Macías, *Mexican American Mojo: Popular Music, Dance, and Urban Culture in Los Angeles, 1935–1968* (Durham, NC: Duke University Press, 2008).

38. We know that approximately 4.6 million guest visas were issued under the Bracero Program, but because many of these workers returned year after year, receiving a new visa each time, we do not have a precise count of how many actually participated.

39. Kitty Calavita, *Inside the State: The Bracero Program, Immigration, and the I.N.S.* (New York: Routledge, 1992), 229–39, 237–38.

40. Two notable interventions in this narrative are Miroslava Chávez-García, *Migrant Longing: Letter Writing across the U.S.-Mexico Borderlands* (Chapel Hill: University of North Carolina Press, 2018); Ana Rosas, *Abrazando el Espíritu: Bracero Families Confront the US-Mexico Border* (Oakland: University of California Press, 2014).

41. I thank Miriam Pawel for sharing this insight with me when discussing the importance of this book. Miriam Pawel, *The Crusades of Cesar Chavez: A Biography* (New York: Bloomsbury Press, 2014).

42. This approach to focusing more on the processes of everyday life can be traced to the 1960s. For example, the work of the Annales School of history that emphasized microhistory and studying the lives of everyday people (e.g., workers' history instead of a union's history).

43. Many historians studying these transnational ties rely on the records of the foreign consulate in Los Angeles, which are housed at the Secretaría de Relaciones Exteriores in Mexico City. However, the consulate did not play as active a role during the period of this study as it did in the 1920s and 1930s, before the mass deportations of Mexicans during the Great Depression. Nonetheless, as discussed in chapter 5, Nayaritas did connect with the consul, who was from Nayarit. See the consul's autobiography, Raúl González Galarza, *Medio siglo sin sorpresas: 1945–1994* (Mexicali: Gráficos, 1993).

44. Barbara Tomlinson and George Lipsitz, *Insubordinate Spaces: Improvisation and Accompaniment for Social Justice* (Philadelphia, PA: Temple University Press,

2019), 8. Similarly, the historian Kelly Lytle Hernández's concept "rebel archives" highlights the ways in which we can center sources and stories that exist outside of the "official record," particularly when they are part of the record officials sought to silence. Kelly Lytle Hernández, *City of Inmates: Conquest, Rebellion, and the Rise of Human Caging in Los Angeles, 1771-1965* (Chapel Hill: University of North Carolina Press, 2017).

45. These two monographs are important models of how to draw on family histories to illuminate larger histories, such as racialized violence, transnational capitalism, and labor migration: Monica Muñoz Martinez, *The Injustice Never Leaves You: Anti-Mexican Violence in Texas* (Cambridge, MA: Harvard University Press, 2018); Monica Perales, *Smeltertown: Making and Remembering a Southwest Border Community* (Chapel Hill: University of North Carolina Press, 2010).

46. It is not uncommon to find such omissions in oral interviews. An example is the classic *All God's Dangers*. Beginning in 1968 and for several years thereafter, Theodore Rosengarten conducted interviews with Ned Cobb (a.k.a. Nate Shaw, 1885-1973), a Black Alabama sharecropper. These interviews reveal what was important to Cobb: guano, how to handle mules, the danger of boll weevils—rather than discussions of electoral politics. This slow-paced, detailed biography reveals what was important in the life of a sharecropper and tenant farmer. Nate Shaw and Theodore Rosengarten, *All God's Dangers: The Life of Nate Shaw* (New York: Knopf, 1974).

47. On the politics of the archive and their effect on producing silences in the narrative, see Antoinette M. Burton, ed., *Archive Stories: Facts, Fictions, and the Writing of History* (Durham, NC: Duke University Press, 2005); Michel-Rolph Trouillot, *Silencing the Past: Power and the Production of History* (Boston: Beacon Press, 1995). On reading archival silences, see Catherine Ramírez, *The Woman in the Zoot Suit: Gender, Nationalism, and the Cultural Politics of Memory* (Durham, NC: Duke University Press, 2009); Miroslava Chávez-García, *States of Delinquency: Race and Science in the Making of California's Juvenile Justice System* (Berkeley: University of California Press, 2012).

48. Alessandro Portelli, *The Order Has Been Carried Out: History, Memory, and Meaning of Nazi Massacre in Rome* (New York: Palgrave Macmillan, 2003), 15. On oral histories, see Alessandro Portelli, *The Battle of Valle Giulia: Oral History and the Art of Dialogue* (Madison: University of Wisconsin Press, 1997); Alessandro

Portelli, *The Death of Luigi Trastulli, and Other Stories: Form and Meaning in Oral History* (Albany: State University of New York Press, 1991); Horacio N. Roque Ramírez, "A Living Archive of Desire: Teresita La Campesina and the Embodiment of Queer Latino Community Histories," in Burton, *Archive Stories*, 111–35.

49. As the historian Nayan Shah, for example, has powerfully shown, archives related to immigrants often privilege settlement over transience, thus posing a special challenge to those wishing to write histories of transient migrants. See Nayan Shah, *Stranger Intimacy: Contesting Race, Sexuality, and the Law in the North American West* (Berkeley: University of California Press, 2011), 6–7.

50. The records of the US government's Immigration and Naturalization Service give us snapshots as people crossed into the United States, were deported from the United States, or came under the scrutiny of the Boards of Special Inquiry, which reviewed each exclusion case, primarily to determine who was likely to become a public charge. Because the majority of Mexican immigrants who crossed at this time were men, this rich source does not provide much insight into the lives of women. Similarly, Manuel Gamio, considered the father of Mexican anthropology, gives us insight into the lives of Mexican immigrants through dozens of oral interviews published in his 1930 book, *Mexican Immigration to the United States*, archived with other works at UC Berkeley's Bancroft Library. A few women are represented in this source set, yet men continue to be the central actors in the interviews. This does not mean that we cannot read these sources against the grain; indeed, these collections offer some priceless archival shards if we are patient enough. On how to contextualize a shard of evidence, see Jill Lepore, *Book of Ages: The Life and Opinions of Jane Franklin* (New York: Vintage, 2014); Tiya Miles, *Ties That Bind: The Story of an Afro-Cherokee Family in Slavery and Freedom* (Berkeley: University of California Press, 2005); Kevin J. Mumford, *Interzones: Black/White Sex Districts in Chicago and New York in the Early Twentieth Century* (New York: Columbia University Press, 1997); George Chauncey, *Gay New York: Gender, Urban Culture, and the Makings of the Gay Male World, 1890–1940* (New York: Basic Books, 1994).

CHAPTER ONE. FINDING A PLACE IN ECHO PARK

1. Vicki L. Ruiz, *From out of the Shadows: Mexican Women in Twentieth-Century America* (New York: Oxford University Press, 1998), 11.

2. We know from personal narratives and decades of research that families make decisions about immigration together—what some scholars refer to as the "household strategy model." But as the sociologist Pierrette Hondagneu-Sotelo points out, the unequal distribution of power within most families affects these decisions, often along gendered lines. Pierrette Hondagneu-Sotelo, *Gendered Transitions: Mexican Experiences of Immigration* (Berkeley: University of California Press, 1994).

3. "Natalia Barraza: Nayarita pionera en L.A.," in *Nayarit en California* (Los Angeles: Asociación de Nayaritas en California), 1993, 16-19.

4. Kelly Lytle Hernández, *Migra! A History of the U.S. Border Patrol* (Berkeley: University of California, 2010).

5. These important studies also argue for the importance of understanding multiethnic and racial communities at the neighborhood level. See Albert Camarillo, "Black and Brown in Compton: Demographic Change, Suburban Decline, and Intergroup Relations in a South Central Los Angeles Community, 1950-2000," in *Not Just Black and White: Historical and Contemporary Perspectives on Immigration, Race, and Ethnicity in the United States*, ed. Nancy Foner and George M. Fredrickson (New York: Russell Sage Foundation, 2004), 358-75; Cheng, *The Changs Next Door to the Díazes*; Abigail Rosas, *South Central Is Home: Race and the Power of Community Investment in Los Angeles* (Stanford, CA: Stanford University Press, 2019); George J. Sánchez, *Boyle Heights: How a Los Angeles Neighborhood Became the Future of American Democracy* (Oakland: University of California Press, 2021).

6. Lisbeth Haas, *Conquests and Historical Identities in California, 1769-1936* (Berkeley: University of California Press, 1995).

7. Richard Griswold del Castillo, *The Treaty of Guadalupe Hidalgo: A Legacy of Conflict* (Norman: University of Oklahoma Press, 1990); Chávez, *The U.S. War with Mexico*.

8. Kelly Lytle Hernández, *City of Inmates: Conquest, Rebellion, and the Rise of Human Caging in Los Angeles, 1771-1965* (Chapel Hill: University of North Carolina Press, 2017), 30. For more on Los Angeles's racialized power structures and practices, see David Torres-Rouff, *Before L.A.: Race, Space, and Municipal Power in Los Angeles, 1781-1894* (New Haven, CT: Yale University Press, 2013).

9. Unlike comparable cities in the Midwest and East, which grew upward, Los Angeles grew outward, and population density remained low. By 1930, New

York reported a central city population per square mile of 23,179; Chicago, 16,723; and Boston, 17,795. Los Angeles, in comparison, had a central city population per square mile of only 2,812 in 1930. Robert M. Fogelson, *The Fragmented Metropolis: Los Angeles, 1850–1930* (Berkeley: University of California Press, 1967), 143.

10. In 1900, Los Angeles's total population was 102,479. See US Census Office, *United States Census of Population, 1900* (Washington, DC: Government Printing Office, 1901–3), vol. 1, 796–803. The same year, Los Angeles eclipsed Chicago as the nation's fastest growing city. Just ten years later, Los Angeles's population had increased by another 211 percent. See Janet Abu-Lughod, *New York, Chicago, Los Angeles: America's Global Cities* (Minneapolis: University of Minnesota Press, 1999), 5–15.

11. Verónica Castillo-Muñoz, *The Other California: Land, Identity, and Politics on the Mexican Borderlands* (Oakland: University of California Press, 2017), ch. 1, "Building the Mexican Borderlands."

12. In 1900, foreign-born residents totaled 19,964, compared to 82,515 native-born. Forty-one percent, or 8,266, of the foreign-born were English-speaking, including immigrants from England, Canada, Ireland, Wales, and Australia. The non-English-speaking foreign-born were German, Chinese, French, Italian, Mexican, Slavic, and Japanese (in descending order from highest to lowest percentage). *US Census of Population*, 796–803. For histories of Los Angeles that trace the city's socioeconomic development, see Fogelson, *The Fragmented Metropolis*; Abu-Lughod, *New York, Chicago, Los Angeles*.

13. Ricardo Romo, *History of a Barrio* (Austin: University of Austin Press, 1983), 61. George J. Sánchez, *Becoming Mexican American: Ethnicity, Culture, and Identity in Chicano Los Angeles, 1900–1945*, 70–72.

14. Albert Camarillo refers to this movement to the Eastside as the barrioization of the Mexican community. Albert Camarillo, *Chicanos in a Changing Society: From Mexican Pueblos to American Barrios in Santa Barbara and Southern California, 1848–1930* (Cambridge, MA: Harvard University Press, 1979), 53. For other histories of East Los Angeles, see Rodolfo Acuña, *A Community under Siege: A Chronicle of Chicanos East of the Los Angeles River, 1945–1975* (Los Angeles: Chicano Studies Research Center Publications, 1984); Richard Griswold del Castillo, *The Los Angeles Barrio, 1850–1890: A Social History* (Berkeley: University of California Press, 1979).

15. Sánchez, *Becoming Mexican American*, 224–25.

16. Marla Ramírez, "Contested Illegality: Three Generations of Exclusion through Mexican 'Repatriation' and the Politics of Immigration Law, 1920–2005" (PhD diss., University of California, Santa Barbara, 2015). On deporting citizens, see also Natalia Molina, "Deportable Citizens: The Decoupling of Race and Citizenship in the Construction of the 'Anchor Baby,'" in *Deportation in the Americas: Histories of Exclusion*, ed. Kenyon Zimmer and Cristina Salinas (Arlington: Texas A&M Press, 2018), 164–91.

17. The 1930 census was found on ancestry.com.

18. Report to the Board of Supervisors from the Superintendent of Charities, 8/7/33, 4, Box 64, 14 a, bb, aaa (1), John Anson Ford Papers (JAF), The Huntington Library, San Marino, California. The County Charity Department did not track medical and charity cases separately.

19. For more on the use of the "public charge" label to deport Mexican immigrants, as well as Mexican American children, during the Depression, see Molina, "Deportable Citizens."

20. Many growers used contractors to provide them with agricultural workers. These contractors were in charge of supervising field operations, as well as providing workers with room and board. They often cheated the laborers, not paying them what they were promised and overcharging them for room and board, knowing that workers had no other option but to accept this treatment. US Congress, Senate, Committee on Education and Labor, *Violations of Free Speech and Rights of Labor. Digest of Report of the Committee on Education and Labor Pursuant to S. Res. 266, a Resolution to Investigate Violations of the Right of Free Speech and Assembly and Interference with the Right of Labor to Organize and Bargain Collectively* (Washington, DC: US Government Printing Office, 1939).

21. See, e.g., García, *Strategies of Segregation*; Menchaca, *The Mexican Outsiders*.

22. Latinx businesses and entrepreneurs are understudied in American history, but they have much to teach us. Latinx entrepreneurs have played significant roles in revitalizing the commercial districts of neighborhoods. They have used their businesses to establish upward mobility for themselves and their coethnics, and their businesses have served as nodes in social networks. See Mike Amezcua, "Beautiful Urbanism: Gender, Landscape, and Contestation in Latino Chicago's Age of Urban Renewal," *Journal of American History* 104, no. 1

(2017): 97–119; Barraclough, *Charros*; Geraldo L. Cadava, *Standing on Common Ground: The Making of a Sunbelt Borderland* (Cambridge, MA: Harvard University Press, 2013); A. K. Sandoval-Strausz, *Barrio America: How Latino Immigrants Saved the American City* (New York: Basic Books, 2019). Also see the following on the important work of immigrant entrepreneurs and their important role in shaping foodways and food culture through their establishment of restaurants: Ray Krishnendu, *The Ethnic Restaurateur* (London: Bloomsbury Academic, 2016); Padoongpatt, *Flavors of Empire*.

23. As the sociologist Leo Gebler has pointed out, citing the history of some well-known department stores, "Historically, entrepreneurship has enabled some of the immigration groups to make extraordinary progress despite poor schooling." Leo Grebler, Joan W. Moore, Ralph C. Guzman, and Jeffrey Lionel Berlant, *The Mexican-American People, the Nation's Second Largest Minority* (New York: Free Press, 1970), 15.

24. Details of Natalia Barraza and the restaurant are derived from María Molina, interview by Natalia Molina, March 8, 2014; and "Natalia Barraza."

25. Kropp, *California Vieja*, 233–34. See also William D. Estrada, *The Los Angeles Plaza: Sacred and Contested Space* (Austin: University of Texas Press, 2008).

26. Paul V. Coates, "Dining Around Town," *Mirror News*, February 15, 1949, 32.

27. For more on the politics of race and Methodist schools and settlement houses, see Ruiz, *From out of the Shadows*. On the politics of these institutions, see Julie T. Cohen, "Pedagogies for 'Productive Citizenship': The Cultural Politics of Child Welfare in Early Twentieth-Century Southern California" (PhD diss., University of California, Irvine, 2009). Cohen interviewed María for this dissertation.

28. Here I build on what the scholar Genevieve Carpio calls a "racial broker," in reference to Latinx real estate agents in 1960s Los Angeles who broke through the profession's color line and used their position to help other Latinx go from renters to buyers (and even helped some become real estate agents themselves). I use the term "cultural broker" to emphasize the cultural capital that these brokers had and gave immigrants like Doña Natalia access to, as well as to make the term more capacious as cultural brokers did not necessarily share the same ethnic or racial background. Carpio, *Collisions at the Crossroads*, 195–200.

29. David Roediger, *Working toward Whiteness. How America's Immigrants Became White: The Strange Journey from Ellis Island to the Suburbs* (New York: Basic

Books, 2005), 12. See also Thomas A. Guglielmo, *White on Arrival: Italians, Race, Color, and Power in Chicago, 1890-1945* (New York: Oxford University Press, 2003); Matthew Frye Jacobson, *Whiteness of a Different Color: European Immigrants and the Alchemy of Race* (Cambridge, MA: Harvard University Press, 1998); Karen Brodkin, *How Jews Became White Folks and What That Says about Race in America* (New Brunswick, NJ: Rutgers University Press, 1998).

30. Roediger, *Working toward Whiteness*.

31. Nahama's biographical details courtesy of ancestry.com; accessed November 9, 2018. On Jews moving to Los Angeles's Westside, see George J. Sánchez, "'What's Good for Boyle Heights Is Good for the Jews': Creating Multiracialism on the Eastside during the 1950s," *American Quarterly* 56, no. 3 (2004): 633-61.

32. Anthea Raymond, "Lionel Rolfe: Bookseller Jake Zeitlin's Echo Park Days—Part One," *Patch*, February 20, 2012, https://patch.com/california/echo-park/lionel-rolfe-remembering-echo-park-s-jake-zietlin-part-one. See also Burt Folkart, "Jacob Zeitlin, Authors' Friend and Noted Book Seller, 84, Dies," *Los Angeles Times*, August 31, 1987.

33. *Red Hill*, documentary created by the Echo Park Film Center Youth Filmmaking Project, Echo Park Film Center, 2006.

34. How to trace something that did not happen, in this case segregation in Echo Park, is difficult to research. I thank Wade Graham, who is writing a book on Echo Park, for sharing this argument on why Echo Park did not develop as a segregated planned community.

35. Davis, *City of Quartz*, 214 n. 23.

36. Ibid., 399.

37. Carina Monica Montoya, *Los Angeles's Historic Filipinotown* (Charleston, SC: Arcadia Publishing, 2009).

38. Carol Jacques, interview by Natalia Molina, July 8, 2016.

39. Rosemary Castillo, interview by Natalia Molina, August 19, 2017. The theater, a beloved institution founded in 1963, became an official Los Angeles Historic Cultural Monument in 2009.

40. Tom Sitton, "Another Generation of Urban Reformers: Los Angeles in the 1930s," *Western Historical Quarterly* 18, no. 3 (1987): 321, 324; Daniel Hurewitz, *Bohemian Los Angeles and the Making of Modern Politics*; Kevin Starr, *Material Dreams: Southern California through the 1920s* (New York: Oxford University Press, 1990),

221, 329, 60. In his study of Boyle Heights, George J. Sánchez also found a unique bedrock of radical politics brought by waves of Jewish, Italian, Russian, Molokan, and Mexican immigrants, as well as African Americans, to Boyle Heights. Sánchez, *Boyle Heights*.

41. Jim Walker, *Pacific Electric Red Cars* (Charleston, SC: Arcadia Publishing, 2006), 59, 67, 68; "Echo Park Lake 1945 to 1980," Echo Park Historical Society, http://historicechopark.org/history-landmarks/places-landmarks/echo-park-lake/#toggle-id-2; accessed October 18, 2018.

42. Raymond, "Lionel Rolfe: Bookseller Jake Zeitlin's Echo Park Days—Part One."

43. Originally quoted in Barbara Marinacci and Rudy Marinacci, *Take Sunset Boulevard! A California Guide* (San Rafael, CA: Presidio Press, 1981), 87.

44. Quoted in Daniel Mark Epstein, *Sister Aimee: The Life of Aimee Semple McPherson* (New York: Harcourt Brace Jovanovich, 1993), 380.

45. Marinacci and Marinacci, *Take Sunset Boulevard!*, 83–87; Hadley Meares, "How America's First Megachurch Changed LA's Echo Park," *Curbed LA*, April 21, 2014.https://la.curbed.com/2014/4/21/10112432/how-americas-first-megachurch-changed-las-echo-park-1.

46. Shire's sons, Billy and Peter, went on to be part of Echo Park history, as a business and gallery owner and an artist and sculptor, respectively. Jessica Goodheart, "One for the Neighborhood: Art: Sculptor Peter Shire's Hilltop Creation Near His Home Will Honor Frank Glass and Grace E. Simons," *Los Angeles Times*, October 29, 1992. The documentary *Red Hill* features interviews with about a dozen such residents who describe Echo Park as one of Los Angeles's "bohemian and politically active spots" and a "place where you are allowed to be somewhat different."

47. Daniel Hurewitz, in *Bohemian Los Angeles and the Making of Modern Politics*, richly documents the radical politics of the area.

48. Edward J. Escobar, "Bloody Christmas and the Irony of Police Professionalism: The Los Angeles Police Department, Mexican Americans, and Police Reform in the 1950s," *Pacific Historical Review* 72, no. 2 (2003): 171–99.

49. This was not an isolated incident of the ways in which ethnic Mexicans were treated in the press. See also Bob Will, "5000 L.A. Hoodlums Belong to Violence-Dealing Gangs," *Los Angeles Times*, December 17, 1953, 2. On the crimi-

nalization and racialization of ethnic Mexican youth in the post–World War II period, see Miroslava Chávez-García, *States of Delinquency: Race and Science in the Making of California's Juvenile Justice System* (Berkeley: University of California Press, 2012); Edward J. Escobar, *Race, Police, and the Making of a Political Identity: Mexican Americans and the Los Angeles Police Department, 1900–1945* (Berkeley: University of California Press, 1999).

50. "**KNOW YOUR RIGHTS!**" flyer, Box 12, folder 22, Civil Rights Congress, Los Angeles, Southern California Library for Social Studies and Research, Los Angeles.

51. Luis Alvarez, *The Power of the Zoot: Youth Culture and Resistance during World War II* (Berkeley: University of California Press, 2008).

52. Alice Greenfield McGrath, "Sleepy Lagoon Case—Chronology," 1983, Department of Special Collections, UCLA, www.library.edu/special/scweb, accessed July 29, 2011; Margot Roosevelt, "Alice McGrath Dies at 92," *Los Angeles Times*, November 29, 2009.

53. Carey McWilliams, *North from Mexico: The Spanish-Speaking People of the United States*, updated by Matt S. Meier (New York: Praeger, 1990), 206. Cited in Scott Kurashige, *The Shifting Grounds of Race: Black and Japanese Americans in the Making of Multiethnic Los Angeles* (Princeton, NJ: Princeton University Press, 2008), 150.

54. Carey McWilliams, *Brothers under the Skin* (Boston: Little, Brown, 1944); *Prejudice: Japanese-Americans: Symbol of Racial Intolerance* (Boston: Little, Brown, 1944); *A Mask for Privilege: Anti-Semitism in America* (Boston: Little, Brown, 1948); *Factories in the Field: The Story of Migratory Farm Labor in California* (Hamden, CT: Archon Books, 1969); *North from Mexico*.

55. McWilliams, *Brothers under the Skin*, 90, 96.

56. Carey McWilliams, *The Education of Carey McWilliams* (New York: Simon and Schuster, 1979).

57. George J. Sánchez, "Edward R. Roybal and the Politics of Multiracialism," *Southern California Quarterly* 92, no. 1 (Spring 2010): 51–54.

58. Albert M. Camarillo, "Navigating Segregated Life in America's Racial Borderhoods, 1910s–1950s," *Journal of American History* 100, no. 3 (2013): 645–62.

59. Javier Aguilar, "Consistency of Change: A Compendium of Data for Echo Park" (Master's thesis, University of California Los Angeles, 1998), 7. The creation

of the East Los Angeles Interchange in the Boyle Heights area, for example, divided neighborhoods, displaced 10,000 people, and destroyed 29,000 homes, Mary S. Pardo, *Mexican American Women Activists: Identity and Resistance in Two Los Angeles Communities* (Philadelphia, PA: Temple University Press, 1998), 265. Today, half a million cars pass through the East Los Angeles Interchange every day, and the freeways continue to wreak environmental and health havoc on East Los Angeles residents. For an overview of the wholesale destruction of neighborhoods in Boyle Heights, see Betsy Kalin, *East LA Interchange* (Clearwater, FL: Media Bluewater, 2015).

60. "Statement regarding Echo Park swimming pool," by Supervisor John Anson Ford, August 1954, ii, 10, Box 42, JAF.

61. Biography sheet, no title, Municipal Reference Library, City Hall, Los Angeles, June 30, 1971, Los Angeles Public Library Reference Files.

62. "Your City Parks and Recreation Centers," *Los Angeles Times*, September 4, 1957; "Senior Citizens Get Clubhouse in Echo Park," *Los Angeles Times*, March 22 1960; Carlton Williams, "Councilman Sworn in Soon after His Election," May 28, 1959.

63. Biography sheet, no title, Municipal Reference Library, City Hall, Los Angeles, June 30, 1971, Los Angeles Public Library Reference Files.

64. Paul Lamport file, ONE Subject File collection, Coll2012-001, ONE National Gay & Lesbian Archives, Los Angeles, CA. See also Lillian Faderman and Stuart Timmons, *Gay L.A.: A History of Sexual Outlaws, Power Politics, and Lipstick Lesbians* (New York: Basic Books, 2006), 165.

65. In addition to bearing the brunt of freeway construction (as in the case of Boyle Heights and the East Los Angeles Interchange), countless poor and minority neighborhoods have been on the losing end of NIMBY (Not In My Backyard) campaigns in which undesirable projects—like prisons and garbage incinerators—end up in poor neighborhoods, because other, wealthier neighborhoods have more resources and political clout to block them. Pardo, *Mexican American Women Activists*; Pulido, *Environmentalism and Economic Justice*; George J. Sánchez, "Disposable People, Expendable Neighborhoods," in *A Companion to Los Angeles*, ed. William Francis Deverell and Greg Hise (Chichester: Wiley-Blackwell, 2010).

66. Donald Craig Parsons, *Making a Better World: Public Housing, the Red Scare, and the Direction of Modern Los Angeles* (Minneapolis: University of Minnesota

Press, 2005); Avila, *Popular Culture in the Age of White Flight*; John H. Laslett, *Shameful Victory: The Los Angeles Dodgers, the Red Scare, and the Hidden History of Chavez Ravine* (Tucson: University of Arizona Press, 2015), 122. On Latinx and urban renewal, see also Sandoval-Strausz, *Barrio America*; Eduardo Contreras, "Voice and Property: Latinos, White Conservatives, and Urban Renewal in 1960s San Francisco," *Western Historical Quarterly* 45, no. 3 (2014): 253–76; Lydia R. Otero, *La Calle: Spatial Conflicts and Urban Renewal in a Southwest City* (Tucson: University of Arizona Press, 2010); Lilia Fernandez, *Brown in the Windy City: Mexicans and Puerto Ricans in Postwar Chicago* (Chicago: University of Chicago Press, 2012); Amezcua, "Beautiful Urbanism."

67. Hector Becerra, "Decades Later, Bitter Memories of Chavez Ravine," *Los Angeles Times*, April 5, 2012.

68. Boyle Heights is a signal example of the impact these policies had on communities. See Sánchez, *Boyle Heights*.

69. Robert O. Self, *American Babylon: Race and the Struggle for Postwar Oakland* (Princeton, N.J.: Princeton University Press, 2003); George Lipsitz, "The Possessive Investment in Whiteness: Racialized Social Democracy and the 'White' Problem in American Studies," *American Quarterly* 47, no. 3 (1995): 369–87; Thomas Sugrue, *The Origins of the Urban Crisis: Race and Inequality in Postwar Detroit* (Princeton, NJ: Princeton University Press, 1996).

70. George Lipsitz has reminded us that many still fail to recognize the ways in which such programs institutionalized inequality and "widened the gap between the resources available to whites and those available to aggrieved racial communities." Lipsitz, "The Possessive Investment in Whiteness," 373.

71. Security map of Los Angeles County, Edendale, D-31; Security Map of Los Angeles, D-34, http://salt.unc.edu/T-RACES/holc.html, accessed February 21, 2014. See reports for D-33 and D-34, which have very similar language and descriptions.

72. According to Philip Ethington et al., who compiled the data used for the demographic charts based on Los Angeles County census data, the category "Other" "includes all non-white but also non-black population. Since 'Mexicans' and 'Central and South Americans' were classified as 'white' in 1940–1960, this variable effectively represents Asians, who comprised the vast majority of remaining nonwhites, although Native Americans were also included."

Ethington et al. "Los Angeles County Union Census Tract Data Series, 1940–1990, Version 1.01, p. 46.

73. "Grace E. Simons: The Defender of Elysian Park," http://historicechopark .org/history-landmarks/people/grace-e-simons.

74. Andrea Thabet, "Culture as Urban Renewal: Postwar Los Angeles and the Remaking of Public Space" (PhD diss., University of California, Santa Barbara, 2013).

75. William Overend, "Lawyers: Two Sides of a Spectrum," *Los Angeles Times*, May 9, 1976, D1; Karen Gillingham, "Taking a Bite out of Shopping: How and Where You Can Join the Food Co-op Movement," *Los Angeles Times*, January 10, 1978, G8; Lori Grange, "Day-Care Center Teaches Commitment," *Los Angeles Times*, May 3, 1990, G1.

76. Larry Gordon, "Echo Park Merchants See Boom in Store: Rebuilt Pioneer Market Spurs New Business around Sunset Boulevard," *Los Angeles Times*, January 17, 1985, 1; Doug Smith, "'You're Not the Most Popular Person in Echo Park. William Toro Is,'" *Los Angeles Times*, August 2, 1990; Iris Yokoi, "Echo Park: Finer's Prepares for a Final Sale," *Los Angeles Times*, March 14, 1993.

77. George Christy, "Looking for Good Food?" *Los Angeles Times*, November 18, 1973, V24.

78. Kate Linthicum, "An Appetite for Service: Three Restaurant Staffers Mark 50 Years on the Job," *Los Angeles Times*, February 29, 2012.

CHAPTER TWO. TASTING HOME

1. "Colorful L.A. Boxer in the '40s and '50s," *Los Angeles Times*, March 26, 2008; "Classic American West Coast Boxing," https://boxrec.com/forum/view-topic.php?t=78351&start=38450.

2. "Aragon, Salas in Savage 45-Minute Barroom Brawl," *Daily News*, December 8, 1951, 1; interview with María Molina.

3. The Cultural historian Robin D. G. Kelley reminds us that such an action is "an assertion of dignity and resistance [that] should not be dismissed as peripheral to the 'real struggles.'" Robin D. G. Kelley, *Race Rebels: Culture, Politics, and the Black Working Class* (New York: Free Press, 1994), 51.

4. Kun, *To Live and Dine in L.A.*, 71–72. Also see Kun, *To Live and Dine in L.A.*, for an overview of Mexican food in the second half of the nineteenth century in

Los Angeles, 71–77; Gustavo Arellano, "Tamales, L.A.'s Original Street Food," *Los Angeles Times*, September 8, 2011.

5. Neil Foley, *The White Scourge: Mexicans, Blacks, and Poor Whites in Texas Cotton Culture* (Berkeley: University of California Press, 1997), 41–42; David Montejano, *Anglos and Mexicans in the Making of Texas, 1836–1986* (Austin: University of Texas Press, 1987), 223–25.

6. Los Angeles County Health Department (LACHD) Annual Health Report (AHR) 1920, 35, Public Health Library, Los Angeles. Hereafter LACHD AHR 1920.

7. LACHD AHR 1920, 20.

8. Pearl Ellis, *Americanization through Homemaking* (Los Angeles: Wetzel, 1929). On the origins on the domestic reform movement, see Laura Shapiro, *Perfection Salad: Women and Cooking at the Turn of the Century* (New York: Farrar, Straus and Giroux, 1986).

9. Colman Andrews, *My Usual Table: A Life in Restaurants* (New York: Ecco, 2014), 59.

10. Ibid., 54.

11. Olvera Street, www.casalagolondrinacafe.com/.

12. Estrada, *The Los Angeles Plaza*, 200.

13. Kropp, *California Vieja*, 353.

14. Coyote Cafe, http://elcoyotecafe.com/; accessed January 6, 2016.

15. Andrews, *My Usual Table*, 65.

16. Ibid., 112.

17. Mary Rourke, "Waitress Credited with Introducing L.A. to Nachos," *Los Angeles Times*, October 17, 2008; Barbara Hansen, "Border Line: Head Chef Adapts Mexican Fare to California Taste," *Los Angeles Times*, June 30, 1977, I33.

18. As the anthropologist Mary Douglas writes, food is "a system of communication" that reveals much about social relationships. Mary Douglas, *In the Active Voice* (New York: Routledge & K. Paul, 1982), 82–124.

19. On food and authenticity, see Perales, "The Food Historian's Dilemma"; Donna R. Gabaccia, *We Are What We Eat: Ethnic Food and the Making of Americans* (Cambridge, MA: Harvard University Press, 1998); Arjun Appadurai, "How to Make a National Cuisine: Cookbooks in Contemporary India." *Comparative Studies in Society and History* 30, no. 1 (1988): 3–24; Marie Sarita Gaytán, "From Sombreros

to Sincronizadas: Authenticity, Ethnicity, and the Mexican Restaurant Industry," *Journal of Contemporary Ethnography* 37, no. 3 (2008): 314-41.

20. Ruiz, *From out of the* Shadows, 50.

21. Dawn Bohulano Mabalon, "As American as Jackrabbit Adobo: Cooking, Eating and Becoming Filipina/o American before World War II," in *Eating Asian America: A Food Studies Reader*, ed. Robert Ji-Song Ku, Martin Manalansan, and Anita Mannur (New York: New York University Press, 2013). 147-76.

22. "A Place Everybody Is High On," "Roundabout with Art Ryon," *Los Angeles Times*, June 21, 1964, S32. The review featured the Nayarit II, which opened that same year.

23. "Nayarit en Los Angeles," *El Eco*, August 26, 1964, 21.

24. Sherryll Mleynek, interview by Natalia Molina, June 8, 2021, Portland, OR, via phone.

25. Ana Raquel Minian, *Undocumented Lives: The Untold Story of Mexican Migration* (Cambridge, Massachusetts: Harvard University Press, 2018), 23, 38, 92, 105.

26. "Natalia Barraza: Nayarita pionera en L.A.," 17.

27. Alexis McSweyn, interview by Natalia Molina, August 13, 2018, Monterey Park, CA.

28. Rodolfo Lora, interview by Natalia Molina, March 29, 2018, Novillero, Nayarit.

29. For more on the beloved owner of El Tepeyac, see www.latimes.com /archives/la-xpm-2013-feb-13-la-me-manuel-rojas-20130214-story.html.

30. The term "politics of respectability" was originally coined by Elizabeth Higginbotham to describe black women's strategies for reform during the Progressive Era. Since then, this term has been taken up by many scholars to show how women's behavior, especially as it pertained to sexuality, was intimately tied to acceptance of all kinds, including both cultural citizenship and actual citizenship, beginning with the ability to migrate to the United States. See Higginbotham, *Religious Discontent*. See also Celeste R. Menchaca, "Staging Crossings: Policing Intimacy and Performing Respectability at the U.S.-Mexico Border, 1907-1917," *Pacific Historical Review* 89, no. 1 (2020): 16-43.

31. Michael Urban, *New Orleans Rhythm and Blues after Katrina: Music, Magic and Myth* (London: Palgrave Macmillan, 2016), 50.

32. On Mexican immigrant employment in the 1960s, see Grebler et al., *The Mexican-American People*, ch. 9, "Occupations and Jobs."

33. *Ralph Story's Los Angeles*, Film and Television Archive, University of California, Los Angeles.

34. Aurelia Guijarro Preciado, conversation with Natalia Molina, January 20, 2020.

35. Francine Rodriguez, email correspondence, December 23, 2020.

36. Evelia Pack, interview by Natalia Molina, August 14, 2015, Los Angeles, CA.

37. McSweyn, interview.

38. Óscar López, interview by Natalia Molina, December 17, 2020, Los Angeles, CA.

39. Ildefonso García, interview by Natalia Molina, August 14, 2015, Los Angeles, CA.

40. On L.A.'s rich Latinx sonic landscape in the 1950s and 1960s, see Macias, *Mexican American Mojo*; Josh Kun, ed., *The Tide Was Always High: The Music of Latin America in Los Angeles* (Oakland: University of California Press, 2017); Gaye Theresa Johnson, *Spaces of Conflict, Sounds of Solidarity: Music, Race, and Spatial Entitlement in Los Angeles* (Berkeley: University of California Press, 2013).

41. According to the historian Matt Garcia, the first Latin American band to perform at the city of Pomona's popular Rainbow Gardens was booked for a Wednesday for exactly this reason. To the owner's surprise, the dance drew over 750 people despite its midweek time slot, and the Rainbow Gardens began holding Latin dances on Friday and Saturday nights as well. Matt Garcia, *A World of Its Own: Race, Labor, and Citrus in the Making of Greater Los Angeles, 1900–1970* (Chapel Hill: University of North Carolina Press, 2001), ch. 6.

42. Guadalupe ("Lupe") Reyes, interview by Natalia Molina, August 5, 2017, Baldwin Hills, CA.

43. The sociologist Tomás Jiménez coined the term "replenished ethnicity." He writes, "When immigrants continually replenish the native-born coethnics, as has occurred with the Mexican-origin population, access to the symbols and practices that epitomize the expression of ethnicity is abundant." Tomás R. Jiménez, *Replenished Ethnicity: Mexican Americans, Immigration, and Identity* (Berkeley: University of California Press, 2010).

44. "Romance Singer Celebrates 100 Year Milestone," *Eastern Group Publications/EGPNews*, http://egpnews.com, accessed March 23, 2014; "KWKW Slates Mexico Programs," *Los Angeles Times*, September 16, 1965, C20.

45. These events were covered not just in the Spanish press but also in the *Los Angeles Times*. Pepe Arciga, "Variety Bill Offered at Million Dollar Theater," *Los Angeles Times*, November 23, 1967; Pepe Arciga, "Manzanero Performs at Million Dollar Theater," *Los Angeles Times*, May 8, 1969; G. K., "Gala Premiere Reopens Million Dollar Theater," *Los Angeles Times*, August 31, 1950, 16; Pepe Arciga, "Million Dollar Theater Program Expanded," *Los Angeles Times*, July 7, 1967, C6; "Mexican Stars Dance, Sing at Million Dollar," *Los Angeles Times*, February 8, 1956, B7.

46. Jaime Jarrín biography, http://losangeles.dodgers.mlb.com/team/broadcasters.jsp?c_id=la; accessed May 19, 2017.

47. Jaime Jarrín, interview by Natalia Molina, September 11, 2020, San Marino, CA, via phone.

48. David Gutierréz, ed. *The Columbia History of Latinos in the United States since 1960* (New York: Columbia University Press, 2004), 2. See also Lorena García and Mérida Rúa, "Processing Latinidad: Mapping Latino Urban Landscapes through Chicago Ethnic Festivals," *Latino Studies* 5, no. 3 (2007): 317–39; Frances R. Aparicio, "Jennifer as Selena: Rethinking Latinidad in Media and Popular Culture," *Latino Studies*, no. 1 (2003): 90–105.

49. Felix M. Padilla, *Latino Ethnic Consciousness: The Case of Mexican Americans and Puerto Ricans in Chicago* (Notre Dame, IN: University of Notre Dame Press, 1985).

50. Clara E. Rodriguez, *Changing Race: Latinos, the Census, and the History of Ethnicity in the United States* (New York: New York University Press, 2000).

51. Thank you to Frances Aparicio for making the point that examining the types of relationships that could form at the Nayarit is also an important way to historicize Latinidad.

52. Roberto Tejada, email correspondence, September 1, 2015.

53. I was fortunate to have Ana Celia Zentella as a colleague; from her I first learned the importance of using language as an analytic lens, as well as its role in identity and community formation. See, e.g., Ana Celia Zentella, "Latin@ Languages and Identities," in *Latinos: Remaking America*, ed. Marcelo M. Suárez-

Orozco and Mariela Páez (Berkeley: University of California Press, 2002). On the intersections of language, politics, and community formation, see also Dolores Ines Casillas, *Sounds of Belonging U.S. Spanish-Language Radio and Public Advocacy* (New York: New York University Press, 2014); Frances R. Aparicio, *Listening to Salsa: Gender, Latin Popular Music, and Puerto Rican Cultures* (Hanover, NH: Wesleyan University Press, 1998).

54. Gaye Teresa Johnson, *Spaces of Conflict, Sounds of Solidarity: Music, Race, and Spatial Entitlement in Los Angeles* (Berkeley: University of California Press, 2013), 8.

55. Ramón Pack II, interview by Natalia Molina, November 14, 2015, San Diego, CA.

56. The concept of Latinidad can be empowering as it helps establish common links between Latinx people. But it can also be disempowering when it is overshadowed by one numerically dominant national group. For example, despite the presence of other Latinx groups in L.A., because Mexicans were numerically dominant, "Mexican" was the default category/description of Latinx in Los Angeles until the 1980s, when the demographics of the city, as well as public spaces and neighborhoods, changed with the influx of Central American immigrants fleeing civil wars in their home countries. Even then, "Mexican" continued to be a default identity category that obfuscated the diversity of this community in part because they remained the dominant national Latinx group in the area and the country and because of their long history in the region.

57. When Rosa Porto relocated to Los Angeles from Cuba via Miami, she began to bake and sell her cakes, based on a family recipe, out of her home. In 1976, with a $5,000 loan, she opened a 300-square-foot bakery in a strip mall on Sunset Boulevard in Silver Lake. The family business eventually opened its flagship store in Glendale in 1982. Maria Elena Fernandez, "L.A. at Large; Cuban Cafecitos and All the Comforts of Home," *Los Angeles Times*, February 6, 2001.

58. See Edward J. Escobar, *Race, Police, and the Making of a Political Identity: Mexican Americans and the Los Angeles Police Department, 1900-1945* (Berkeley: University of California Press, 1999).

59. Macías, *Mexican American Mojo*, 340 n. 89. Macías discusses these musicians and the cultural politics of the music scene in Los Angeles at the time. It should also be noted that these Latino musicians represented diverse musical

genres. Cugat, for example, was known for introducing Latin music, like the rumba, to mainly well-heeled white audiences, in particular, when he was bandleader at the Warldorf Astoria in New York City for sixteen years starting in 1933. Some of the lesser-known performers from Club Virginia's and Club Havana, however, played music that appealed more to Mexican American and other youths of color; often this music blended genres and styles across the color line. John S. Wilson, Obituary, "Xavier Cugat, 90, the Bandleader Who Rose on the Rumba's Tide," *New York Times*, October 28, 1990.

60. Ramón Pack II, interview.

61. On Latino baseball players in the major leagues, see Adrian Burgos, *Playing America's Game: Baseball, Latinos, and the Color Line* (Berkeley: University of California Press, 2007).

62. *The Negro Motorist Green Book* (1936–64), known popularly as the *Green Book*, was an annual guidebook for African American travelers designed to help them navigate a racist, and often dangerous, landscape. Named after its author, Victor Green, the *Green Book* listed restaurants, hotels, gas stations, and miscellaneous other businesses like beauty salons, barbershops, repair shops, and pharmacies across America and the world that served African Americans. Candacy Taylor has referred to the *Green Book* as "the overground railroad," a counterpart to the "underground railroad" of safe houses used to help escaped slaves travel to the North.

63. Thanks to Judith Smith for this observation. Rita Moreno, *Rita Moreno: A Memoir* (New York: Celebra, 2013).

64. See, e.g., Vicki L. Ruiz, "Citizen Restaurant: American Imaginaries, American Communities," *American Quarterly* 60, no. 1 (2008): 1–21; Deverell, *Whitewashed Adobe*.

65. Nathan Masters, "When Hollywood Boulevard Became Santa Claus Lane," December 20, 2012, www.kcet.org/shows/lost-la/when-hollywood-boulevard-became-santa-claus-lane.

66. Peter Standish, *The States of Mexico: A Reference Guide to History and Culture* (Westport, CT: Greenwood Press, 2009), 242.

67. Both William Deverell and Lon Kurashige provide excellent examples of how we can read parades as a historical source that gets at the racial and cultural politics of the day. Deverell, *Whitewashed Adobe*; Lon Kurashige, *Japanese Ameri-*

can Celebration and Conflict: A History of Ethnic Identity and Festival in Los Angeles, 1934–1990 (Berkeley: University of California Press, 2002).

68. Although the Treaty of Guadalupe Hidalgo established Mexicans' eligibility for citizenship in 1848, attempts to establish Mexicans as ineligible for citizenship continued for decades. According to the Naturalization Act of 1790 and its revision in 1870, only those who were deemed white or Black could become citizens; attempts were made to legally categorize Mexicans as "Indian" (or Indigenous), which would have made them ineligible to naturalize.

CHAPTER THREE. THE EMOTIONAL LIFE OF IMMIGRATION

1. Grebler et al., *The Mexican-American People*, ch. 9; Secretaría de Economía, *Censo general de población*, 1950.

2. Robert Alvarez, *Familia: Migration and Adaptation in Baja and Alta California, 1800–1975* (Berkeley: University of California Press, 1987), 56–57, 133.

3. Similarly, in her investigation of Cambodian-owned donut shops in Los Angeles, Erin Curtis has found that the proprietors see their business as a means to earn a living for themselves and as a way to provide opportunities for their children. Erin Curtis, "Cambodian Donut Shops and the Negotiation of Donut Shops in Los Angeles," in Ku, Manalansan, and Mannur, *Eating Asian America*, 13–29.

4. Scholars have studied the processes of settlement in great detail. Key works include Richard D. Alba and Victor Nee, *Remaking the American Mainstream: Assimilation and Contemporary Immigration* (Cambridge, MA: Harvard University Press, 2003); Douglas S. Massey, *Return to Aztlan: The Social Process of International Migration from Western Mexico* (Berkeley: University of California Press, 1987); Alejandro Portes and Rubén G. Rumbaut, *Legacies: The Story of the Immigrant Second Generation* (Berkeley: University of California Press, 2001); Cecilia Menjívar, *Fragmented Ties: Salvadoran Immigrant Networks in America* (Berkeley: University of California Press, 2000).

5. On the importance of social networks for settlement, two excellent books are Leisy J. Abrego, *Sacrificing Families: Navigating Laws, Labor, and Love across Borders* (Stanford, CA: Stanford University Press, 2014); Hondagneu-Sotelo, *Gendered Transitions*. There has been little work on examining the Mexican American

middle class, historically or in the contemporary period. On the growth of the Mexican middle class after World War II, due in part to entrepreneurs, see Barraclough, *Charros*, ch. 2. In addition, Jody Aguis Vallejo's study shows us how resources, such as education and middle-class mentors, provide key pathways to the middle class. Barraza provided such resources, discussed in this chapter. Jody Agius Vallejo, *Barrios to Burbs: The Making of the Mexican American Middle Class* (Stanford, CA: Stanford University Press, 2012).

6. Heather Lee, "A Life Cooking for Others: The Work and Migration Experience of a Chinese Restaurant Worker in New York City, 1920–1946," in Ku, Manalansan, and Mannur, *Eating Asian America*, 55.

7. Heather Lee, "Entrepreneurs in the Age of Chinese Exclusion: Transnational Capital, Migrant Labor, and Chinese Restaurants in New York City, 1850–1943" (PhD diss., Brown University, 2014).

8. American Immigration Lawyers Association, "Green Card Background," www.aila.org/infonet/ins-green-card-background; accessed September 2, 2017.

9. Minian, *Undocumented Lives*.

10. Nicholas De Genova, *Working the Boundaries: Race, Space, and "Illegality" in Mexican Chicago* (Durham, NC: Duke University Press, 2005).

11. Abrego, *Sacrificing Families*; Pierrette Hondagneu-Sotelo and Ernestine Avila, "'I'm Here, but I'm There': The Meanings of Latina Transitional Motherhood," *Gender & Society* 11, no. 5 (1997): 548–59; Rhacel Salazar Parrenas, *Servants of Globalization: Women, Migration, and Domestic Work* (Stanford, CA: Stanford University Press, 2001); Lila Soto, "The Preludes to Migration: Anticipation and Imaginings of Mexican Immigrant Adolescent Girls," *Girlhood Studies: An Interdisciplinary Journal* 3, no. 2 (December 2010): 30–48.

12. Abrego, *Sacrificing Families*, 75–76.

13. US Congress, House, Committee on the Judiciary, *Study of Population and Immigration Problems* (Washington, DC: US Government Printing Office, 1962), 51.

14. Frank L. Auerbach, *Immigration Laws of the United States: A Textbook Integrating Statute, Regulations, Administrative Practice, and Leading Administrative Decisions, with A Comprehensive Index, Citation Guide, and Bibliography* (Indianapolis, IN: Bobbs-Merrill Co., 1955).

15. Secretaría de Economía, *Censo general de población*, 1950.

16. The Tijuana office was particularly busy. Charles Hillinger, "U.S. Consulate at Tijuana Claims World's Busiest Title," *Los Angeles Times*, May 31, 1967, 2. Ana Rosas, *Abrazando el Espíritu*, 63, also describes how immigrants could obtain counterfeit crossing documents in Tijuana.

17. Virginia ("Vicky") Lizárraga Tamayo, interview by Natalia Molina, January 9, 2018, via phone.

18. Eduwiges ("Vicky") Cueva Tavares, interview by Natalia Molina, August 13, 2015, Los Angeles, CA.

19. The legal scholar Ian Haney-López has chronicled how judicial discrimination continued to operate in the Los Angeles Superior Court and its grand jury system in two 1968 cases related to the Chicanx movement. Ian Haney-López, *Racism on Trial: The Chicano Fight for Justice* (Cambridge, MA: Belknap Press of Harvard University Press, 2003); see also Escobar, *Race, Police, and the Making of a Political Identity*.

20. See the following articles in the *Los Angeles Times*: "Carlos Teran to Take Post as Newest Judge," January 3, 1958, C3; "Civic Leaders Honor Superior Judge Teran," February 26, 1960, B2; "Judge Teran Sworn in for Superior Court," January 1, 1960, B2; "Teran Raised to Superior Court Bench," December 31, 1959, B1; "Judge Teran Commended by Council," January 28, 1960, 18; "600 Honor Judge Teran at Testimonial Dinner," January 30, 1958, 19.

21. "Mother, Children Found Starving in Motel Room," *Los Angeles Times*, November 29, 1954, 12; "Mrs. Gilliland Divorces Mate," *Los Angeles Times*, June 14, 1956, A12.

22. Rodolfo Lora, interview.

23. Cybelle Fox, "Unauthorized Welfare: The Origins of Immigrant Status Restrictions in American Social Policy," *Journal of American History* 102, no. 4 (2016): 1058–59.

24. Conversation with Ramón Barragan, August 15, 2019.

25. Grebler et al., *The Mexican-American People*, 87.

26. Erasmo Gamboa has shown the many ways in which braceros' vulnerability was often entrenched by social isolation, including lack of mobility and leisure options. Erasmo Gamboa, *Mexican Labor and World War II: Braceros in the Pacific Northwest, 1942–1947* (Austin: University of Texas Press, 1990).

27. According to the historian Alina Méndez, employers tried to keep any "vice-related" activities out of their camps, and thus farmworkers in the border towns of the Imperial Valley sought these activities outside the camps, on the other side of the segregated town and even on the other side of the border, in Mexicali. Alina Méndez, "Cheap for Whom? Migration, Farm Labor, and Social Reproduction in the Imperial Valley–Mexicali Borderlands, 1942–1969" (PhD diss., University of California, San Diego, 2017).

28. Lori A. Flores, *Grounds for Dreaming: Mexican Americans, Mexican Immigrants, and the California Farmworker Movement* (New Haven, CT: Yale University Press, 2016), 57–61.

29. Railroad workers who lived in camps and brick workers who lived in company towns experienced similar isolation. See Deverell, *Whitewashed Adobe*; Jeffrey Marcos Garcilazo, "Traqueros: Mexican Railroad Workers in the United States, 1870 to 1930" (PhD diss., University of California, Santa Barbara, 1995).

30. Alicia R. Schmidt Camacho, *Migrant Imaginaries: Latino Cultural Politics in the U.S.-Mexico Borderlands* (New York: New York University Press, 2008), 91.

31. Lupe Reyes, interview.

32. Blanca Arrevillaga, interview by Natalia Molina, December 11, 2020, Los Angeles, CA.

33. Abrego, *Sacrificing Families*, 11.

34. Sarah Lynn Lopez, *The Remittance Landscape: Spaces of Migration in Rural Mexico and Urban USA* (Chicago: University of Chicago Press, 2014).

35. I do not have knowledge of any lesbians who worked at the restaurant. This may suggest that while gay men were to some degree accepted at the restaurant or within the broader society, lesbians were not. On gay Latin in Los Angeles during this period, see Faderman and Timmons, *Gay L.A.* They discuss the Redhead in East Los Angeles, a bar that catered to Mexican American lesbians, and the M&M bar, which catered primarily to Latinas, both working-class and pink-collar workers, near West Lake/MacArthur Park (89).

36. Ethnic enclaves have much to offer. Though de facto and de jure residential segregation tend to limit opportunities in ethnic enclaves, they inspire profound affection, as places rich with history and culture where residents are less likely to experience discrimination among their coethnics. The affection for such neighborhoods is a theme that has fueled many a memoir, novel, and Hollywood

movie. See, e.g., Rosa Linda Fregoso, *meXicana Encounters: The Making of Social Identities on the Borderlands* (Berkeley: University of California Press, 2003); Raúl H. Villa, *Barrio-Logos: Space and Place in Urban Chicano Literature and Culture* (Austin: University of Texas Press, 2000).

37. See Héctor Carrillo, *Pathways of Desire: The Sexual Migration of Mexican Gay Men* (Chicago: University of Chicago Press, 2017); Lionel Cantú Jr., *The Sexuality of Migration: Border Crossings and Mexican Immigrant Men*, ed. Nancy A. Naples and Salvador Vidal-Ortiz (New York: New York University Press, 2009). In her study of the small town of Nochistlán, Zacatecas, Ana Minian found that queer men migrated to the United States at lower rates than heterosexual men. Minian, *Undocumented Lives*, 91.

38. Chauncey, *Gay New York*.

39. Ildefonso "Poncho" García, interview by Natalia Molina, August 13, 2015.

40. Ramón Pack II, interview.

41. George Chauncey's *Gay New York*, a study of gay life across four neighborhoods in New York, and Daniel Hurewitz's, *Bohemian Los Angeles and the Making of Modern Politics*, a look at mainly white gay political life in Edendale (which encompasses Echo Park), are foundational texts, but queer Latinx histories are more difficult to ascertain. For some exemplary work, in terms of both methodologies and findings, see Ernesto Chávez, "'Ramon Is Not One of These': Race and Sexuality in the Construction of Silent Film Actor Ramón Novarro's Star Image," *Journal of the History of Sexuality* 20, no. 3 (2011): 520–44; Deena J. González, *Refusing the Favor: The Spanish-Mexican Women of Santa Fe, 1820–1880* (New York: Oxford University Press, 1999); Eithne Luibhéid, *Entry Denied: Controlling Sexuality at the Border* (Minneapolis: University of Minnesota Press, 2002); Emma Pérez, *The Decolonial Imaginary: Writing Chicanas into History* (Bloomington: Indiana University Press, 1999); Emma Pérez, "Queering the Borderlands: The Challenges of Excavating the Invisible and Unheard," *Frontiers: A Journal of Women Studies* 24, no. 2-3 (2003): 122–31; Roque Ramírez, "A Living Archive of Desire."

42. Insightful accounts that have been produced in these fields are Héctor Carrillo, *The Night Is Young: Sexuality in Mexico in the Time of AIDS* (Chicago: University of Chicago Press, 2002); Matthew C. Gutmann, *The Meanings of Macho: Being a Man in Mexico City* (Berkeley: University of California Press, 1996); Cantú, *The Sexuality of Migration*.

43. Faderman and Timmons, *Gay L.A.*, 166.

44. This has changed since the 2000s as a result of gentrification.

45. Mireya Loza has pinpointed one source of such silence in her impressive study of braceros, describing how the oral history guide the research team used prevented her from getting at experiences the guide's designers had not imagined, causing her to retool it. Mireya Loza, *Defiant Braceros: How Migrant Workers Fought for Racial, Sexual, and Political Freedom* (Chapel Hill: University of North Carolina Press, 2016), 21. A small but growing number of scholars—including Nayan Shah, Margot Canaday, Eithne Luibhéid, Siobhan Somerville, and Julio Capó—have demonstrated how we might combine our research of sexuality with immigration history.

46. For example, Cantú found that while gay men may form their own social networks with each other that help them as new immigrants, gay men often find a niche in their ethnic enclaves even more than in the gay community. Cantú, *The Sexuality of Migration*, 18.

47. Margot Canaday, *The Straight State: Sexuality and Citizenship in Twentieth-Century America* (Princeton, NJ: Princeton University Press, 2009); Shah, *Stranger Intimacy*; Siobhan B. Somerville, "Notes toward a Queer History of Naturalization," *American Quarterly* 57, no. 3 (2005): 659–75; Julio Capó, *Welcome to Fairyland: Queer Miami Before 1940* (Chapel Hill: University of North Carolina Press, 2017).

48. María Molina, interview, August 14, 2015; Ildefonso "Poncho" García, interview; Evelia Díaz Barraza Pack, interview, August 14, 2015, Los Angeles, CA.

49. María Molina, interview.

50. On "sexual silence," see Carrillo, *The Night Is Young*, 139–50, esp. 139–40; Carrillo, *Pathways of Desire*, 73–74, 207.

51. Name withheld to protect privacy.

52. In his landmark study, Chauncey demonstrates that restaurants' treatment of gay customers ranged widely, from refusing them service to fully accepting them, though the latter was not advertised to the straight world given that the gay community was policed and targeted. Chauncey, *Gay New York*, 19, 163–67, 73, 76.

53. Theresa Wang et al., *Lavender Los Angeles* (Charleston, SC: Arcadia Publishing, 2011), 46–47.

54. In the 2000s, under new ownership but the same name, the Nayarit hosted a gay club (Klub Fantasy) on Sunday nights. E-mail correspondence with Karen Tongson, December 10, 2020.

55. Rosa Blanca Arrevillaga Sánchez, interview, August 6, 2017, Los Angeles, CA.

56. Steven Osuna, interview, June 12, 2017, Los Angeles, CA.

57. Eve Kosofsky Sedgwick, *Epistemology of the Closet* (Berkeley: University of California Press, 1990); Chauncey, *Gay New York*.

58. Christine Stansell, *City of Women: Sex and Class in New York, 1789–1860* (New York: Knopf, 1986); Joanne J. Meyerowitz, *Women Adrift: Independent Wage Earners in Chicago, 1880–1930* (Chicago: University of Chicago Press, 1988).

59. Rarely do studies capture the interior lives of immigrant women. On important contributions, see Chávez-García, *Migrant Longing*; Rosas, *Abrazando el Espíritu*; Ruiz, *From out of the Shadows*.

60. Key works include Elizabeth R. Escobedo, *From Coveralls to Zoot Suits: The Lives of Mexican American Women on the World War II Home Front* (Chapel Hill: University of North Carolina Press, 2013); Douglas Monroy, *Rebirth: Mexican Los Angeles from the Great Migration to the Great Depression* (Berkeley: University of California Press, 1999); George J. Sánchez, "'Go after the Women': Americanization and the Mexican Immigrant Woman, 1915–1929," in *A Multi-Cultural Reader in U.S. Women's History*, ed. Ellen DuBois and Vicki Ruiz (New York: Routledge, 1990), 250–63; Ruiz, *From out of the Shadows*.

61. Hondagneu-Sotelo, *Gendered Transitions*, ch. 4.

62. Vicki Ruiz has described how in ethnic Mexican families in the United States, young people were often mobilized by parents into serving as chaperones for their siblings in the hope of ensuring young women conformed to social and sexual mores. Ruiz, *From out of the Shadows*, 51–71.

63. Rosa Blanca Arrevillaga Sanchez, interview.

64. "Rueda Ferris," *El Eco*, March 26, 1964, 4.

65. Evelia Díaz Barraza Pack, interview.

66. Ramón Pack II, interview.

67. "Rueda Ferris," *El Eco*, February 22, 1953, 1. "Gringo" is slang for white people from the United States.

68. Nelly Díaz Barraza Casillas, interview by Natalia Molina, July 7, 2016, Los Angeles, CA.

69. The surname Wongpec comes from Irene's father, who emigrated from what she referred to as "Canton," now referred to as the Guangdong region of China. After the passage of the 1882 Exclusion Act barred Chinese immigrants from entering the United States, Chinese began to immigrate to Mexico in larger numbers seeking opportunity. See Robert Chao Romero, *The Chinese in Mexico, 1882–1940* (Tucson: University of Arizona Press, 2010).

70. Irene Wongpec, interview by Natalia Molina, December 16, 2015, Los Angeles, CA.

71. "Mujeres Destacadas: Irene Wongpec," *La Opinión*, March 27, 2014, 10A.

72. Garment work was unfortunately not something that Mexican women found enjoyable, and it usually did not pay well. See Lori A. Flores, "An Unladylike Strike Fashionably Clothed: Mexicana and Anglo Women Garment Workers against Tex-Son, 1959–1963," *Pacific Historical Review* 78, no. 3 (2009): 367–402.

73. Vicky Tavares, interview.

CHAPTER FOUR. VENTURING FORTH

1. Vicky Tavares, conversation with author, March 8, 2014.

2. By 1960, only 12 percent of ethnic Mexicans in the United States could claim a high school degree (as compared to 27.8 percent of whites) and only 5.6 percent had some college education (as compared to 22.1 percent of whites). Grebler et al., *The Mexican-American People*, 143.

3. I draw on a rich body of work that helped lead me to a tradition of immigrants as place-takers, including George Lipsitz's theory of the "black spatial imaginary" and Robin Kelley's the "moving theatre." See Kelley, *Race Rebels*; Lipsitz, *How Racism Takes Place*.

4. Macías, *Mexican American Mojo*.

5. María Molina, interview, Los Angeles, CA, August 14, 2015.

6. Lizabeth Cohen, *Making a New Deal: Industrial Workers in Chicago, 1919–1939* (Cambridge, MA: Harvard University Press, 1990), 99–158, esp. 147.

7. Blanca Arrevillaga, interview.

8. Ildefonso García, interview; Ramón Pack II, interview.

9. For more on O'Malley's hunting adventures, see Michael D'Antonio, *Forever Blue: The True Story of Walter O'Malley, Baseball's Most Controversial Owner, and the Dodgers of Brooklyn and Los Angeles* (New York: Riverhead Books, 2009), 297; Hank Hollingworth, "Safety of Autos: 'Lot of Hot Air,'" *Long Beach Press-Telegram*, April 27, 1966, 45.

10. Ramón Pack II, interview.

11. According to WorldCat, the paper started in November 1964. According to two L.A. city directories (published in 1973 and 1987), Lira lived in East Los Angeles at 2028 City View Ave., 90033; I located Lira's immigration history on ancestry.com.

12. Advertisement, *El Águila*, July 4, 1969, 4.

13. There is only one issue of *El Águila* that has been archived for all of 1969. *El Águila*, San Fernando, CA, July 4, 1969, Julian Nava Collection, box 54, folder 16, Special Collections & Archives, California State University, Northridge.

14. *El Águila*, July 4, 1969.

15. On the history of the "politics of respectability," see Higginbotham, *Righteous Discontent*. On ethnic Mexicans and beauty pageants, see Amezcua, "Beautiful Urbanism." On Japanese Americans and beauty pageants, see Kurashige, *Japanese American Celebration and Conflict*. On the cultural politics of beauty pageants, see Sarah Banet-Weiser, *The Most Beautiful Girl in the World: Beauty Pageants and National Identity* (Berkeley: University of California Press, 1999).

16. Thomas A. Guglielmo, "Fighting for Caucasian Rights: Mexicans, Mexican Americans, and the Transnational Struggle for Civil Rights in World War II Texas," *Journal of American History* 92, no. 4 (2006): 1212–37; David Gutiérrez, *Walls and Mirrors: Mexican Americans, Mexican Immigrants, and the Politics of Identity* (Berkeley: University of California Press, 1995); Vicki L. Ruiz, *Cannery Women, Cannery Lives: Mexican Women, Unionization, and the California Food Processing Industry, 1930-1950* (Albuquerque: University of New Mexico Press, 1987); Sánchez, *Becoming Mexican American*; Zaragosa Vargas, *Labor Rights Are Civil Rights: Mexican American Workers in Twentieth-Century America* (Princeton, NJ: Princeton University Press, 2005).

17. None of my interviewees mentioned such activities.

18. Rodolfo Acuña, *Anything but Mexican: Chicanos in Contemporary Los Angeles* (New York: Verso, 1996), 47.

19. María Molina, interview; Shana Bernstein, *Bridges of Reform: Interracial Civil Rights Activism in Twentieth-Century Los Angeles* (Oxford: Oxford University Press, 2010); Sánchez, "Edward R. Roybal and the Politics of Multiracialism."

20. The FBI's investigation shows that in his four months in Los Angeles, "while some of Ray's activities, such as his enrollment in dancing and bartending school in Los Angeles, brought him into regular contact with others, a close investigation of these activities revealed that significant friendships or associations never developed." US Congress, House, and Select Committee on Assassinations, *Report of the Select Committee on Assassinations, U.S. House of Representatives, Ninety-Fifth Congress, Second Session: Findings and Recommendations* (Washington, DC: US Government Printing Office, 1979).

21. For details of Ray's time in Los Angeles, see Gerald L. Posner, *Killing the Dream: James Earl Ray and the Assassination of Martin Luther King, Jr.*, 1st Harvest ed. (San Diego: Harcourt Brace, 1999).

22. *El Eco*, August 4, 1968, 8.

23. Vega P. Fahey Written Statement: JFK #1, 1997, John F. Kennedy Oral History Collection, John F. Kennedy Presidential Library.

24. Steve Lopez, "Ex-Busboy Will Never Forget Bobby Kennedy," *Los Angeles Times*, June 1, 2003.

25. "Dos nayaritas han figurado en las reseñas de los crímenes mas sonados en los últimos meses," *El Eco*, August 4, 1968, 8.

26. Josh Sides, "Straight into Compton: American Dreams, Urban Nightmares, and the Metamorphosis of a Black Suburb," *American Quarterly* 56, no. 3 (2004): 586.

27. Zora Neale Hurston, "How It Feels to Be Colored Me," *The World Tomorrow*, May 1928, 215–16, 216.

28. Grebler et al., *The Mexican-American People*, 72.

29. Ibid., 271.

30. Philip Deloria's work has been helpful in thinking about what it means to be out of place. See Philip Joseph Deloria, *Indians in Unexpected Places* (Lawrence: University Press of Kansas, 2004). Genevieve Carpio's work is important in showing us how mobility (and the lack of it) shaped how we perceived groups in terms of race and ethnicity. Carpio, *Collisions at the Crossroads*.

31. Vargas, *Labor Rights Are Civil Rights*, 46–54. See also Benny J. Andrés, *Power and Control in the Imperial Valley: Nature, Agribusiness, and Workers on the California Borderland, 1900–1940* (College Station: Texas A&M University Press, 2015); Mark Reisler, "Mexican Unionization in California Agriculture, 1927–1936," *Labor History* 14, no. 4 (1973): 566–67.

32. Deverell, *Whitewashed Adobe*, 33.

33. This "fixing" of Mexicans, of course, continued far into the twentieth century and even until today. To use but one example, the actor Lupe Ontiveros (1942–2012) played a maid over 150 times in her career. She lamented that if she did not audition with a Spanish accent, speaking perfect English instead, she would not get the part—a small but telling illustration of how difficult it is for ethnic Mexicans to break out of the cultural mold in which they are placed. www.huffingtonpost.com/2013/06/21/lupe-ontiveros-maid_n_3480416.html.

34. Luis Alvarez, *The Power of the Zoot: Youth Culture and Resistance During World War Ii* (Berkeley: University of California Press, 2008); Johnson, *Spaces of Conflict, Sounds of Solidarity*; Kurashige, *The Shifting Grounds of Race*; George Lipsitz, *Time Passages: Collective Memory and American Popular Culture* (Minneapolis: University of Minnesota Press, 1990); Macías, *Mexican American Mojo*.

35. Lipsitz, *Time Passages*, 160.

36. Ibid., 150.

37. Ibid., 140.

38. See Peggy Pascoe, *What Comes Naturally: Miscegenation, Law and the Making of Race in America* (Oxford; New York: Oxford University Press, 2009); Dara Orenstein, "Void for Vagueness: Mexicans and the Collapse of Miscegenation Law in California," *Pacific Historical Review* 74 (2005): 367–408.

39. George Lipsitz, *Midnight at the Barrelhouse: The Johnny Otis Story* (Minneapolis: University of Minnesota Press, 2010), 63. Matt Garcia describes the El Monte American Legion Stadium as a site of "cultural convergence and exchange extant among a new generation of Angelenos." Matt Garcia, *A World of Its Own: Race, Labor, and Citrus in the Making of Greater Los Angeles, 1900–1970* (Chapel Hill: University of North Carolina Press, 2001), 188.

40. Faderman and Timmons, *Gay L.A.*, 3.

41. Ibid., 80.

42. Ibid., 80–81.

43. Ibid., 113–14.

44. Ibid., 45.

45. John Rechy, *City of Night* (New York: Grove Press, 1963), 212–13. Faderman and Timmons write that the beach was a "cruising ground . . . where one could legitimately wear minimal clothing and look at others who were similarly unattired"; as such, beaches were "a veritable oasis of gay life . . . where the atmosphere was celebratory, carnival-like, even lawless." Faderman and Timmons, *Gay L.A.*, 72–73.

46. Wang et al., *Lavender Los Angeles*, 48–49.

47. Ildefonso "Poncho" García, interview, August 13, 2015.

48. Cindy Dorn, "Culinary S.O.S.; Enchiladas from La Villa Taxco," *Los Angeles Times*, April 24, 2002; Virginia "Vicky" Lizárraga Tamayo, telephone interview by Natalia Molina, January 9, 2018.

49. Barbara Hansen, "Let's Eat Out: A 'Shocking' Experience," *Los Angeles Times*, October 6, 1983, L37; Grace Navarro (Barragan), interview by Natalia Molina, Vista, CA, October 31, 2015.

50. Lois Dwan, "Roundabout," *Los Angeles Times*, January 6, 1974, M50.

51. Lina Lecaro, "Caliente Kitsch," *Los Angeles Magazine*, May 1, 2012, www.lamag.com/laculture/culturefilesblog/2012/05/01/caliente-kitsch; accessed January 10, 2014.

52. "Silver Lake Bar Recognized for Gay Rights Activism," *Los Angeles Times*, November 8, 2008, B3.

53. Casita del Campo, also in the area, opened in 1961 by Rudy del Campo, a dancer who played one of the Sharks in *West Side Story* (1961), is also a gay urban anchor. The restaurant is now owned and operated by del Campo's son, Robert. Robert del Campo, interview by Natalia Molina, July 8, 2016, Los Angeles, CA.

54. Conor Dougherty, "Influx of Newcomers Changing Sunset Junction Neighborhood," *Los Angeles Business Journal* vol. 24, no. 49 (December 9, 2002): 26.

55. "Market Forces Threaten Market," *Los Angeles Times*, January 23, 2008.

56. Marcia Chatelain, *Franchise: The Golden Arches in Black America* (New York: Liveright, 2020).

57. In the early twentieth century, Mexicans formed *mutualistas* (mutual aid societies) to provide social and medical aid to their communities, but investment capital was not a goal. See ch. 5 for more on mutual aid societies.

1. Some classic studies are Menjívar, *Fragmented Ties*; Sherri Grasmuck and Patricia R. Pessar, *Between Two Islands: Dominican International Migration* (Berkeley: University of California Press, 1991); Aihwa Ong, *Flexible Citizenship: The Cultural Logics of Transnationality* (Durham, NC: Duke University Press, 1999); Hondagneu-Sotelo and Avila, "'I'm Here but I'm There'"; Hondagneu-Sotelo, *Gendered Transitions*; Roger Rouse, "Thinking through Transnationalism: Notes on the Cultural Politics of Class Relations in the Contemporary United States," *Public Culture* 7, no. 2 (1995): 353–402.

2. Michael P. Smith, *Transnational Urbanism: Locating Globalization* (Malden, MA: Blackwell, 2001).

3. As Martha Gonzalez writes, "The term translocal disrupts the social science binaries—global/local, local/national, and transnational—and instead offers a view of the 'social field' that makes visible the material survival strategies of these communities, that abstract theorizations can miss." Martha E. Gonzalez, "Mixing in the Kitchen: Entre Mujeres ('Among Women') Translocal Musical Dialogues," in *Performing Motherhood: Artistic, Activist and Everyday Enactments*, ed. Amber E. Kinser, Kryn Freehling-Burton, and Terri Hawkes (Bradford, ON: Demeter Press, 2014), 69–89. See also Maylei Blackwell, "Geographies of Indigeneity: Indigenous Migrant Women's Organizing and Translocal Politics of Place," *Latino Studies* 15, no. 2 (July 2017): 156–81.

4. On *La Opinión* and *La Prensa*, see Nicolás Kanellos and Helvetia Martell, *Hispanic Periodicals in the United States, Origins to 1960* (Houston, TX: Arte Público Press, 2000).

5. *El Universal*, a major Mexican newspaper, is one year older.

6. *El Eco*, June 17, 1964.

7. Michael C. Meyer, William L. Sherman, and Susan M. Deeds, *The Course of Mexican History* (New York: Oxford University Press, 1995), 639–77.

8. Gutiérrez, *Migración y empoderamiento transnacional*.

9. "Aumenta el número de antenas receptoras de TV," *El Eco*, January 28, 1967, 5; "Hasta en junio próximo tendremos televisión," *El Eco*, February 2, 1967, 1; "En Tecuala están disfrutando de maravillosa proyección televisora: Muchas personas están adquiriendo equipos, pues hay fiebre por esta moderna diversión," *El Eco*, February 1, 1967, 5. This article mentions that Antonio Filippini

Mariscal, who lived in Los Angeles for a few years, brought with him a twenty-five-meter antenna with which he captured signals from Mazatlán and the United States.

10. Antonio Sáizar, interview, November 6, 2015, San Diego, CA; Ramón Pack II, interview.

11. Nick Dunne was a Hollywood insider: when Morales worked for his family, he was a producer for Twentieth Century Fox; later, he wrote books and screenplays, some of them in collaboration with his older brother, John Gregory Dunne, who was married to the writer Joan Didion.

12. Ad in Anniversary section of *El Eco*, August 26, 1967, n.p.

13. Antonio Sáizar, interview.

14. Guillermo ("Willy") Casillas, interview by Natalia Molina, January 10, 2018.

15. Isabel Wilkerson, *The Warmth of Other Suns: The Epic Story of America's Great Migration* (New York: Random House, 2010); Flamming, *Bound for Freedom*; Sides, *L.A. City Limits*.

16. Willy Casillas, interview.

17. Nicolas Avila, "Panoramas Angelinos," *La Opinión*, June 25, 1967, 1.

18. "Notas de Viaje: Los Angeles (1)," *El Eco*, July 17, 1969, 3; "Notas de Viaje: Los Angeles (2)," *El Eco*, July 20, 1969.

19. Sáizar does not give more details about the baseball team or the park.

20. "La Fonda Restaurant," KCET, www.kcet.org/shows/live-the-ford/la-fonda-restaurant; accessed July 16, 2019.

21. El Zarape was not located in a traditionally Mexican ethnic enclave but in Inglewood, a historically African American community, and it catered to both Spanish- and English-speaking customers. The historians Albert Camarillo and Abigail Rosas show that although much of South Central Los Angeles (a.k.a. South L.A.) has been characterized as homogeneously African American, in reality the area has had a long history of ethnic Mexican residents and businesses. Rosas, *South Central Is Home*; Camarillo, "Navigating Segregated Life in America's Racial Borderhoods."

22. Descriptions of the evening can be found in Jesús L. Robles, "Yo ví [*sic*] derramar lágrimas a un director del periódico," *El Eco*, June 29, 1967, 1, 6; August 26, 1967, 13.

23. It is not entirely clear why the Nayarit restaurant and Doña Natalia were not involved in the preparation of the food for the event. It may be because Doña Natalia's health was beginning to fail; by 1967, her rheumatoid arthritis had worsened. It also may be because Doña Natalia never closed her own restaurant, even for a day, and she rarely took a day off. She did, however, host the club that would form after this event at the Nayarit. See, e.g., Martín M. Sáizar, "El Club Social 'NAYARIT' de Los Angeles, Calif., trabaja por este estado," *El Eco*, July 25, 1968.

24. Robles, "Yo ví derramar lágrimas a un director del periódico."

25. The one other mention of Isabel I found is a 1964 announcement in *El Eco* of her marriage to Dee Shisler, which took place in Hollywood, with a reception in the Hollywood Hills.

26. Robles, "Yo ví derramar lágrimas a un director del periódico," 6.

27. Nicolas Avila, "Panoramas Angelinos," *La Opinión*, July 2, 1967, 1, 8; "Panoramas Angelinos por Nicolas Avila, jefe de redacción de 'La Opinión' de Los Angeles," *El Eco*, July 9, 1967, 1, 7.

28. For examples of hometown associations in Los Angeles at this time, see "Diez clubes se unen en esta Cd. para un gran baile," *La Opinión*, March 1, 1968, which lists the various clubs holding a joint dance: Jacotepec (Jalisco), Jalpense (Querétaro), Regional Jalisciense (Jalisco), Santa Barbara Chihuahua (Chihuahua), Guadalupe Victoria, Nayarit, San Vicente, Hidalgo, Chihuahua, Fresnillo (Zacatecas), and Teocaltiche (Jalisco).

29. Minian, *Undocumented Lives*; David Fitzgerald, "Colonies of the Little Motherland: Membership, Space, and Time in Mexican Migrant Hometown Associations," *Comparative Studies in Society and History* 10, no. 1 (2008).

30. For media coverage of the meetings, see "Fue un éxito la junta de Nayaritas," *La Opinión*, July 30, 1967; "El miércoles es la junta de Nayaritas," *La Opinión*, July 23, 1967; "Raul González Galarza, Logra la unificación de los Nayaritas en California," *El Eco*, August 6, 1967, 4.

31. Esmeralda Bermudez, "New Life for an Old Gem in Boyle Heights," *Los Angeles Times*, July 31, 2008, www.latimes.com/local/la-me-casa31-2008jul31-story.html; accessed December 18, 2015.

32. "Fue un éxito la junta de Nayaritas," *La Opinión*, July 30, 1967; "Raul González Galarza, logra la unificación de los Nayaritas en California," *El Eco*, August 6, 1967, 4.

33. "Luto por la muerte de José Inés Jiménez," *La Opinión*, November 3, 1978.

34. "Supervisors Invited to Attend Mexican Fete," *Los Angeles Times*, September 6, 1961, B7. Abraham Hoffman, "Stimulus to Repatriation: The 1931 Federal Deportation Drive and the Los Angeles Mexican Community," *Pacific Historical Review* 42, no. 2 (1973): 205–19.

35. Kenneth C. Burt, *The Search for a Civic Voice: California Latino Politics* (Claremont, CA: Regina Books, 2007), 206.

36. Nicolas Avila, "Panoramas Angelinos," *La Opinión*, July 2, 1967, 1, 8.

37. Thirteen of the people in the photograph were women, but there was no caption and, thus, no names or titles. Martín Sáizar, "El 7 de septiembre cumple un año de fundado el Club Social Nayarit de Los Angeles, California," *El Eco*, August 25, 1968, 26.

38. Martín Sáizar, "El Club Social 'NAYARIT' de Los Angeles, Calif., trabaja por este estado," *El Eco*, July 25, 1968, 1.

39. "Grandes festejos del Club Social NAYARIT de Los Angeles, Calif., en ocasión de su primer aniversario," *El Eco*, September 5, 1968, 3.

40. KALI, which had been broadcasting in Spanish since 1952, estimated that 60 percent of Latinos in L.A. listened to the station. KWKW became KALI's biggest competitor when it started broadcasting in Spanish full-time in 1962. KWKW broadcasts throughout Los Angeles and Orange County and has an estimated one million listeners. David Maciel, Isidro D. Ortiz, and María Herrera-Sobek, *Chicano Renaissance: Contemporary Cultural Trends* (Tucson: University of Arizona Press, 2000), 8.

41. On Robles's ten-year absence from Acaponeta, see "Nos visitaron Estanislao Robles y Victoria León de Robles," *El Eco*, June 23, 1966, 3.

42. "Padrinos y madrinas de nuestra edición especial de aniversario," *El Eco*, August 15, 1965, 7.

43. Biographical details were obtained from *El Eco* and familysearch.com.

44. Antonio Sáizar Quintero, "Notas de Viaje: Los Angeles (1)," *El Eco*, July 13, 1969, 4, 6.

45. "Grandioso baile del Club Social Nayarit en Los Angeles, Calif., el sábado." *El Eco*, June 26, 1969, 4.

46. Antonio Sáizar Quintero, "Notas de Viaje: Los Angeles (1)," *El Eco*, July 17, 1969, 3.

47. "Mr. Alerico D. Ortega un gran amigo de los Nayaritas en Los Angeles, California," *El Eco*, August 26, 1969, 10, 13.

48. Davis, *City of Quartz*, 123–27; Sonenshein, *Politics in Black and White*, 85–86, 222; Burt, *The Search for a Civic Voice*.

49. *El Eco*, August 23, 1970.

EPILOGUE

1. Ben Ehrenreich, "Los Angeles Is Eating Itself," *Los Angeles Magazine*, November 27, 2015.

2. www.urbandisplacement.org/los-angeles/los-angeles-gentrification-and-displacement.

3. Take, for example, the failure to pass rent control at the state level in California (Proposition 10 in California in 2018 and Proposition 21 in Los Angeles County in 2020). Jan Lin, *Taking Back the Boulevard: Art, Activism, and Gentrification in Los Angeles* (New York: New York University Press, 2019); Nicholas Blomley, *Unsettling the City: Urban Land and the Politics of Property* (New York: Routledge, 2004); Alfredo Huante, "Is Boyle Heights 'Worth Saving'? The History of Gentrification in an Immigrant Gateway," *Boom: A Journal of California*, July 10, 2018, https://boomcalifornia.org/2018/07/10/is-boyle-heights-worth-saving/.

4. Rebecca Solnit and Susan Schwartzenberg, *Hollow City: The Siege of San Francisco and the Crisis of American Urbanism* (New York: Verso, 2000), 13–14.

5. Evan Kleinman, "Restaurants: Treacherous Times," *Los Angeles Times*, December 29, 2019.

6. Peter Khoury, "I'm Really Missing Old Familiar Places," *New York Times*, June 24, 2020.

7. Farley Elliott, "California Will Provide $125 Million in Stimulus Checks to Undocumented Workers," *Eater: Los Angeles*, April 15, 2020.

8. www.npr.org/2020/05/26/859982428/new-california-relief-program-for-undocumented-overwhelmed-by-demand.

9. www.npr.org/2020/05/26/859982428/new-california-relief-program-for-undocumented-overwhelmed-by-demand.

10. www.pewresearch.org/fact-tank/2020/03/27/young-workers-likely-to-be-hard-hit-as-covid-19-strikes-a-blow-to-restaurants-and-other-service-sector-jobs/.

11. Bill Esparza, "From Parking Lot Barbacoa to Brick-and-Mortar and Back Again," *Eater: Los Angeles*, June 23, 2020, www.eater.com/2020/6/23/21292248 /la-restaurant-aqui-es-taxco-returns-to-parking-lot-spot-barbacoa-estilo-taxco-guerrero.

12. Ibid.

Bibliography

Archival and Manuscript Collections

Echo Park Film Center, Los Angeles, CA

Hemeroteca Nacional de México, Instituto de Investigaciones Bibliográficas, Universidad Nacional Autónoma de México

El Eco de Nayarit

Henry E. Huntington Library, San Marino, CA

John Anson Ford Collection

John F. Kennedy Presidential Library, Boston, MA

John F. Kennedy Oral History Collection

Los Angeles City Archives

City Council Minutes and Council Petitions

Mayor Sam Yorty's Papers

Los Angeles Public Library

The California File

Shades of LA Collection

Subject Files Collection

ONE National Gay & Lesbian Archives, Los Angeles, CA

Public Health Library, County of Los Angeles

Annual Health Reports

Southern California Library for Social Studies and Research, Los Angeles

Civil Rights Congress, Los Angeles, CA

Special Collections & Archives, California State University, Northridge
Julian Nava Collection
University of California, Los Angeles
    Alice Greenfield McGrath Papers (Collection 1490), Library Special
    Collections
    Los Angeles Times Photographic Archives (Collection 1429), Library Special
    Collections
    Film and Television Archive

INTERVIEWS

María Molina, March 7 and August 14, 2015, Los Angeles, CA
Eduwiges ("Vicky") Cueva Tavares, August 13, 2015, Los Angeles, CA
Ildefonso ("Poncho") García, August 13, 2015
Evelia Díaz Barraza Pack, August 14, 2015, Los Angeles, CA
Ramón Pack III, August 14, 2015, Los Angeles, CA
Grace Navarro (Barragan), October 31, 2015, Vista, CA
Antonio Sáizar, November 6, 2015, San Diego, CA
Ramón Pack II, November 14, 2015, San Diego, CA
Bernard Inchauspe, December 15, 2015, Los Angeles, CA
Irene Wongpec, December 16, 2015, Los Angeles, CA
Nelly Díaz Barraza Casillas, July 7, 2016, Los Angeles, CA
Carol Jacques, July 8, 2016, Los Angeles, CA
Robert del Campo, July 8, 2016, Los Angeles, CA
Steven Osuna, June 12, 2017, Los Angeles, CA
Fran De La Rosa, July 27, 2017, San Marino, CA
Guadalupe ("Lupe") Reyes, August 5, 2017, Baldwin Hills, CA
Rosa Blanca Arrevillaga Sánchez, August 6, 2017, Los Angeles, CA
Rosemary Castillo, August 19, 2017, via phone
Julie Serna, August 11, 2017, Los Angeles, CA
Virginia ("Vicky") Lizárraga Tamayo, January 9, 2018, via phone
Guillermo ("Willy") Casillas, January 10, 2018, via phone
Alexis McSweyn, August 13, 2018, Monterey Park, CA
Rodolfo Lora, March 29, 2018, Novillero, Nayarit
Consuelo Guerrero de Sáizar, March 31, 2018, Acaponeta, Nayarit

Lucena Lau Valle, April 24, 2020, via phone
Jaime Jarrín, September 11, 2020, San Marino, CA, via phone
Blanca Arrevillaga, December 11, 2020, Los Angeles, CA, via phone
Óscar López, December 17, 2020, Los Angeles, CA, via phone
Sherryll Mleynek, June 8, 2021, Portland, OR, via phone

NEWSPAPERS
El Eco de Nayarit
Los Angeles Times
La Opinión

SECONDARY SOURCES

Abrego, Leisy J. *Sacrificing Families: Navigating Laws, Labor, and Love across Borders*. Stanford, CA: Stanford University Press, 2014.

Abu-Lughod, Janet. *New York, Chicago, Los Angeles: America's Global Cities*. Minneapolis: University of Minnesota Press, 1999.

Acuña, Rodolfo. *Anything but Mexican: Chicanos in Contemporary Los Angeles*. New York: Verso, 1996.

———. *A Community under Siege: A Chronicle of Chicanos East of the Los Angeles River, 1945-1975*. Los Angeles: Chicano Studies Research Center Publications, an imprint of the University of California Press, 1984.

Agius Vallejo, Jody. *Barrios to Burbs: The Making of the Mexican American Middle Class*. Stanford, CA: Stanford University Press, 2012.

Aguilar, Javier. "Consistency of Change: A Compendium of Data for Echo Park." Master's thesis, University of California, Los Angeles, 1998.

Alba, Richard D., and Victor Nee. *Remaking the American Mainstream: Assimilation and Contemporary Immigration*. Cambridge, MA: Harvard University Press, 2003.

Aldama, Arturo J. *Disrupting Savagism: Chicana/o, Mexican Immigrant, and Native American Struggles for Self-Representation*. Durham, NC: Duke University Press, 2001.

Alvarez, Luis. *The Power of the Zoot: Youth Culture and Resistance during World War II*. Berkeley: University of California Press, 2008.

Alvarez, Robert. *Familia: Migration and Adaptation in Baja and Alta California, 1800-1975*. Berkeley: University of California Press, 1987.

Amezcua, Mike. "Beautiful Urbanism: Gender, Landscape, and Contestation in Latino Chicago's Age of Urban Renewal." *Journal of American History* 104, no. 1 (2017): 97–119.

Anderson, Kay J. "The Idea of Chinatown: The Power of Place and Institutional Practice in the Making of a Racial Category." *Annals of the Association of American Geographers* 77, no. 4 (1987): 580–98.

Andrés, Benny J., Jr. "'I Am Almost More at Home with Brown Faces than with White': An Americanization Teacher in Imperial Valley, California, 1923–1924." *Southern California Quarterly* 93, no. 1 (2011): 69–107.

———. *Power and Control in the Imperial Valley: Nature, Agribusiness, and Workers on the California Borderland, 1900–1940*. College Station: Texas A&M University Press, 2015.

Andrews, Colman. *My Usual Table: A Life in Restaurants*. New York: Ecco, 2014.

Aparicio, Frances R. "Jennifer as Selena: Rethinking Latinidad in Media and Popular Culture." *Latino Studies* 1, no. 1 (2003): 90–105.

———. *Listening to Salsa: Gender, Latin Popular Music, and Puerto Rican Cultures*. Hanover, NH: Wesleyan University Press, an imprint of University Press of New England, 1998.

Appadurai, Arjun. "How to Make a National Cuisine: Cookbooks in Contemporary India." *Comparative Studies in Society and History* 30, no. 1 (1988): 3–24.

Arciga, Pepe. "Manzanero Performs at Million Dollar Theater," *Los Angeles Times*, May 8, 1969.

———. "Million Dollar Theater Program Expanded." *Los Angeles Times*, July 7, 1967, C6.

———. "Variety Bill Offered at Million Dollar Theater." *Los Angeles Times*, November 23, 1967.

Arellano, Gustavo. "Anthony Bourdain Was the Eternal Compadre of Overlooked Latinos." *Los Angeles Times*, June 8, 2018,

———. *Taco USA: How Mexican Food Conquered America*. New York: Scribner, 2012.

———. "Tamales, L.A.'s Original Street Food." *Los Angeles Times*, September 8, 2011.

Arredondo, Gabriela F. *Mexican Chicago: Race, Identity, and Nation, 1916–39*. Urbana: University of Illinois Press, 2008.

Auerbach, Frank L. *Immigration Laws of the United States: A Textbook Integrating Statute, Regulations, Administrative Practice, and Leading Administrative Decisions, with a Comprehensive Index, Citation Guide, and Bibliography.* Indianapolis, IN: Bobbs-Merrill, 1955.

Auerbach, Jerold S. *Labor and Liberty: The La Follette Committee and the New Deal.* New York: Bobbs-Merrill, 1966.

Avila, Eric. *The Folklore of the Freeway: Race and Revolt in the Modernist City.* Minneapolis: University of Minnesota Press, 2014.

———. "L.A.'s Invisible Freeway Revolt: The Cultural Politics of Fighting Freeways." *Journal of Urban History* 40, no. 5 (2014): 831–42.

———. *Popular Culture in the Age of White Flight: Fear and Fantasy in Suburban Los Angeles.* Berkeley: University of California Press, 2004.

Banet-Weiser, Sarah. *The Most Beautiful Girl in the World: Beauty Pageants and National Identity.* Berkeley: University of California Press, 1999.

Barraclough, Laura R. *Charros: How Mexican Cowboys Are Remapping Race and American Identity.* Oakland: University of California Press, 2019.

———. *Making the San Fernando Valley: Rural Landscapes, Urban Development, and White Privilege.* Athens: University of Georgia Press, 2011.

Becerra, Hector. "Decades Later, Bitter Memories of Chavez Ravine." *Los Angeles Times*, April 5, 2012.

Bermudez, Esmeralda. "New Life for an Old Gem in Boyle Heights." *Los Angeles Times*, July 31, 2008, www.latimes.com/local/la-me-casa31-2008jul31-story.html; accessed December 18, 2015.

Bernstein, Shana. *Bridges of Reform: Interracial Civil Rights Activism in Twentieth-Century Los Angeles.* Oxford: Oxford University Press, 2010.

Blackwell, Maylei. *Chicana Power! Contested Histories of Feminism in the Chicano Movement.* Austin: University of Texas Press, 2011.

———. "Geographies of Indigeneity: Indigenous Migrant Women's Organizing and Translocal Politics of Place." *Latino Studies* 15, no. 2 (July 2017): 156–81.

Blomley, Nicholas. *Unsettling the City: Urban Land and the Politics of Property.* New York: Routledge, 2004.

Bokovoy, Matthew F. *The San Diego World's Fairs and Southwestern Memory, 1880–1940.* Albuquerque: University of New Mexico Press, 2005.

Brilliant, Mark. *The Color of America Has Changed: How Racial Diversity Shaped Civil Rights Reform in California, 1941-1978*. New York: Oxford University Press, 2010.

Brodkin, Karen. *How Jews Became White Folks and What That Says about Race in America*. New Brunswick, NJ: Rutgers University Press, 1998.

Brooks, James, ed. *Confounding the Color Line: The Indian-Black Experience in North America*. Lincoln: University of Nebraska Press, 2002.

Burgos, Adrian. *Playing America's Game: Baseball, Latinos, and the Color Line*. Berkeley: University of California Press, 2007.

Burguière, André. *The Annales School: An Intellectual History*. Translated by Jane Marie Todd. Ithaca, NY: Cornell University Press, 2009.

Burt, Kenneth C. *The Search for a Civic Voice: California Latino Politics*. Claremont, CA: Regina Books, 2007.

Burton, Antoinette M., ed. *Archive Stories: Facts, Fictions, and the Writing of History*. Durham, NC: Duke University Press, 2005.

Cadava, Geraldo L. "Entrepreneurs from the Beginning: Latino Business and Commerce since the 16th Century." In *American Latinos and the Making of the United States: A Theme Study*, 215-29. Washington, DC: National Park System Advisory Board, 2013.

———. *Standing on Common Ground: The Making of a Sunbelt Borderland*. Cambridge, MA: Harvard University Press, 2013.

Calavita, Kitty. *Inside the State: The Bracero Program, Immigration, and the I.N.S.* New York: Routledge, 1992.

Camarillo, Albert. "Black and Brown in Compton: Demographic Change, Suburban Decline, and Intergroup Relations in a South Central Los Angeles Community, 1950-2000." In *Not Just Black and White: Historical and Contemporary Perspectives on Immigration, Race, and Ethnicity in the United States*, edited by Nancy Foner and George M. Fredrickson, 358-75. New York: Russell Sage Foundation, 2004.

———. *Chicanos in a Changing Society: From Mexican Pueblos to American Barrios in Santa Barbara and Southern California, 1848-1930*. Cambridge, MA: Harvard University Press, 1979.

———. "Navigating Segregated Life in America's Racial Borderhoods, 1910s-1950s." *Journal of American History* 100, no. 3 (2013): 645-62.

Canaday, Margot. *The Straight State: Sexuality and Citizenship in Twentieth-Century America*. Princeton, NJ: Princeton University Press, 2009.

Cantor, Nancy, Peter Englot, and Marilyn Higgins. "Making the Work of Anchor Institutions Stick: Building Coalitions and Collective Expertise." *Journal of Higher Education Outreach and Engagement* 17, no. 3 (2013): 17–46.

Cantú, Lionel, Jr. *The Sexuality of Migration: Border Crossings and Mexican Immigrant Men*. Edited by Nancy A. Naples and Salvador Vidal-Ortiz. New York: New York University Press, 2009.

Capó, Julio. *Welcome to Fairyland: Queer Miami before 1940*. Chapel Hill: University of North Carolina Press, 2017.

Carpio, Genevieve. *Collisions at the Crossroads: How Place and Mobility Make Race*. Oakland: University of California Press, 2019.

———. "Unexpected Allies: David C. Marcus and His Impact on the Advancement of Civil Rights in the Mexican-American Legal Landscape of Southern California." In *Beyond Alliances*, edited by Bruce Zuckerman and George J. Sánchez, 1–32. West Lafayette, IN: Purdue University Press, 2012.

Carrillo, Héctor. *The Night Is Young: Sexuality in Mexico in the Time of AIDS*. Chicago: University of Chicago Press, 2002.

———. *Pathways of Desire: The Sexual Migration of Mexican Gay Men*. Chicago: University of Chicago Press, 2017.

Casillas, Dolores Inés. *Sounds of Belonging: U.S. Spanish-Language Radio and Public Advocacy*. New York: New York University Press, 2014.

Castellanos, M. Bianet. "Building Communities of Sentiment: Remittances and Emotions among Maya Migrants." *Chicana/Latina Studies* 8, no. 1–2 (2009): 140–71.

Castillo-Muñoz, Verónica. "Historical Roots of Rural Migration: Land Reform, Corn Credit, and the Displacement of Rural Farmers in Nayarit, Mexico, 1900–1952." *Mexican Studies/Estudios Mexicanos* 29, no. 1 (2013): 36–60.

———. *The Other California: Land, Identity, and Politics on the Mexican Borderlands*. Oakland: University of California Press, 2017.

Certeau, Michel de. *The Practice of Everyday Life*. Berkeley: University of California Press, 1984.

Chafe, William H. *Civilities and Civil Rights: Greensboro, North Carolina, and the Black Struggle for Freedom*. New York: Oxford University Press, 1980.

Chatelain, Marcia. *Franchise: The Golden Arches in Black America*. New York: Liveright, 2020.

Chauncey, George. *Gay New York: Gender, Urban Culture, and the Makings of the Gay Male World, 1890–1940*. New York: Basic Books, 1994.

Chávez, Alex E. *Sounds of Crossing: Music, Migration, and the Aural Poetics of Huapango Arribeño*. Durham, NC: Duke University Press, 2017.

Chávez, Ernesto. *"Mi Raza Primero!" (My People First!): Nationalism, Identity, and Insurgency in the Chicano Movement in Los Angeles, 1966–1978*. Berkeley: University of California Press, 2002.

———. "'Ramon Is Not One of These': Race and Sexuality in the Construction of Silent Film Actor Ramón Novarro's Star Image." *Journal of the History of Sexuality* 20, no. 3 (2011): 520–44.

———. *The U.S. War with Mexico: A Brief History with Documents*. New York: Bedford/St. Martins, 2007.

Chávez-García, Miroslava. *Migrant Longing: Letter Writing across the U.S.-Mexico Borderlands*. Durham: University of North Carolina Press, 2018.

———. *Negotiating Conquest: Gender and Power in California, 1770s to 1880s*. Tucson: University of Arizona Press, 2004.

———. *States of Delinquency: Race and Science in the Making of California's Juvenile Justice System*. Berkeley: University of California Press, 2012.

Chen, Yong. *Chop Suey, USA: The Story of Chinese Food in America*. New York: Columbia University Press, 2014.

Cheng, Wendy. *The Changs Next Door to the Díazes: Remapping Race in Suburban California*. Minneapolis: University of Minnesota Press, 2013.

Christy, George. "Looking for Good Food?" *Los Angeles Times*, November 18, 1973, V24.

Coates, Paul V. "Dining Around Town." *Mirror News*, February 15, 1949, 32.

Cohen, Julie T. "Pedagogies for 'Productive Citizenship': The Cultural Politics of Child Welfare in Early Twentieth-Century Southern California." PhD diss., University of California, Irvine, 2009.

Cohen, Lizabeth. *Making a New Deal: Industrial Workers in Chicago, 1919–1939*. Cambridge, MA: Harvard University Press, 1990.

Contreras, Eduardo. "Voice and Property: Latinos, White Conservatives, and Urban Renewal in 1960s San Francisco." *Western Historical Quarterly* 45, no. 3 (2014): 253–76.

Cresswell, Tim. *Place: An Introduction*. 2nd ed. Malden, MA: Wiley-Blackwell, 2015.

Cuff, Dana. *The Provisional City: Los Angeles Stories of Architecture and Urbanism*. Cambridge, MA: MIT Press, 2000.

Curtis, Erin. "Cambodian Donut Shops and the Negotiation of Donut Shops in Los Angeles." In *Eating Asian America: A Food Studies Reader*, edited by Robert Ji-Song Ku, Martin F. Manalansan, and Anita Mannur, 13–29. New York: New York University Press, 2013.

D'Antonio, Michael. *Forever Blue: The True Story of Walter O'Malley, Baseball's Most Controversial Owner, and the Dodgers of Brooklyn and Los Angeles*. New York: Riverhead Books, 2009.

Dávila, Arlene. *Barrio Dreams: Puerto Ricans, Latinos, and the Neoliberal City*. Berkeley: University of California Press, 2004.

Davis, Mike. *City of Quartz: Excavating the Future in Los Angeles*. London: Verso, 1990.

De Genova, Nicholas. *Working the Boundaries: Race, Space, and "Illegality" in Mexican Chicago*. Durham, NC: Duke University Press, 2005.

Deloria, Philip Joseph. *Indians in Unexpected Places*. Lawrence: University Press of Kansas, 2004.

Deverell, William. *Whitewashed Adobe: The Rise of Los Angeles and the Remaking of Its Mexican Past*. Berkeley: University of California Press, 2004.

Dorn, Cindy. "Culinary S.O.S.; Enchiladas from La Villa Taxco." *Los Angeles Times*, April 24, 2002.

Dougherty, Conor. "Influx of Newcomers Changing Sunset Junction Neighborhood." *Los Angeles Business Journal* 24, no. 49 (December 9, 2002): 26.

Douglas, Mary. *In the Active Voice*. New York: Routledge & K. Paul, 1982.

DuBois, Ellen Carol, and Vicki L. Ruiz. *Unequal Sisters: A Multicultural Reader in U.S. Women's History*. New York: Routledge, 1990.

Durand, Jorge, Douglas S. Massey, and Fernando Charvet. "The Changing Geography of Mexican Immigration to the United States: 1910–1996." *Social Science Quarterly* 81, no. 1 (2000): 1–15.

Dwan, Lois. "Roundabout." *Los Angeles Times*, January 6, 1974.

Echo Park Historical Society News. "Echo Park Lake: The Historic Heart of Echo Park: Echo Park Lake, 1945 to 1980." http://historicechopark.org/history-landmarks/places-landmarks/echo-park-lake.

———. "Grace E. Simons: The Defender of Elysian Park." http://historicechopark
.org/history-landmarks/people/grace-e-simons/.

Ehlenz, Meagan M. "Gown, Town, and Neighborhood Change: An Examination
of Urban Neighborhoods with University Revitalization Efforts." *Journal of
Planning Education and Research* 39, no. 3 (2019): 285–99.

Elliott, Farley. "California Will Provide $125 Million in Stimulus Checks to
Undocumented Workers." *Eater: Los Angeles*, April 15, 2020.

Ellis, Pearl I. *Americanization through Homemaking*. Los Angeles: Wetzel, 1929.

Emler, Ron. *Ghosts of Echo Park: A Pictorial History*. Los Angeles: Echo Park Publishing, 1999.

Epstein, Daniel Mark. *Sister Aimee: The Life of Aimee Semple McPherson*. New York:
Harcourt Brace Jovanovich, 1993.

Escobar, Edward J. "Bloody Christmas and the Irony of Police Professionalism:
The Los Angeles Police Department, Mexican Americans, and Police Reform
in the 1950s." *Pacific Historical Review* 72, no. 2 (2003): 171–99.

———. *Race, Police, and the Making of a Political Identity: Mexican Americans and the
Los Angeles Police Department, 1900–1945*. Berkeley: University of California
Press, 1999.

———. "The Unintended Consequences of the Carceral State: Chicana/o Political
Mobilization in Post–World War II America." *Journal of American History* 102,
no. 1 (2015): 174–84.

Escobedo, Elizabeth R. *From Coveralls to Zoot Suits: The Lives of Mexican American
Women on the World War II Home Front*. Chapel Hill: University of North Carolina Press, 2013.

Esparza, Bill. "From Parking Lot Barbacoa to Brick-and-Mortar and Back Again."
Eater: Los Angeles, June 23, 2020. www.eater.com/2020/6/23/21292248
/la-restaurant-aqui-es-taxco-returns-to-parking-lot-spot-barbacoa-estilo-
taxco-guerrero.

Estrada, William D. *The Los Angeles Plaza: Sacred and Contested Space*. Austin: University of Texas Press, 2008.

Ethington, Philip J., Anne Marie Kooistra, and Edward DeYoung. "Los Angeles
County Union Census Tract Data Series, 1940–1990, Version 1.01." Created
with the support of the John Randolph Haynes and Dora Haynes Foundation.
University of Southern California, Los Angeles, 2000.

Faderman, Lillian, and Stuart Timmons. *Gay L.A.: A History of Sexual Outlaws, Power Politics, and Lipstick Lesbians*. New York: Basic Books, 2006.

Fernández, Lilia. *Brown in the Windy City: Mexicans and Puerto Ricans in Postwar Chicago*. Chicago: University of Chicago Press, 2012.

Fernandez, Maria Elena. "L.A. At Large; Cuban Cafecitos and All the Comforts of Home." *Los Angeles Times*, February 6, 2001.

FitzGerald, David. "Colonies of the Little Motherland: Membership, Space, and Time in Mexican Migrant Hometown Associations." *Comparative Studies in Society and History* 10, no. 1 (2008): 145–69.

Flamming, Douglas. *Bound for Freedom: Black Los Angeles in Jim Crow America*. Berkeley: University of California Press, 2005.

Flores, Lori A. *Grounds for Dreaming: Mexican Americans, Mexican Immigrants, and the California Farmworker Movement*. New Haven, CT: Yale University Press, 2016.

———. "An Unladylike Strike Fashionably Clothed: Mexicana and Anglo Women Garment Workers against Tex-Son, 1959–1963." *Pacific Historical Review* 78, no. 3 (2009): 367–402.

Fogelson, Robert M. *The Fragmented Metropolis: Los Angeles, 1850–1930*. Berkeley: University of California Press, 1967.

Foley, Neil. *The White Scourge: Mexicans, Blacks, and Poor Whites in Texas Cotton Culture*. Berkeley: University of California Press, 1997.

Folkart, Burt. "Jacob Zeitlin, Authors' Friend and Noted Book Seller, 84, Dies." *Los Angeles Times*, August 31, 1987.

Fox, Cybelle. "Unauthorized Welfare: The Origins of Immigrant Status Restrictions in American Social Policy." *Journal of American History* 102, no. 4 (2016): 1051–74.

Freedman, Paul. *Ten Restaurants That Changed America*. New York: Liveright, 2016.

Fregoso, Rosa Linda. *meXicana Encounters: The Making of Social Identities on the Borderlands*. Berkeley: University of California Press, 2003.

Gabaccia, Donna R. *We Are What We Eat: Ethnic Food and the Making of Americans*. Cambridge, MA: Harvard University Press, 1998.

Gabaccia, Donna R., and Jeffrey M. Pilcher. "'Chili Queens' and Checkered Tablecloths: Public Dining Cultures of Italians in New York City and

Mexicans in San Antonio, Texas, 1870s–1940s." *Radical History Review* 110 (2011): 109–26.

Gabbert, Laura, dir. *City of Gold*. 2015; New York: MPI Media Group, 2016. DVD.

Gamboa, Erasmo. *Mexican Labor and World War II: Braceros in the Pacific Northwest, 1942–1947*. Austin: University of Texas Press, 1990.

García, David G. "Listening across Boundaries: Soundings from the Paramount Ballroom and Boyle Heights." In *The Tide Was Always High: The Music of Latin America in Los Angeles*, edited by Josh Kun, 153–162. Oakland: University of California Press, 2017.

———. *Strategies of Segregation: Race, Residence, and the Struggle for Educational Equality*. Oakland: University of California Press, 2018.

García, Lorena, and Mérida Rúa. "Processing Latinidad: Mapping Latino Urban Landscapes through Chicago Ethnic Festivals." *Latino Studies* 5, no. 3 (2007): 317–39.

García, Mario T. *The Chicano Movement: Perspectives from the Twenty-First Century*. New York: Routledge, 2014.

———. *Memories of Chicano History: The Life and Narrative of Bert Corona*. Berkeley: University of California Press, 1994.

Garcia, Matt E. "Setting the Table: Historians, Popular Writers, and Food History." *Journal of American History* 103, no. 3 (2016): 656–78.

———. *A World of Its Own: Race, Labor, and Citrus in the Making of Greater Los Angeles, 1900–1970*. Chapel Hill: University of North Carolina Press, 2001.

Garcia, Matt E., Melanie DuPuis, and Don Mitchell. *Food across Borders*. New Brunswick, NJ: Rutgers University Press, 2017.

Garcilazo, Jeffrey Marcos. "Traqueros: Mexican Railroad Workers in the United States, 1870 to 1930." PhD diss., University of California, Santa Barbara, 1995.

———. *Traqueros: Mexican Railroad Workers in the United States, 1870 to 1930*. Edited by Vicki L. Ruiz. Denton: University of North Texas Press, 2012.

Gaytán, Marie Sarita. "From Sombreros to Sincronizadas: Authenticity, Ethnicity, and the Mexican Restaurant Industry." *Journal of Contemporary Ethnography* 37, no. 3 (2008): 314–41.

Gieseking, Jen Jack, William Mangold, Cindi Katz, Setha Low, and Susan Saegert, eds. *The People, Place, and Space Reader*. New York: Routledge, Taylor & Francis, 2014.

Gillingham, Karen. "Taking a Bite out of Shopping: How and Where You Can Join the Food Co-op Movement." *Los Angeles Times,* January 10, 1978, G8.

G. K. "Gala Premiere Reopens Million Dollar Theater." *Los Angeles Times*, August 31, 1950, 16.

Gold, Jonathan. *Counter Intelligence: Where to Eat in the Real Los Angeles*. New York: LA Weekly Books, 2000.

Gómez, Laura E. *Manifest Destinies: The Making of the Mexican American Race*. New York: New York University Press, 2007.

Gómez-Quiñones, Juan, and Irene Vásquez. *Making Aztlán: Ideology and Culture of the Chicana and Chicano Movement, 1966-1977*. Albuquerque: University of New Mexico Press, 2014.

González, Deena J. *Refusing the Favor: The Spanish-Mexican Women of Santa Fe, 1820-1880*. New York: Oxford University Press, 1999.

González, Jerry. *In Search of the Mexican Beverly Hills: Latino Suburbanization in Postwar Los Angeles*. New Brunswick, NJ: Rutgers University Press, 2017.

González, Martha E. "Mixing in the Kitchen: Entre Mujeres ('Among Women') Translocal Musical Dialogues." In *Performing Motherhood: Artistic, Activist and Everyday Enactments,* edited by Amber E. Kinser, Kryn Freehling-Burton, and Terri Hawkes, 69-89. Bradford, ON: Demeter Press, 2014.

González Galarza, Raúl. *Medio siglo sin sorpresas: 1945-1994*. Mexicali: Gráficos, 1993.

Goodheart, Jessica. "One for the Neighborhood: Art: Sculptor Peter Shire's Hilltop Creation Near His Home Will Honor Frank Glass and Grace E. Simons." *Los Angeles Times*, October 29, 1992.

Gordon, Larry. "Echo Park Merchants See Boom in Store: Rebuilt Pioneer Market Spurs New Business around Sunset Boulevard." *Los Angeles Times*, January 17, 1985.

Grange, Lori. "Day-Care Center Teaches Commitment Echo Park." *Los Angeles Times*, May 3, 1990.

Grasmuck, Sherri, and Patricia R. Pessar. *Between Two Islands: Dominican International Migration*. Berkeley: University of California Press, 1991.

Grebler, Leo, Joan W. Moore, Ralph C. Guzman, and Jeffrey Lionel Berlant. *The Mexican-American People, the Nation's Second Largest Minority*. New York: Free Press, 1970.

Griswold del Castillo, Richard. *The Los Angeles Barrio, 1850-1890: A Social History.* Berkeley: University of California Press, 1979.

———. *The Treaty of Guadalupe Hidalgo: A Legacy of Conflict.* Norman: University of Oklahoma Press, 1990.

Guglielmo, Thomas A. "Fighting for Caucasian Rights: Mexicans, Mexican Americans, and the Transnational Struggle for Civil Rights in World War II Texas." *Journal of American History* 92, no. 4 (2006): 1212–37.

———. *White on Arrival: Italians, Race, Color, and Power in Chicago, 1890-1945.* New York: Oxford University Press, 2003.

Gutiérrez, Abel Gómez. *Migración y empoderamiento transnacional: Los Nayaritas en el sur de California.* Bloomington, IN: Palibrio, 2013.

Gutiérrez, David, ed. *The Columbia History of Latinos in the United States since 1960.* New York: Columbia University Press, 2004.

———. *Walls and Mirrors: Mexican Americans, Mexican Immigrants, and the Politics of Identity.* Berkeley: University of California Press, 1995.

Gutiérrez, Ramón A., and Richard J. Orsi, eds. *Contested Eden: California before the Gold Rush.* Berkeley: University of California Press, 1998.

Gutmann, Matthew C. *The Meanings of Macho: Being a Man in Mexico City.* Berkeley: University of California Press, 1996.

Haas, Lisbeth. *Conquests and Historical Identities in California, 1769-1936.* Berkeley: University of California Press, 1995.

Hall, Stuart, Chas Critcher, Tony Jefferson, John Clarke, and Brian Roberts. *Policing the Crisis: Mugging, the State, and Law and Order.* London: Macmillan, 1978.

Hall, Stuart, Jennifer Daryl Slack, and Lawrence Grossberg. *Cultural Studies 1983: A Theoretical History.* Durham, NC: Duke University Press, 2016.

Haney-López, Ian. *Racism on Trial: The Chicano Fight for Justice.* Cambridge, MA: Belknap Press of Harvard University Press, 2003.

Hansen, Barbara. "Border Line: Head Chef Adapts Mexican Fare to California Taste." *Los Angeles Times,* June 30, 1977, I33.

———. "Let's Eat Out: A 'Shocking' Experience." *Los Angeles Times,* October 6, 1983, L37.

Harvey, Steve. "People and Events." *Los Angeles Times,* September 21, 1988.

Hayden, Dolores. *The Power of Place: Urban Landscapes as Public History.* Cambridge, MA: MIT Press, 1995.

Heap, Chad C. *Slumming: Sexual and Racial Encounters in American Nightlife, 1885–1940*. Chicago: University of Chicago Press, 2009.

Higginbotham, Evelyn Brooks. *Righteous Discontent: The Women's Movement in the Black Baptist Church, 1880–1920*. Cambridge, MA: Harvard University Press, 1993.

Hillinger, Charles. "U.S. Consulate at Tijuana Claims World's Busiest Title." *Los Angeles Times*, May 31, 1967, 2–a1.

Hise, Greg. "Border City: Race and Social Distance in Los Angeles." *American Quarterly* 56, no. 3 (2004): 545–58.

Hochschild, Arlie. "Global Care Chains and Emotional Surplus Value." In *On the Edge: Living with Global Capitalism*, edited by Anthony Giddens and Will Hutton, 130–46. London: Jonathan Cape, 2000.

Hoelscher, Steven. "Making Place, Making Race: Performances of Whiteness in the Jim Crow South." *Annals of the Association of American Geographers* 93, no. 3 (2003): 657–86.

Hoffman, Abraham. "Stimulus to Repatriation: The 1931 Federal Deportation Drive and the Los Angeles Mexican Community." *Pacific Historical Review* 42, no. 2 (1973): 205–19.

Hollingworth, Hank. "Safety of Autos: 'Lot of Hot Air.'" *Long Beach Press-Telegram*, April 27, 1966, 45.

Holloway, Jonathan Scott. *Jim Crow Wisdom: Memory and Identity in Black America since 1940*. Chapel Hill: University of North Carolina Press, 2013.

Hondagneu-Sotelo, Pierrette. *Gender and U.S. Immigration: Contemporary Trends*. Berkeley: University of California Press, 2003.

———. *Gendered Transitions: Mexican Experiences of Immigration*. Berkeley: University of California Press, 1994.

Hondagneu-Sotelo, Pierrette, and Ernestine Avila. "'I'm Here, but I'm There': The Meanings of Latina Transitional Motherhood." *Gender & Society* 11, no. 5 (October 1997): 548–59.

HoSang, Daniel Martinez. *Racial Propositions: Ballot Initiatives and the Making of Postwar California*. Berkeley: University of California Press, 2010.

Hsu, Madeline Y. "On the Possibilities of Food Writing as a Bridge between the Popular and the Political." *Journal of American History* 103, no. 3 (2016): 682–85.

Huante, Alfredo. "Is Boyle Heights 'Worth Saving?': The History of Gentrification in an Immigrant Gateway." *Boom: A Journal of California*, July 10, 2018. https://boomcalifornia.org/2018/07/10/is-boyle-heights-worth-saving/.

———. "A Lighter Shade of Brown? Racial Formation and Gentrification in Latino Los Angeles." *Social Problems* 68, no. 1 (2021): 63–79.

Hurewitz, Daniel. *Bohemian Los Angeles and the Making of Modern Politics*. Berkeley: University of California Press, 2007.

Hurston, Zora Neale. "How It Feels to Be Colored Me." *The World Tomorrow* 11 (1928): 215–16.

Instituto Nacional de Estadística y Geografía de México. Septimo Censo General de Población: 6 de Junio, 1950. Mexico City: Coordinación General de los Servicios Nacionales de Estadística, Geografía e Informática, 1953.

Jacobs-Huey, Lanita. *From the Kitchen to the Parlor: Language and Becoming in African American Women's Hair Care*. New York: Oxford University Press, 2006.

Jacobson, Matthew Frye. *Whiteness of a Different Color: European Immigrants and the Alchemy of Race*. Cambridge, MA: Harvard University, 1998.

Jayaraman, Sarumathi, and Eric Schlosser. *Behind the Kitchen Door*. Ithaca, NY: ILR Press, 2013.

Jiménez, Tomás R. *Replenished Ethnicity: Mexican Americans, Immigration, and Identity*. Berkeley: University of California Press, 2010.

Johnson, Gaye Theresa. *Spaces of Conflict, Sounds of Solidarity: Music, Race, and Spatial Entitlement in Los Angeles*. Berkeley: University of California Press, 2013.

Kalin, Betsy. *East LA Interchange*. Clearwater, FL: Media Bluewater, 2015.

Kanellos, Nicolás, and Helvetia Martell. *Hispanic Periodicals in the United States, Origins to 1960: A Brief History and Comprehensive Bibliography*. Houston, TX: Arte Público Press, 2000.

Kelley, Robin D. G. *Race Rebels: Culture, Politics, and the Black Working Class*. New York: Free Press, 1994.

———. "'We Are Not What We Seem': Rethinking Black Working-Class Opposition in the Jim Crow South." *Journal of American History* 80, no. 1 (1993): 75–112.

Kennedy, Elizabeth Lapovsky, and Madeline D. Davis. *Boots of Leather, Slippers of Gold: The History of a Lesbian Community*. New York: Routledge, 1993.

Khoury, Peter. "I'm Really Missing Old Familiar Places," *New York Times*, June 24, 2020.

Kleinman, Evan. "Restaurants: Treacherous Times," *Los Angeles Times*, December 29, 2019.

Kobayashi, Audrey, and Linda Peake. "Racism out of Place: Thoughts on Whiteness and an Antiracist Geography in the New Millennium." *Annals of the Association of American Geographers* 90, no. 2 (2000): 392–403.

Krishnendu, Ray. *The Ethnic Restaurateur*. London: Bloomsbury Academic, 2016.

Kropp, Phoebe. *California Vieja: Culture and Memory in a Modern American Place*. Berkeley: University of California Press, 2006.

Ku, Robert Ji-Song, Martin Manalansan, and Anita Mannur, eds. *Eating Asian America: A Food Studies Reader*. New York: New York University Press, 2013.

Kun, Josh. *To Live and Dine in L.A.: Menus and the Making of the Modern City*. Santa Monica, CA: Angel City Press, 2015.

———, ed. *The Tide Was Always High: The Music of Latin America in Los Angeles*. Oakland: University of California Press, 2017.

Kurashige, Lon. *Japanese American Celebration and Conflict: A History of Ethnic Identity and Festival in Los Angeles, 1934–1990*. Berkeley: University of California Press, 2002.

Kurashige, Scott. T*he Shifting Grounds of Race: Black and Japanese Americans in the Making of Multiethnic Los Angeles*. Princeton, NJ: Princeton University Press, 2008.

Lara, Juan D. De. *Inland Shift: Race, Space, and Capital in Southern California*. Oakland: University of California Press, 2018.

Laslett, John H. M. *Shameful Victory: The Los Angeles Dodgers, the Red Scare, and the Hidden History of Chavez Ravine*. Tucson: University of Arizona Press, 2015.

Leal, Jorge. "Las Plazas of South Los Ángeles." In *Post-Ghetto: Reimagining South Los Angeles*, edited by Josh Sides, 11–32. San Marino, CA: Huntington Library and University of California Press, 2012.

Lecaro, Lina. "Caliente Kitsch." *Los Angeles Magazine*, May 1, 2012. http://www.lamag.com/laculture/culturefilesblog/2012/05/01/caliente-kitsch.

Lee, Heather. "Entrepreneurs in the Age of Chinese Exclusion: Transnational Capital, Migrant Labor, and Chinese Restaurants in New York City, 1850–1943." PhD diss., Brown University, 2014.

———. "A Life Cooking for Others: The Work and Migration Experience of a Chinese Restaurant Worker in New York City, 1920–1946." In *Eating Asian America:*

A *Food Studies Reader*, edited by Robert Ji-Song Ku, Martin F. Manalansan, and Anita Mannur, 53–77. New York: New York University Press, 2013.

Lefebvre, Henri. *The Production of Space*. Cambridge, MA: Blackwell, 1991.

———. *The Survival of Capitalism: Reproduction of the Relations of Production*. New York: St. Martin's Press, 1976.

Lepore, Jill. *Book of Ages: The Life and Opinions of Jane Franklin*. New York: Vintage, 2014.

Lewis, Earl. *In Their Own Interests: Race, Class, and Power in Twentieth-Century Norfolk, Virginia*. Berkeley: University of California Press, 1991.

Lin, Jan. *Taking Back the Boulevard: Art, Activism and Gentrification in Los Angeles*. New York: New York University Press, 2019.

Linthicum, Kate. "An Appetite for Service: Three Restaurant Staffers Mark 50 Years on the Job." *Los Angeles Times*, February 29, 2012.

Lipsitz, George. "Cruising around the Historical Bloc: Postmodernism and Popular Music in East Los Angeles." *Cultural Critique*, no. 5 (1986): 157–77.

———. *How Racism Takes Place*. Philadelphia, PA: Temple University Press, 2011.

———. *Midnight at the Barrelhouse: The Johnny Otis Story*. Minneapolis: University of Minnesota Press, 2010.

———. *The Possessive Investment in Whiteness: How White People Profit from Identity Politics*. Philadelphia, PA: Temple University Press, 1998.

———. "The Possessive Investment in Whiteness: Racialized Social Democracy and the 'White' Problem in American Studies." *American Quarterly* 47, no. 3 (1995): 369–87.

———. *Time Passages: Collective Memory and American Popular Culture*. Minneapolis: University of Minnesota Press, 1990.

Lira, Natalie. "'Of Low Grade Mexican Parentage': Race, Gender and Eugenic Sterilization in California, 1928–1952." PhD diss., University of Michigan, 2015.

Lira, Natalie, and Alexandra Minna Stern. "Mexican Americans and Eugenic Sterilization." *Aztlán: A Journal of Chicano Studies* 39, no. 2 (2014): 9–34.

Liu, Haiming. *From Canton Restaurant to Panda Express: A History of Chinese Food in the United States*. New Brunswick, NJ: Rutgers University Press, 2015.

Lopez, Bricia, and Javier Cabral. *Oaxaca: Home Cooking from the Heart of Mexico*. New York: Abrams, 2019.

Lopez, Steve. "Ex-Busboy Will Never Forget Bobby Kennedy." *Los Angeles Times*, June 1, 2003.

———. "Market Forces Threaten Market." *Los Angeles Times*, January 23, 2008.

Lopez, Sarah Lynn. *The Remittance Landscape: Spaces of Migration in Rural Mexico and Urban USA*. Chicago: University of Chicago Press, 2014.

Loza, Mireya. *Defiant Braceros: How Migrant Workers Fought for Racial, Sexual, and Political Freedom*. Chapel Hill: University of North Carolina Press, 2016.

Luibhéid, Eithne. *Entry Denied: Controlling Sexuality at the Border*. Minneapolis: University of Minnesota Press, 2002.

Lytle Hernández, Kelly. *City of Inmates: Conquest, Rebellion, and the Rise of Human Caging in Los Angeles, 1771-1965*. Chapel Hill: University of North Carolina Press, 2017.

———. *Migra! A History of the U.S. Border Patrol*. Berkeley: University of California, 2010.

Mabalon, Dawn Bohulano. "As American as Jackrabbit Adobo: Cooking, Eating and Becoming Filipina/o American before World War II." In *Eating Asian America: A Food Studies Reader*, edited by Robert Ji-Song Ku, Martin Manalansan, and Anita Mannur, 147-76. New York: New York University Press, 2013.

Macías, Anthony F. *Mexican American Mojo: Popular Music, Dance, and Urban Culture in Los Angeles, 1935-1968*. Durham, NC: Duke University Press, 2008.

Maciel, David, Isidro D. Ortiz, and María Herrera-Sobek. *Chicano Renaissance: Contemporary Cultural Trends*. Tucson: University of Arizona Press, 2000.

Manalansan, Martin. "Beyond Authenticity: Rerouting the Filipino Culinary Diaspora." In *Eating Asian America: A Food Studies Reader*, edited by Robert Ji-Song Ku, Martin Manalansan, and Anita Mannur, 288-302. New York: New York University Press, 2013.

Marinacci, Barbara, and Rudy Marinacci. *Take Sunset Boulevard! A California Guide*. San Rafael, CA: Presidio Press, 1981.

Mariscal, George. *Brown-Eyed Children of the Sun: Lessons from the Chicano Movement, 1965-1975*. Albuquerque: University of New Mexico Press, 2005.

Massey, Doreen B. *Space, Place, and Gender*. Minneapolis: University of Minnesota Press, 1994.

Massey, Douglas. *Return to Aztlan: The Social Process of International Migration from Western Mexico*. Berkeley: University of California Press, 1987.

Massey, Douglas, and Nancy Denton. *American Apartheid: Segregation and the Making of the Underclass*. Cambridge, MA: Harvard University Press, 1993.

Mayhew, Susan. *A Dictionary of Geography*. Oxford: Oxford University Press, 2015.

McKay, Deirdre. "'Sending Dollars Shows Feeling'—Emotions and Economies in Filipino Migration." *Mobilities* 2, no. 2 (2007): 175–94.

McKittrick, Katherine, and Clyde Adrian Woods, eds. *Black Geographies and the Politics of Place*. Toronto: Between the Lines, 2007.

McWilliams, Carey. *Brothers under the Skin*. Boston: Little, Brown, 1943.

———. *The Education of Carey McWilliams*. New York: Simon and Schuster, 1979.

———. *Factories in the Field: The Story of Migratory Farm Labor in California*. Hamden, CT: Archon Books, 1969.

———. *A Mask for Privilege: Anti-Semitism in America*. Boston: Little, Brown, 1948.

———. *North from Mexico: The Spanish-Speaking People of the United States*. Updated by Matt S. Meier. New York: Praeger, 1990.

———. *Prejudice: Japanese-Americans: Symbol of Racial Intolerance*. Boston: Little, Brown, 1944.

———. *Southern California: An Island on the Land*. Salt Lake City, UT: Peregrine Smith Books, 1946.

Meares, Hadley. "How America's First Megachurch Changed LA's Echo Park." *Curbed LA*, April 21, 2014. https://la.curbed.com/2014/4/21/10112432/how-americas-first-megachurch-changed-las-echo-park-1.

Menchaca, Celeste R. "Staging Crossings: Policing Intimacy and Performing Respectability at the U.S.-Mexico Border, 1907–1917." *Pacific Historical Review* 89, no. 1 (2020): 16–43.

Menchaca, Martha. "Chicano Indianism: A Historical Account of Racial Repression in the United States." *American Ethnologist* 20, no. 3 (1993): 583–603.

———. *The Mexican Outsiders: A Community History of Marginalization and Discrimination in California*. Austin: University of Texas Press, 1995.

Méndez, Alina. "Cheap for Whom? Migration, Farm Labor, and Social Reproduction in the Imperial Valley-Mexicali Borderlands, 1942–1969." PhD diss., University of California, San Diego, 2017.

Menjívar, Cecilia. *Fragmented Ties: Salvadoran Immigrant Networks in America*. Berkeley: University of California Press, 2000.

Meyer, Michael C., William L. Sherman, and Susan M. Deeds. *The Course of Mexican History*. New York: Oxford University Press, 1995.

Meyerowitz, Joanne J. *Women Adrift: Independent Wage Earners in Chicago, 1880–1930*. Chicago: University of Chicago Press, 1988.

Miles, Tiya. *Ties That Bind: The Story of an Afro-Cherokee Family in Slavery and Freedom*. Berkeley: University of California Press, 2005.

Minian, Ana Raquel. *Undocumented Lives: The Untold Story of Mexican Migration*. Cambridge, MA: Harvard University Press, 2018.

Mitchell, Pablo. *Coyote Nation: Sexuality, Race, and Conquest in Modernizing New Mexico, 1880–1920*. Chicago: University of Chicago Press, 2005.

———. *West of Sex: Making Mexican America, 1900–1930*. Chicago: University of Chicago Press, 2012.

Molina, Natalia. "Borders, Laborers, and Racialized Medicalization: Mexican Immigration and US Public Health Practices in the 20th Century." *American Journal of Public Health* 101, no. 6 (2011): 1024–31.

———. "The Construction of the East Los Angeles Freeway." Undergraduate thesis, University of California, Los Angeles, 1993.

———. "Deportable Citizens: The Decoupling of Race and Citizenship in the Construction of the 'Anchor Baby.'" In *Deportation in the Americas: Histories of Exclusion*, edited by Kenyon Zimmer and Cristina Salinas, 164–91. Arlington: Texas A&M Press, 2018.

———. *Fit to Be Citizens? Public Health and Race in Los Angeles, 1879–1939*. Berkeley: University of California Press, 2006.

———. *How Race Is Made in America: Immigration, Citizenship, and the Historical Power of Racial Scripts*. Berkeley: University of California, 2014.

Molina, Natalia, Daniel HoSang Martinez, and Ramón Gutiérrez, eds. *Relational Formations of Race: Theory, Method and Practice*. Oakland: University of California Press, 2019.

Monroy, Douglas. *Rebirth: Mexican Los Angeles from the Great Migration to the Great Depression*. Berkeley: University of California Press, 1999.

Montejano, David. *Anglos and Mexicans in the Making of Texas, 1836–1986*. Austin: University of Texas Press, 1987.

Montoya, Carina Monica. *Los Angeles's Historic Filipinotown*. Charleston, SC: Arcadia Publishing, 2009.

Moreno, Rita. *Rita Moreno: A Memoir*. New York: Celebra, 2013.

Mumford, Kevin J. *Interzones: Black/White Sex Districts in Chicago and New York in the Early Twentieth Century*. New York: Columbia University Press, 1997.

Muñoz Martinez, Monica. *The Injustice Never Leaves You: Anti-Mexican Violence in Texas*. Cambridge, MA: Harvard University Press, 2018.

"Natalia Barraza: Nayarita pionera en L.A." In *Nayarit en California*, 16–19. Los Angeles: Asociación de Nayaritas en California, 1993.

Ngai, Mae M. *Impossible Subjects: Illegal Aliens and the Making of Modern America*. Princeton, NJ: Princeton University Press, 2004.

Nicolaides, Becky M. *My Blue Heaven: Life and Politics in the Working-Class Suburbs of Los Angeles, 1920–1965*. Chicago: University of Chicago Press, 2002.

Ocegueda, Mark. "Sol y Sombra: San Bernardino's Mexican Community, 1880–1960." PhD diss., University of California, Irvine, 2017.

O'Neill, Molly. "New Mainstream: Hot Dogs, Apple Pie and Salsa." *New York Times*, March 11, 1992, C1.

Ong, Aihwa. *Flexible Citizenship: The Cultural Logics of Transnationality*. Durham, NC: Duke University Press, 1999.

Ono, Kent A., and John M. Sloop. *Shifting Borders: Rhetoric, Immigration, and California's Proposition 187*. Philadelphia, PA: Temple University Press, 2002.

Orenstein, Dara. "Void for Vagueness: Mexicans and the Collapse of Miscegenation Law in California." *Pacific Historical Review* 74 (2005): 367–408.

Otero, Lydia R. *La Calle: Spatial Conflicts and Urban Renewal in a Southwest City*. Tucson: University of Arizona Press, 2010.

Overend, William. "Lawyers: Two Sides of a Spectrum." *Los Angeles Times*, May 9, 1976, D1.

Padilla, Felix M. *Latino Ethnic Consciousness: The Case of Mexican Americans and Puerto Ricans in Chicago*. Notre Dame, IN: University of Notre Dame Press, 1985.

Padoongpatt, Mark. *Flavors of Empire: Food and the Making of Thai America*. Oakland: University of California Press, 2017.

Pardo, Mary S. *Mexican American Women Activists: Identity and Resistance in Two Los Angeles Communities*. Philadelphia, PA: Temple University Press, 1998.

Parrenas, Rhacel Salazar. *Servants of Globalization: Women, Migration, and Domestic Work*. Stanford, CA: Stanford University Press, 2001.

Parsons, Donald Craig. *Making a Better World: Public Housing, the Red Scare, and the Direction of Modern Los Angeles*. Minneapolis: University of Minnesota Press, 2005.

Pascoe, Peggy. *What Comes Naturally: Miscegenation, Law and the Making of Race in America*. Oxford: Oxford University Press, 2009.

Patiño, Jimmy. *Raza Sí, Migra No: Chicano Movement Struggles for Immigrant Rights in San Diego*. Chapel Hill: University of North Carolina Press, 2017.

Patterson, Kelly L., and Robert Mark Silverman, eds. *Schools and Urban Revitalization: Rethinking Institutions and Community Development*. New York: Routledge, 2013.

Pawel, Miriam. *The Crusades of Cesar Chavez: A Biography*. New York: Bloomsbury Press, 2014.

Perales, Monica. "The Food Historian's Dilemma: Reconsidering the Role of Authenticity in Food Scholarship." *Journal of American History* 103, no. 3 (2016): 690–93.

———. *Smeltertown: Making and Remembering a Southwest Border Community*. Chapel Hill: University of North Carolina Press, 2010.

Pérez, Emma. *The Decolonial Imaginary: Writing Chicanas into History*. Bloomington: Indiana University Press, 1999.

———. "Queering the Borderlands: The Challenges of Excavating the Invisible and Unheard." *Frontiers: A Journal of Women Studies* 24, no. 2–3 (2003): 122–31.

Pilcher, Jeffrey M. *Planet Taco: A Global History of Mexican Food*. New York: Oxford University Press, 2012.

Pitti, Stephen J. *The Devil in Silicon Valley: Northern California, Race, and Mexican Americans*. Princeton, NJ: Princeton University Press, 2003.

Portelli, Alessandro. *The Battle of Valle Giulia: Oral History and the Art of Dialogue*. Madison: University of Wisconsin Press, 1997.

———. *The Death of Luigi Trastulli, and Other Stories: Form and Meaning in Oral History*. Albany: State University of New York Press, 1991.

———. *The Order Has Been Carried Out: History, Memory, and Meaning of Nazi Massacre in Rome*. New York: Palgrave Macmillan, 2003.

Portes, Alejandro, and Rubén G. Rumbaut. *Legacies: The Story of the Immigrant Second Generation*. Berkeley: University of California Press, 2001.

Portnoy, Sarah J. *Food, Health, and Culture in Latino Los Angeles*. Lanham, MD: Rowman & Littlefield, 2017.

Posner, Gerald L. *Killing the Dream: James Earl Ray and the Assassination of Martin Luther King, Jr.* San Diego: Harcourt Brace, 1999.

Price, Patricia L. "At the Crossroads: Critical Race Theory and Critical Geographies of Race." *Progress in Human Geography* 34, no. 2 (2010): 147–74.

Pugmire, Lance. "Colorful L.A. Boxer in the '40s and '50s." *Los Angeles Times*, March 26, 2008.

Pulido, Laura. *Environmentalism and Economic Justice: Two Chicano Struggles in the Southwest*. Tucson: University of Arizona Press, 1996.

Pulido, Laura, Laura R. Barraclough, and Wendy Cheng. *A People's Guide to Los Angeles*. Berkeley: University of California Press, 2012.

Ramírez, Catherine. *The Woman in the Zoot Suit: Gender, Nationalism, and the Cultural Politics of Memory*. Durham, NC: Duke University Press, 2009.

Ramírez, Marla. "Contested Illegality: Three Generations of Exclusion through Mexican 'Repatriation' and the Politics of Immigration Law, 1920–2005." PhD diss., University of California, Santa Barbara, 2015.

Ray, Krishnendu. *The Ethnic Restaurateur*. New York: Bloomsbury Academic, 2016.

Raymond, Anthea. "Lionel Rolfe: Bookseller Jake Zeitlin's Echo Park Days—Part One." *Patch*, February 20, 2012. https://patch.com/california/echopark/lionel-rolfe-remembering-echo-park-s-jake-zietlin-part-one.

Razack, Sherene. *Race, Space, and the Law: Unmapping a White Settler Society*. Toronto: Between the Lines, 2002.

Rechy, John. *City of Night*. New York: Grove Press, 1963.

Red Hill. Echo Park Film Center Youth Documentary Project, 2006. https://vimeo.com/287149046.

Reisler, Mark. *By the Sweat of Their Brow: Mexican Immigrant Labor in the United States, 1900–1940*. Westport, CT: Greenwood Press, 1976.

———. "Mexican Unionization in California Agriculture, 1927–1936." *Labor History* 14, no. 4 (1973): 562–79.

Reyes, Luis, and Peter Rubie. *Hispanics in Hollywood: A Celebration of 100 Years in Film and Television*. Hollywood, CA: Lone Eagle, 2000.

Rodríguez, Clara E. *Changing Race: Latinos, the Census, and the History of Ethnicity in the United States*. New York: New York University Press, 2000.

Roediger, David. *Working toward Whiteness: How America's Immigrants Became White: The Strange Journey from Ellis Island to the Suburbs*. New York: Basic Books, 2005.

Romero, Robert Chao. *The Chinese in Mexico, 1882–1940*. Tucson: University of Arizona Press, 2010.

Romo, Ricardo. *History of a Barrio*. Austin: University of Austin Press, 1983.

Roosevelt, Margot. "Alice McGrath Dies at 92." *Los Angeles Times*, November 29, 2009.

Roque Ramírez, Horacio N. "A Living Archive of Desire: Teresita La Campesina and the Embodiment of Queer Latino Community Histories." In *Archive Stories: Facts, Fictions, and the Writing of History*, edited by Antoinette M. Burton, 111–35. Durham, NC: Duke University Press, 2005.

Rosas, Abigail. "Banking on the Community: Mexican Immigrants' Experiences in a Historically African American Bank in South Central Los Angeles, 1970." In *Black and Brown in Los Angeles: Beyond Conflict and Coalition*, edited by Josh Kun and Laura Pulido, 67–89. Berkeley: University of California Press, 2014.

———. *South Central Is Home: Race and the Power of Community Investment in Los Angeles*. Stanford, CA: Stanford University Press, 2019.

Rosas, Ana. *Abrazando el Espíritu: Bracero Families Confront the US-Mexico Border*. Oakland: University of California Press, 2014.

Rothstein, Richard. *The Color of Law: A Forgotten History of How Our Government Segregated America*. New York: Liveright, 2017.

Rourke, Mary. "Waitress Credited with Introducing L.A. to Nachos." *Los Angeles Times*, October 17, 2008.

Rouse, Roger. "Thinking through Transnationalism: Notes on the Cultural Politics of Class Relations in the Contemporary United States." *Public Culture* 7, no. 2 (1995): 353–402.

Ruiz, Vicki L. *Cannery Women, Cannery Lives: Mexican Women, Unionization, and the California Food Processing Industry, 1930–1950*. Albuquerque: University of New Mexico Press, 1987.

———. "Citizen Restaurant: American Imaginaries, American Communities." *American Quarterly* 60, no. 1 (2008): 1–21.

———. *From out of the Shadows: Mexican Women in Twentieth-Century America*. New York: Oxford University Press, 1998.

———. "'We Always Tell Our Children They Are American': *Mendez v. Westminster* and the California Road to *Brown*." *College Board Review*, no. 200 (Fall 2003): 21–27.

Rumbaut, Rubén G. "Paradoxes (and Orthodoxies) of Assimilation." *Sociological Perspectives* 40, no. 3 (1997): 483–511.

St. John, Rachel C. *Line in the Sand: A History of the Western U.S.-Mexico Border.* Princeton, NJ: Princeton University Press, 2011.

Sáizar, Martín. "El Club Social 'NAYARIT' de Los Angeles, Calif., trabaja por este estado." *El Eco*, July 25, 1968, 1.

———. "El 7 de septiembre cumple un año de fundado el Club Social Nayarit de Los Angeles, California." *El Eco*, August 25, 1968, 26.

Sánchez, George J. *Becoming Mexican American: Ethnicity, Culture, and Identity in Chicano Los Angeles, 1900–1945.* New York: Oxford University Press, 1993.

———. *Boyle Heights: How a Los Angeles Neighborhood Became the Future of American Democracy.* Oakland: University of California Press, 2021.

———. "Disposable People, Expendable Neighborhoods." In *A Companion to Los Angeles*, edited by William Deverell and Greg Hise, 129–46. Malden, MA: Wiley-Blackwell, 2010.

———. "Edward R. Roybal and the Politics of Multiracialism." *Southern California Quarterly* 92, no. 1 (Spring 2010): 51–73.

———. "'Go after the Women': Americanization and the Mexican Immigrant Woman, 1915–1929." In *A Multi-Cultural Reader in U.S. Women's History*, edited by Ellen DuBois and Vicki L. Ruiz, 250–63. New York: Routledge, 1990.

———. "'What's Good for Boyle Heights Is Good for the Jews': Creating Multiracialism on the Eastside during the 1950s." *American Quarterly* 56, no. 3 (2004): 633–61.

Sandoval-Strausz, A. K. *Barrio America: How Latino Immigrants Saved the American City.* New York: Basic Books, 2019.

Sassen, Saskia. *The Global City: New York, London, Tokyo.* 2nd ed. Princeton, NJ: Princeton University Press, 2001.

Schmidt Camacho, Alicia R. *Migrant Imaginaries: Latino Cultural Politics in the U.S.-Mexico Borderlands.* New York: New York University Press, 2008.

Scott, A.O. "Tastes of Los Angeles in 'City of Gold.'" *New York Times*, March 10, 2016.

Scott, James C. *Domination and the Arts of Resistance: Hidden Transcripts*. New Haven, CT: Yale University Press, 1990.

Sedgwick, Eve Kosofsky. *Epistemology of the Closet*. Berkeley: University of California Press, 1990.

Self, Robert O. *American Babylon: Race and the Struggle for Postwar Oakland*. Princeton, NJ: Princeton University Press, 2003.

Shah, Nayan. *Contagious Divides: Epidemics and Race in San Francisco's Chinatown*. Berkeley: University of California Press, 2001.

———. *Stranger Intimacy: Contesting Race, Sexuality, and the Law in the North American West*. Berkeley: University of California Press, 2011.

Shapiro, Laura. *Perfection Salad: Women and Cooking at the Turn of the Century*. New York: Farrar, Straus and Giroux, 1986.

Shaw, Nate, and Theodore Rosengarten. *All God's Dangers: The Life of Nate Shaw*. New York: Knopf, 1974.

Sides, Josh. *L.A. City Limits: African Americans in Los Angeles from the Great Depression to the Present*. Berkeley: University of California Press, 2003.

———. "Straight into Compton: American Dreams, Urban Nightmares, and the Metamorphosis of a Black Suburb." *American Quarterly* 56, no. 3 (2004): 583–605.

Sifuentez, Mario Jimenez. *Of Forests and Fields: Mexican Labor in the Pacific Northwest*. New Brunswick, NJ: Rutgers University Press, 2016.

Sitton, Tom. "Another Generation of Urban Reformers: Los Angeles in the 1930s." *Western Historical Quarterly* 18, no. 3 (1987): 315–32.

Slocum, Rachel B., and Arun Saldanha, eds. *Geographies of Race and Food: Fields, Bodies, Markets*. Burlington, VT: Ashgate, 2013.

Smith, Anna Deavere. *Twilight: Los Angeles, 1992. On the Road: A Search for American Character*. New York: Anchor Books, 1994.

Smith, Doug. "'You're Not the Most Popular Person in Echo Park. William Toro Is.'" *Los Angeles Times*, August 2, 1990.

Smith, Michael P. *Transnational Urbanism: Locating Globalization*. Malden, MA: Blackwell, 2001.

Smith, R.J. *The Great Black Way: L.A. In the 1940s and the Lost African-American Renaissance*. New York: Public Affairs, 2006.

Smith, Suzanne E. *To Serve the Living: Funeral Directors and the African American Way of Death*. Cambridge, MA: Belknap Press of Harvard University Press, 2010.

Soja, Edward W. *Thirdspace: Journeys to Los Angeles and Other Real-and-Imagined Places*. Cambridge, MA: Blackwell, 1996.

Solnit, Rebecca, and Susan Schwartzenberg. *Hollow City: The Siege of San Francisco and the Crisis of American Urbanism*. New York: Verso, 2000.

Somerville, Siobhan B. "Notes toward a Queer History of Naturalization." *American Quarterly* 57, no. 3 (2005): 659–75.

Sonenshein, Raphael. *Politics in Black and White: Race and Power in Los Angeles*. Princeton, NJ: Princeton University Press, 1993.

Soto, Lilia. "The Preludes to Migration: Anticipation and Imaginings of Mexican Immigrant Adolescent Girls." *Girlhood Studies: An Interdisciplinary Journal* 3, no. 2 (December 2010): 30–48.

Stack, Carol B. *All Our Kin: Strategies for Survival in a Black Community*. New York: Harper & Row, 1974.

Standish, Peter. *The States of Mexico: A Reference Guide to History and Culture*. Westport, CT: Greenwood Press, 2009.

Stansell, Christine. *City of Women: Sex and Class in New York, 1789–1860*. New York: Knopf, 1986.

Starr, Kevin. *Americans and the California Dream, 1850–1915*. New York: Oxford University Press, 1973.

———. *Inventing the Dream: California through the Progressive Era*. New York: Oxford University Press, 1985.

———. *Material Dreams: Southern California through the 1920s*. New York: Oxford University Press, 1990.

Stern, Alexandra Minna. *Eugenic Nation: Faults and Frontiers of Better Breeding in Modern America*. Berkeley: University of California Press, 2005.

———. "Sterilized in the Name of Public Health and Population Policy: Race, Immigration, and Reproductive Control in Modern California." *American Journal of Public Health* 95, no. 7 (2005): 1128–38.

Stevenson, Brenda E. *The Contested Murder of Latasha Harlins: Justice, Gender, and the Origins of the LA Riots*. Oxford: Oxford University Press, 2013.

Stoler, Ann Laura. "Colonial Archives and the Arts of Governance." *Archival Science* 2, no. 2 (2002): 87–109.

Strum, Philippa. *Mendez v. Westminster: School Desegregation and Mexican-American Rights*. Lawrence: University Press of Kansas, 2010.

Sugrue, Thomas. *The Origins of the Urban Crisis: Race and Inequality in Postwar Detroit*. Princeton, NJ: Princeton University Press, 1996.

Taylor, Candacy, *Overground Railroad: The Green Book and Roots of Black Travel in America*. New York: Abrams Books, 2020.

Taylor, Diana. *The Archive and the Repertoire: Performing Cultural Memory in the Americas*. Durham, NC: Duke University Press, 2003.

Tchen, John Kuo Wei. *New York before Chinatown: Orientalism and the Shaping of American Culture, 1776–1882*. Baltimore, MD: Johns Hopkins University Press, 1999.

Thabet, Andrea. "Culture as Urban Renewal: Postwar Los Angeles and the Remaking of Public Space." PhD diss., University of California, Santa Barbara, 2013.

Tomlinson, Barbara, and George Lipsitz. *Insubordinate Spaces: Improvisation and Accompaniment for Social Justice*. Philadelphia, PA: Temple University Press, 2019.

Tompkins, Kyla Wazana. *Racial Indigestion: Eating Bodies in the Nineteenth Century*. New York: New York University Press, 2012.

Tongson, Karen. "The Light That Never Goes Out: Butch Intimacies and Sub-Urban Sociabilities in 'Lesser Los Angeles.'" In *A Companion to Lesbian, Gay, Bisexual, Transgender, and Queer Studies*, edited by George E. Haggerty and Molly McGarry, 355–76. Malden, MA: Blackwell, 2007.

Torres-Rouff, David. *Before L.A.: Race, Space, and Municipal Power in Los Angeles, 1781–1894*. New Haven, CT: Yale University Press, 2013.

Trouillot, Michel-Rolph. *Silencing the Past: Power and the Production of History*. Boston: Beacon Press, 1995.

US Census Office. *United States Census of Population, 1900*. Washington, DC: US Government Printing Office, 1901–3.

US Congress. House. Committee on the Judiciary. *Study of Population and Immigration Problems*. Washington, DC: US Government Printing Office, 1962.

———. House. Select Committee on Assassinations. Report of the Select Committee on Assassinations, U.S. House of Representatives, Ninety-Fifth Congress, Second Session: Findings and Recommendations. Washington, DC: US Government Printing Office, 1979.

———. Senate. Committee on Education and Labor. *Violations of Free Speech and Rights of Labor. Digest of Report of the Committee on Education and Labor Pursuant to S. Res. 266, a Resolution to Investigate Violations of the Right of Free Speech and Assembly and Interference with the Right of Labor to Organize and Bargain Collectively*. Washington, DC: US Government Printing Office, 1939.

Urban, Michael. *New Orleans Rhythm and Blues after Katrina: Music, Magic and Myth*. London: Palgrave Macmillan, 2016.

Vargas, Zaragosa. *Labor Rights Are Civil Rights: Mexican American Workers in Twentieth-Century America*. Princeton, NJ: Princeton University Press, 2005.

Villa, Raúl H. *Barrio-Logos: Space and Place in Urban Chicano Literature and Culture*. Austin: University of Texas Press, 2000.

Villa, Raúl H., and George J. Sánchez. *Los Angeles and the Future of Urban Cultures: A Special Issue of American Quarterly*. Baltimore, MD: Johns Hopkins University Press, 2005.

Villarreal, Mary Ann. *Listening to Rosita: The Business of Tejana Music and Culture, 1930–1955*. Norman: University of Oklahoma Press, 2015.

Viruell-Fuentes, Edna A. "'My Heart Is Always There': The Transnational Practices of First-Generation Immigrant and Second-Generation Mexican American Women." *Identities* 13, no. 3 (2006): 335–62.

Walker, Jim. *Pacific Electric Red Cars*. Charleston, SC: Arcadia Publishing, 2006.

Wang, Theresa, et al. *Lavender Los Angeles*. Charleston, SC: Arcadia Publishing, 2011.

Weems, Robert E. *Desegregating the Dollar: African American Consumerism in the Twentieth Century*. New York: New York University Press, 1998.

Widener, Daniel. *Black Arts West: Culture and Struggle in Postwar Los Angeles*. Durham, NC: Duke University Press, 2010.

Wilkerson, Isabel. *The Warmth of Other Suns: The Epic Story of America's Great Migration*. New York: Random House, 2010.

Will, Bob. "5000 L.A. Hoodlums Belong to Violence-Dealing Gangs." *Los Angeles Times*, December 17, 1953.

Williams, Carlton. "Councilman Sworn in Soon after His Election." *Los Angeles Times*, May 28, 1959.

Williams-Forson, Psyche A. *Building Houses out of Chicken Legs: Black Women, Food, and Power*. Chapel Hill: University of North Carolina Press, 2006.

Williams-Forson, Psyche A., and Carole Counihan. *Taking Food Public: Redefining Foodways in a Changing World*. New York: Routledge, 2011.

Wolcott, Victoria W. *Race, Riots, and Roller Coasters: The Struggle over Segregated Recreation in America*. Philadelphia: University of Pennsylvania Press, 2012.

Wollenberg, Charles. *All Deliberate Speed: Segregation and Exclusion in California Schools, 1855–1975*. Berkeley: University of California Press, 1978.

Wood, Denis, and John Fels. *The Power of Maps*. New York: Guilford Press, 1992.

Woods, Clyde. *Development Arrested: The Blues and Plantation Power in the Mississippi Delta*. London: Verso, 1998.

Yokoi, Iris. "Echo Park: Finer's Prepares for a Final Sale." *Los Angeles Times*, March 14, 1993.

Zavella, Patricia. *I'm Neither Here nor There: Mexicans' Quotidian Struggles with Migration and Poverty*. Durham, NC: Duke University Press, 2011.

Zentella, Ana Celia. "Latin@ Languages and Identities." In *Latinos: Remaking America*, edited by Marcelo M. Suárez-Orozco and Mariela Páez, 321–38. Berkeley: University of California Press, 2002.

Index

Barraza, Natalia (Doña Natalia), *11, 33, 112,* *119;* overview, 4–5, 26; adoption of children (Carlos and María), 32, *33,* 34; as agricultural camp worker, 34–35; appearance and dress of, 64, 79; boldness of her dream of entrepreneurship, 35, 199–200nn22–23; certainty that differences in wealth or status did not determine individual worth, 133; character of, 4, 76; daughter of (*see* Molina, María); death of, 6, 178; discrimination faced by, 27; discrimination not faced by, due to Echo Park location, 53–54; dish pattern collected by (Franciscan Ivy), 184–85; as divorced/single woman, 26, 98, 113; Doña Natalia as address for, 4; as fair and respectful employer, 108–9; first (name unknown) restaurant of, 31–32, 34, 35; health of, 76, 227n23; homes owned by, 40; hosting parties and weddings, 165, *166, 167,* 176; immigration to the US (1922), 26–27; patriarchal role of, 98, 127; as permanent resident, 101; and religion, 78, 117; in reviews, 75; as sharing her middle-class comforts, 99, 132; as skeptical of the Spanish fantasy past, 14; supervision of the front-of-house service, 77; supervision of the kitchen, 76–77. *See also* emotional ties; employees of the Nayarit; exploration of the city by Nayarit employees, DN's encouragement of; immigration sponsorship by DN; Nayarit restaurant (1951–76); placemaking—via the Nayarit restaurant

barrio/ghetto: Echo Park dismissed as, 7, 58; as label, and perception of the people who live there, 8; Mexican move to East Los Angeles as barrioization, 30, 198n14

bars: placemaking and, 9; as sites of everyday resistance, 12; straight, as tolerating conventional-acting gay customers, 151; as urban anchors, 10. *See also* gay bars and clubs

baseball players: as clientele of the Nayarit, 90–91; discrimination faced by, 91. *See also* Dodger Stadium and the Dodgers

beauty salons, 9

Becerra, Martín, 85

Belmar Café, 140

Belmont High School, 126

belonging: seeking, as resistance, 19; urban anchors and, 66, 91

Beverly Hills, 165

Beverly Wilshire, 82, 83

birthdays, 87, 136, 137

Black capitalism, 159

Black Cat bar, 158

Black spatial imaginary, 189n11

B'nai B'rith, 149

Bob Baker Marionette Theater, 46, 201n39

Bogart, Humphrey, 71

bohemianism, 47–48, 115

Bohemian Los Angeles and the Making of Modern Politics (Hurewitz), 188n6

bookstores, 9, 42

Border Patrol, 27, 147–48

Borquez, Alejandro and Rosa, 72–73

Boston, 197–98n9

Bourdain, Anthony, 13

bowling alleys, 9

Boyle Heights: diversity and radical politics of, 201–2n40; freeways and destruction of, 203–4n59; gentrification of, 7, 181; and racist government

Chicanx movement, 18-19, 21-22, 142, 148-49, 187-88n4, 215n19

Chilean immigrants, 19

Chinese immigrants: "chop suey" menus in restaurants of, 14; in Echo Park, 46; excluded from the US, 27, 53, 220n69; in Mexico, 220n69; restaurants as sponsors for, 100; settlements of, 30

Choi, Roy, 191n19

Christmas season and the Nayarit, 92, 92-93, 95, 136, 173

Chumash (Indigenous), 28

Citizens Committee to Save Elysian Park, 60-61

citizenship status: arrest for homosexual behavior as interfering in application for, 150; banishment of Mexican American citizens, 30-31; Communist Party membership and stripping of naturalized citizenship, 101, 142; and differential racialization, 15; DN as permanent resident, 101; Indigenous identity as placing in jeopardy, 93-94, 213n68; and lack of political engagement, 142; of Mexicans after US conquest of Mexico, 28-29; naturalization limited to white or Black people, 213n68

Civil Rights Congress (CRC), 49-50

Civil Rights movement: the Chicanx movements and, 18; Greensboro Four, 11-12; integration of public facilities and, 12; nonviolent protest and, 12; post-WWII organizing by ethnic Mexicans, 141. *See also* social justice

Club Havana (Silver Lake), 90, 211-12n59

Club Nayarit (Club Social Nayarita en Los Angeles): celebration of native heritage, 173; dances of, 175-77,

228n37; disbursements by, 174, 175; dues for, 174; first meeting of, 173-74; first president of (José Inés Jiménez), 174; fund-raising activities, 174, 175; goal of strengthening mainstream Los Angeles political connections, 176-78; as hosted by DN, 227n23; launched at the retirement banquet for Martín Sáizar, 172, 173; as open to all, 174, 175; second president (Estanislao "Tani" López Robles), 176-77

Club Virginia's (MacArthur Park), 90, 211-12n59

Coates, Paul, 38

coffee shops, 9

Cohen, Lizabeth, 136

Cold War: and abandonment of public housing, 57; McCarthyism and anti-Communism, 49, 50, 142; and punitive laws against the undocumented, 101; and the spatial metaphor of "the closet," 123

Cole, Nat King, 44

Colombian immigrants, 86

Communist Party members: anti-Communist campaigns as thinly veiled anti-union campaigns, 142; blacklisting of, 49, 50; Civil Rights Congress (CRC), 49-50; deportation of, 101, 142; McCarthyism, 49, 50, 142; and social justice work, 50; stripped of naturalized citizenship, 101, 142; vilification of, 142. *See also* Echo Park, progressive and radical politics of

Community Service Organization (CSO), 141

compadrazgo relationships, 98

Compton, 146

institutions due to, 173, 174; juridical, 51, 106, 215n19; Latinx baseball players experiencing, 91; Latinx celebrities experiencing, 90; pan-Latinx identity and shared experience of, 88; police discrimination, 50, 51; refusal to seat ethnic Mexicans in restaurants, 148, 169; service-entrance, requirement to use, 90; WWII scapegoating, 51–52. *See also* press coverage of ethnic Mexicans; racially restrictive covenants; racism; segregation

diversity: as redlining gauge, 57, 58. *See also* Echo Park—diversity of; Nayarit restaurant (1951–76)—clientele, diversity of

DN. *See* Barraza, Natalia (Doña Natalia)

documented immigration: ability to return home to visit family, 103–4; costs and risk as lower than for undocumented immigrants, 103–4; driver's license eligibility, 103; family members living with undocumented workers, 103; fees for, 104; green card (Form I-151), 101, 103, 104, 107, 150; health exams, 102; as increasingly difficult without a family connection, 101–2, 104; registration after 1940, 101; as relieving the burdens of illegality, 104–5; visa application process, 105, 215n16. *See also* Bracero Program; immigration; immigration sponsorship by DN; visas

Dodger Stadium and the Dodgers: built in Elysian Park after displacement of Chavez Ravine residents, 56–57; and Echo Park as geographical crossroads, 42; and Nikola's as hangout, 62–63; passes to the Stadium Club, 138–39;

players and fans as Nayarit clientele, 81, 85–86, 90–91; restaurant workers moonlighting in food service at, 137–39; Spanish-language broadcasts of, 85, 175

Dominican Republic, 90–91

Doña Natalia. *See* Barraza, Natalia (Doña Natalia)

Douglas, Mary, 207n18

Dunne, Dominick, 165, 226n11

East Los Angeles: attorney of DN from (Carlos Teran), 106; choice of DN not to open restaurant in, 39; commuting to work from, 146–47; El Águila (newspaper), 139–40, 221n13; and "families of resemblance," forging, 148–49; lesbian bar in, 216n35; Mexican Independence Day parade, 93, *94*, 128, 174; Mexican movement to (barrioization), 30, 198n14; Nayarit Furniture, 174. *See also* ethnic enclaves

Echo (club), 179

Echo Park: archival silence about, 54–55; City Council District 13 representatives, 54, 55–56; development of, 44, 47; dismissed as a "bad part of town"/ghetto, 7, 58; ethnic Mexican community formed by former Nayarit employees opening businesses, 153, 160; first (name unknown) restaurant of DN in, 31–32, 34, 35; gay community visibility and opportunities in, 113, 115–17, 150; as geographic crossroads, 42, 153; government resources not provided to, 54, 55; home values, increase in, 180; lack of overarching histories written about, 7, 188n6; location and size of, 42; as

Echo Park *(continued)*

location for the Nayarit, 40, 53–54, 81; map of, *43*; public swimming pool, 16; redlining practices and, 57–58, 205nn68,70; rents, increase in, 180; services available within the neighborhood, 62–63; and Sunset Boulevard, 42, 47, 62, 81, 160; and urban renewal practices, avoidance of, 54, 56; white flight and, 23, 57–60. *See also* gentrification—of Echo Park; transportation

—DIVERSITY OF: as attraction for and threatened by gentrification, 7, 179; and comfort crossing color lines, 46–47, 54, 201–2n40; educational exchange programs and, 126; lack of planned segregation and, 44, 53, 54, 201n34; population percentages, 45; postwar increase in, 23; and race as a relational concept, 46–47; statistics showing changes over time in, 59, *59–60*, 205n72

—AS MULTIETHNIC AND MULTICULTURAL: overview, 6, 17, 23, 27–28; Angelus Temple/Aimee Semple McPherson and, 48–49; artists and other creatives attracted to, 47; and attorney for DN, 106–7; bohemianism and, 47–48, 115; as cosmopolitan, 17; and customer/worker encounters at the Nayarit, 130; different sensibility of, 42; gay men's community and, 47; and segregation, lack of, 44, 53, 54, 201n34

—PROGRESSIVE AND RADICAL POLITICS OF: overview, 49, 202n46; and friendly welcome to DN's restaurant, 53; and outsiders/others, common cause among, 46, 47, 53, 201–2n40;

placemaking and, 61–62; and race as a relational concept, 51–53; social justice work, 49–51, 53, 60–61; white residents and, 46, 47, 59

Echo Park Food Conspiracy (cooperative), 61

Echo Park Lake, 47, 58, 89

Edendale, 47, 58

education: attainment of ethnic Mexicans (1960), 220n2; exchange programs and diversity of Echo Park, 126; and underestimation of young ethnic Mexican women, 123–24. *See also* school segregation

Ehrenreich, Ben, 179–80

El Águila (newspaper), 139–40, 221n13

El Batey (market), 158–59, 169, 179

El Carmelo Bakery, 6, 89, 179–80

El Chavo restaurant, 6, 156, 157

El Cholo restaurant, 69, 72–73

El Comité de Beneficiencia Mexicana (Mexican Charity Committee), 174

El Congreso de Pueblos de Habla Española, 141, 142

El Conquistador restaurant, 6, 131, 156–58, 160, 179

El Coyote Mexican Cafe, 71–72, 73

El Eco de Nayarit: advertisement for *The Nayarit* placed by Doña Natalia, 1–2, *3*, 84, 165; anniversary issues and ads, 165; as archival source, 20–21; and Club Nayarit, 173, 175, 176; and cultural priming, 168; death of DN honored in, 178; DN covered by, 165, *167*; family members sending to LA, 166; founding of, 163; fundraising activities via, 164; gossip column, "Rueda Ferris" (Ferris Wheel), 126, 127, 164, 165, *167*; independence of, 163; Robert Kennedy assassination reported in, 145–46; maintaining ties between LA and Nayarit, 161–62, 163, 165–67; the Nayarit restaurant covered in, 170; Martín Sáizar as editor of, 164–65, 168–69, 170–72; ordinary people as focus of, 163, 164, 165; publishing schedule, 164; retirement banquet for Martín Sáizar, and coverage of, 170–72, 227n23; saving old issues in LA, 167; subscriptions to, in LA, 166; translocal connection, in-person contact as developing, 168–70; as translocal placemaker, 164–68, 170–72; as ubiquitous among LA Nayaritas, 166–67, 170

El Farolito, 142

Ellis, Pearl, 69

El Mercado de Los Ángeles, 140

El Monte American Legion Stadium, 149, 223n39

El Río Club el Kikiriki Place, 140

El Salvador, immigrants from, 104

El Tepeyac Cafe, 79

El Trópico Club, 140

Elysian Park, 42, 56–57; movement to preserve, 60–61

El Zarape restaurant, 170, 171, 176, 226n21

Emler, Ron, 188n6

emotional ties: DN as understanding, 105; placemaking as driven by, 99, 100, 113; remittances and, 112–13; as strengthened by the business, 108; training of employees as commitment, 100, 108, 111–12

employees of the Nayarit: branching out to become placemakers, 128–29; the business as means to earn a living and to provide help to, 99, 100, 213n3; Echo Park and LA as home to,

134; English language learning and speaking, 110, 112; gossip about, DN refusal to hear, 118; housed with DN, 97, 117; housing, DN renting to, 40, 117; moonlighting elsewhere, 137–38; number of, 108, 113; political connection of, via events that unfolded in and near the restaurant, 142–46, 222n20; political organizing not engaged in, 141–42; precarity of alternatives to the Nayarit, 109–10, 215n26; relationships between employees, 121, 123, 129–30, 151–53, 184; relationships with regular customers, 110, 121, *122*, 130, 151, 154; remittances not expected of, 112–13, 129; and sense of obligation to help one another in the settlement process, 99; stability of the work-force/low turnover of, 108–9; staff meal, 110–11; tipping, 135; training of, 100, 107–8, 111–12; undocu-mented workers, 107–8. *See also* exploration of the city by Nayarit employees, DN's encouragement of; gay men—as employees at the Nayarit; immigration sponsorship by DN; place-taking by employees of the Nayarit; restaurants and businesses opened by former Nayarit employees; women—as employees of the Nayarit

English language learning and speaking: documented workers, 103; employees of the Nayarit, 110, 112–13, 126, 128; *I Love Lucy* and, 185

English-only laws, 80

entrepreneurship. *See* ethnic entrepreneurship

Esparza, Bill, 191n19

Ethington, Philip, 205–6n72

ethnic enclaves: affection for, 216–17n36; cultural crossroads of Echo Park as offering greater opportunity than, 61–62, 113; gay men finding a preferred niche in, 218n46; gay men's opportunities as more constrained in, 113, 131; Latinx presence as the rule in, 80; mass culture as building bridges to, 136; the nature of ethnic entrepreneurship in, 62; placemakers of, as allowing segregation to become congregation, 17; segregation as limiting opportunities in, 216–17n36. *See also* multiethnic and multicultural neighborhoods

ethnic entrepreneurship: boldness of DN's dream, 35, 199–200nn22–23; Echo Park as location for, 62; ethnic enclaves as main location of, 62; foodways and food culture shaped by, 199–200n22; importance of Latinx, 199–200n22; as pathway to success for immigration groups, 200n23. *See also* ethnic restaurants; urban anchors

ethnicity, as term, 8. *See also* racialized groups

ethnic Mexicans. *See* Mexican ethnics

ethnic restaurants: as bringing together people across divides of race, class, or politics, 12–13; and culinary tourism vs. restaurant regulars, 13; exoticization of cuisines, 13

exoticization: of ethnic cuisines, 13; long-standing relationships between restaurants and customers as replaced by, 182; representation of Latinx in films, 148; in restaurant reviews, 38

exploration of the city by Nayarit employees, DN's encouragement of:

bravery required to venture out, 149, 151; building knowledge as goal of, 133; crossing geographic and cultural boundaries, 134, 149; dressing up for, 132, 133, *138*; English-language ability as aid to, 110; gay male employees and, 137, *138*, 150–53, 224n45; María as the cultural broker for, 132–33; moonlighting for other food services, 137–39; motivations of DN for, 133–34; and the multicultural urban civility of mid-20th-century LA, 134; sharing of cultural capital gained through, 135; time off given for, 132; women employees and, 132–33, *138*. *See also* place-taking by employees of the Nayarit; restaurants and businesses opened by former Nayarit employees

Faderman, Lillian, 116, 150, 151, 216n35, 224n45

"families of resemblance," forging, 148–49

family: chaperonage expectations of, 124–25, 219n62; desire of women to escape the expectations of, 123; of gay men, as limiting person conduct, 114; gender in decisions about immigration, 124, 197n2; immigration sponsorship of, by DN, 99–100, 111, 129; parental worries about daughters abandoning their culture, 124; place-taking Nayarit employees sharing cultural capital with friends and, 135, 137, 138–39. *See also* fictive kinship

Federal Housing Administration (FHA), redlining as racist policy of, 57–58, 205n70

gay bars and clubs *(continued)*
of, 150; gentrification and loss of,
180; Klub Fantasy at the Nayarit
under new ownership, 219n54;
lesbian bars, 216n35; police harassment and raids of, 55–56, 117, 120,
150–51, 153, 158, 218n52; Stonewall
Inn (NYC), 158; as urban anchors,
158; working-class, 150, 216n35

gay community: and the AIDS epidemic,
117, 181; and the freedom and
anonymity of LA, 150; gay liberation
movement, 158; number of community institutions started in LA, 150;
political mobilization of, 55–56;
urban anchors of, 156–58, 224n53;
visibility of and opportunities for, in
Echo Park, 113, 115–17, 150; and the
WWII economic boom, 149–50. *See
also* gay bars and clubs; gay men;
homophobia; lesbians

gay men: and boardinghouses, 114;
bravery of place-taking by, 149, 151;
and the complexity of immigrant
sexuality, 116–17, 218nn45–46;
cross-dressers, arrests of, 153; danger
of the legal system for, 150–51;
entrapment by police, 120, 150–51;
families of, as limiting personal
conduct, 114; finding preferred niche
in ethnic enclaves, 218n46; and fluid
situational identities vs. the static
spatial metaphor of "the closet," 123;
immigration decisions of, 114,
217n37; and Mexican culture of
sexual silence, 118; the Nayarit as safe
space for, 120–21, 218n52, 219n54;
and oral histories, silences in, 22,
116–17, 118, 218n45; police harassment and abuse of, 55–56, 117, 120,

150–51, 153, 158, 218n52; prison
sentences for consensual sexual
behavior, 151; restaurants opened by,
156–58, 224n53; restaurants'
treatment of, generally, 218n52; and
the Santa Monica beach, 152–53,
224n45; sex offender registration,
151, 158

—AS EMPLOYEES AT THE NAYARIT:
acceptance of sexual identities of, 22,
120; affection of DN for, 119–20;
affinity with, DN and, 113; appearance and conduct of, DN as con-
straining, 115, 117–18, 120, 130–31;
cutting loose when DN was not
present, 118, 120; exploration of the
city encouraged by DN, 137, 150–53,
224n45; as fictive kin, 98, 121;
friendships with straight women, 121,
122, 151; gendered naming as
evidence of acceptance of, 120;
homophobia as less limiting for, 98;
housed with DN, 97, 117; housing
assistance from DN, 115; immigration
sponsorship from DN, 97–98, 130;
married with children, 22, 120;
number of, 113; opportunities
available to, as much greater, 99, 113,
115–16, 130–31; and silences in oral
histories, 22; socializing with straight
men, 121, 123, 151, *152*; as tethered to
the Nayarit community, 184

gender: and family decisions about
immigration, 124, 197n2; and
nicknames for gay men, 120. *See also*
women

gentefication, 181

gentrification: close resemblance of those
moving in with those who are
displaced (*gentefication*), 181; and

homophobia *(continued)*
    gay community mobilization against,
    56; as less limiting in Los Angeles,
    114; as less limiting working at the
    Nayarit, 98; in Mexico, 97, 98, 114;
    police harassment of gay bars and
    meeting places, 55–56, 117, 120,
    150–51, 153, 158, 218n52
Hondagneu-Sotelo, Pierrette, 124, 197n2
housekeeper/nanny work, 147, 165
House Un-American Activities Commit-
    tee (HUAC), 49
housing: demand for, and displacement of
    Mexican immigrants, 30; gentrifica-
    tion and loss of affordable, 180–81;
    loan policies as allowing gentrifica-
    tion, 180. *See also* housing
    segregation
housing segregation: redlining and white
    flight, 57–59, 205nn68,70; tech-
    niques used by white home owners to
    intimidate buyers of color, 44, *45*,
    146. *See also* racially restrictive
    covenants
Huajicori, Nayarit, Mexico, 175
Huichol (Indigenous), 93, 161, 164
Huntington Park, 44
Hurewitz, Daniel, 47, 188n6
Hurston, Zora Neale, 146

identity, situational and fluid, 123
I Love Lucy (TV), 185
immigrants: children of, gentrification as
    displacing, 180; definition and use of
    term, 187–88n4; diseases blamed
    upon, 41, 68; elderly, gentrification as
    displacing, 180; "good immigrants,"
    and deviancy/normalcy, 117
—MEXICAN: definition of term, 187–88n4;
    doing jobs that others reject, 183;

early 20th-century increase in, and
    welcome as laborers only, 147;
    gentrification as displacing, 180–81;
    hiring of, through cheaper channels
    than Bracero, 18; as *los de afuera*,
    187n1; men as majority of, 18, 19, 24,
    124, 196n50; mutual aid societies,
    172, 174, 224n57; as percentage of all
    immigrants, 17–18; reinscription of
    ethnic Mexicans as noncitizens, by
    mainstream politicians, 177–78. *See
    also* Bracero Program; documented
    immigration; hometown associations
    (HTAs, *clubes de oriundos*); immigra-
    tion sponsorship by DN; labor,
    Mexican low-wage; remittances;
    translocal connections; undocu-
    mented workers
immigration: Chinese restaurants and
    sponsorship of, 100; circular, laws
    and policies reducing, 27; gendered
    expectation that migration was a role
    for the head of household, 124, 197n2;
    household strategy model, 197n2;
    increases in, and pan-Latinx
    identity, 86. *See also* documented
    immigration; immigration sponsor-
    ship by DN; undocumented workers
Immigration and Naturalization Service
    (INS): as archival source, 196n50;
    collusion to deport union members,
    147–48; registration with, 101
immigration sponsorship by DN:
    overview, 97–98; affidavit stating the
    immigrant had a job, 104; attorney
    assistance, 105–7; care packages, 105;
    documentation process, 101, 104–5;
    emotional needs, 105; families
    sponsored, 99–100, 111, 129; fees and
    costs covered, 104, 105; and freedom

from burdens of illegality, 104–5; gay men sponsored, 97–98, 130; immigrants as coming from families with some means, 113, 126; jobs provided as stable employment, 97, 108–9; living quarters with DN, 97, 117; and the Nayarit as urban anchor, 100–101; number of immigrants assisted, 98–99; visa application process, 105, 215n16; women sponsored, 99–100, 123–27, 128, 130. *See also* employees of the Nayarit

Imperial Valley, 109–10, 216n27

Inchauspe, Bernard, 63

income and wage inequality in Mexico, 104, 133, 164

Indigenous peoples: Club Nayarit as celebrating native identity, 173; dispossession of lands, 28; legal attempts to classify Mexican ethnics as, 213n68; mission system imposed on, 28; the Nayarit's Christmas parade float emphasizing native identity, 93–94, 95, 173; right to naturalized citizenship, 93–94, 213n68; the "Spanish fantasy past" as erasing histories of, 14

Individual Taxpayer Identification numbers, taxes paid into, 183

industry, low-wage Mexican labor in, 29–30

Inés Jiménez, José, 174, 176

Inglewood, 170, 176, 226n21

INS. *See* Immigration and Naturalization Service

institutional racism and inequality: redlining and resultant white flight, 57–59, 205nn68,70; and wealth accumulation, lack of, 58, 205n70. *See also* structural inequalities

International School of Bartending, 115, 143–44, 170

interracial relationships: banning of rock íní roll to prevent, 149; moral panics about, 149; overturning of laws banning, 15, 149

Italian community, 14, 41, 175

Jacques, Carol, 46

Jaimes, Julio and Micaela, 183–84

Japanese and Japanese Americans: immigrants excluded from the US, 27; internment during WWII, 51–52; and segregation, 45

Jarrín, Jaime, 85–86, 94

jazz clubs, 10, 17

Jewish community: in fight against laws and policies banning interracial relationships, 149; racially restrictive covenants and, 44; redlining and, 58; and relational concept of race, 51–52. *See also* Jewish immigrants

Jewish immigrants: discrimination against, 41; as legally classified as white, 41; and race as a relational concept, 51

Jim Crow ("Jaime Crow"), 54

Jiménez, Tomás, 85, 209n43

Johnson, Gaye, 87

jury duty, Mexican Americans excluded from, 106

KALI (Spanish-language radio), 175, 176, 228n40

Kelley, Robin D. G., 206n3

Kelley, Thomas, 47

Kennedy, Ethel, 145

Kennedy, Jackie, 144

Kennedy, John F., 144

Kennedy, Robert "Bobby," 144–46

thinking of themselves as, 19; as more likely to report a pay cut or lost job due to COVID-19, 183; as real estate agents, 200n28. *See also* pan-Latinx spaces

Lau, Tomás, 115, 144, 170

La Villa Taxco/Casa Vallarta restaurants, 6, 154–55, 156

laws. *See* California—state and local laws; federal laws

League of United Latin American Citizens (LULAC), 141

Lee, Heather, 100

Lefebvre, Henri, 8

leftist politics. *See* Communist Party members; Echo Park, progressive and radical politics of

legal system: danger for gay immigrants, 150–51; DN's attorneys accompanying sponsees to traffic court, 105–6; first Mexican American serving as California Superior Court judge, 106; illegality as burden for immigrants, 104–5; juridical discrimination against ethnic Mexicans, 51, 106, 215n19; juries, Mexican Americans excluded from serving on, 106; police discrimination against ethnic Mexicans, 50, 51. *See also* California—state and local laws; federal laws

lesbians: bars catering to, 216n35; and the complexity of immigrant sexuality, 116–17, 218n45. *See also* gay community

Les Freres Taix restaurant, 63

Lewis, Earl, 17

LGBTQ+ community. *See* gay community

libraries, as anchor institutions and as urban anchors, 10

Lipsitz, George, 8, 21, 148–49, 189n11, 205n70

liquor and entertainment licenses, and gentrification, 180

Lira, Carlos Estrada, 139, 221n11

Little Manila (Historic Filipinotown), 45

local laws. *See* California—state and local laws

López, Óscar, 83

López, Rigoberto Robles, 171, 176

López, Tanis, 178

Lora, Rodolfo, 77, 107

Los Angeles: banning of rock íní roll concerts to avoid interracial relationships, 149; Club Nayarit and goal of strengthening connections with mainstream political establishment, 176–78; as featured in print ad for the Nayarit, 1–2, 3; Great Depression and deportation of Mexicans, 30–31, 32, 49, 194n43; history of welcoming immigrants as laborers but restricting them through laws and practices, 30; name under Spanish rule (Nuestra Señora la Reina de los Ángeles de Porceúncula), 28, 72; Office of Latin American Affairs (Yorty), 177–78; population of, 29, 197–98nn9–10; population of, foreign-born, 198n12; population of, Mexican, 29–30; the railroad and, 29, 30; World War II economic boom, 35, 149–50. *See also* Echo Park; gastronomic landscape of Los Angeles; gentrification; neighborhoods; placemaking; police; politics; racism; segregation; tourism development; translocal connections; urban anchors; *other entries at Los Angeles*; *specific neighborhoods*

Los Angeles City Archives, 54–55

Los Angeles City Council: gay community mobilized by homophobia of, 55–56;

mented lives, 20, 24; women's lives as difficult to find archival sources about, 24, 123–24, 196n50, 219n59. *See also El Eco de Nayarit*

Mexican American Bar Association, 142–43

Mexican Americans: banishment of citizens during "repatriation" campaigns, 30–31; voter registration of (1960), 142; Sam Yorty crediting, for reelection, 177. *See also* Mexican ethnics

Mexican Chamber of Commerce, 174

Mexican Civic Patriotic Committee, 174

Mexican ethnics: at Angelus Temple, 48–49; definition of and use of term, 187–88n4; and John F. and Jackie Kennedy, 144; and Robert Kennedy, 144–46; legal attempts to classify as Indigenous, 213n68; as legally classified as white, 16–17, 103, 205n72; mainstream view of as racialized subjects, 16; reinscribed as noncitizen immigrants by mainstream politicians, 177–78. *See also* citizenship status; discrimination—against ethnic Mexicans; employees of the Nayarit; family; fictive kin; immigrants—Mexican; immigration; labor, Mexican low-wage; Latinx people; placemaking; political resistance; politics; press coverage of ethnic Mexicans; resistance; Spanish language; working class

Mexican food in Los Angeles: and "authentic" as vexed term, 73; and cultural coalescence, 73; as historically working class, 13; mainstream popularity of, 13, 69–73; mom-and-pop establishments, 13; and the "Spanish fantasy past," 14; and standardization of Mexican service people, 14; street vendors, 13, 67, 183–84; traditional diet condemned as unhealthy by public health officials and assimilationists, 68–69, 70. *See also* gastronomic landscape of Los Angeles; Mexican food menus; restaurants

Mexican food menus: American-friendly, 75, 155; "California-style," 73; at restaurants started by former Nayarit employees, 154, 155, 156–57, 160; simplified and homogenized for white clientele, 13–14, 69–70, 73, 171; and the "Spanish fantasy past," 14, 38, 71, 73; of street vendors, 67; unmistakably of Nayarit, 184

—AT THE NAYARIT: concessions to American tastes, 75; desserts, 136; dishes served, 36, 38, 74–75; employees encouraged to taste all the dishes, 111; ingredient procurement, 74; late-night menu, 81; as portal to home in Mexico, 76; refusal to whitewash, 14, 38, 73, 75–76, 207n18; staff meal, 110–11

Mexican Independence Day celebrations and parades, 92, 93, 94, 128, 174

Mexico: Chinese immigration to, 220n69; consulate and consul, 170, 173–74, 194n43; culture of sexual silence, 118; homophobia in, 97, 98, 114; income and wage inequality in, 104, 133, 164; independence from Spain (1821), 28; John F. and Jackie Kennedy visit to, 144; Mexican Revolution, 29, 147, 174; US conquest of/war with (1846–48), 14, 28–29, 147, 192n25; US Foreign Service offices, 105, 215n16; Vacant

Mexico *(continued)*
Lands Law and displacement from the land, 29; working class as left out of the "Mexican miracle," 163–64; working-class disaffection for the government, 164. *See also* Nayarit, Mexico; *patria chica*; Spanish fantasy past

middle class: comforts of, shared by DN, 99, 132; Cuban exiles, 87; gays and lesbians, 150; *La Opinión* as focused on, 163, 165; Mexican food catering to, 13–14; Mexican, growth of, 177, 213–14n5; political organizations, 141. *See also* assimilation

migrants, definition and use of term, 187–88n4

Miller, Loren, 15

Million Dollar Theater, 85

miners, 147

Minian, Ana, 172–73, 217n37

misogyny, and ethnic Mexican women, 124

mission system, 28

Mleynek, Sherryll and Darryl, 76

Molina, Héctor (husband of María), 121, 123, 135, 136–37, 145

Molina, María: adoption by DN, 32, *33*, 34; appearance and dress of, *11*, 78–79, 129–30, *166*; in bartending school, 143–44; childhood work in the restaurants, 39; curfew for, 125; on the death of DN, 178; education of, 38–39; and extended community up and down Sunset Boulevard, 160; finding interviewees for the study, 21; friendships with gay men, 121; Nayarita pride of, 85; as outgoing and chatting with clientele, 78, 80, 170; and James Earl Ray, 143–44, 222n20;

in reviews, 75; as right-hand assistant in the business, 4; as running the business after DN's death, 6; and the Salas/Aragón fistfight, 66; as translator, 110; work duties of, 77–78, 108

Montezuma's (dance club, Sunset Blvd.), 129

Morales Díaz, Carmen, 165, 226n11

Moreno, Rita, 90, 91, 148

Movimiento Estudiantil Chicano de Aztlán (MEChA), 18

multicultural urban civility, 17, 134

multiethnic and multicultural neighborhoods: as cosmopolitan, 17; Latinx presence as unusual in, 80–81. *See also* Echo Park

music and musicians: banning of rock íní roll concerts to avoid interracial relationships, 149; at Club Nayarit dances, 175, 176; ethnic Mexican performers booked midweek, 84, 209n41; and "families of resemblance," forging, 148–49; at La Fonda, 19; mariachi bands, significance of, 170; midweek audiences as late-night Nayarit clientele, 84; musicians as Nayarit clientele, 90, 91; musicians employed by the Nayarit, 97–98; music scene in LA, 211–12n59; at the retirement banquet for Martín Sáizar, 170, 171; rock music brought to Mexico by returning immigrants, 126

music stores, 10

mutual aid societies (*mutualistas*), 172, 174, 224n57

NAACP, 15, 17

NAACP (National Association for the Advancement of Colored People), 149

Nayarit restaurant *(continued)*
following midweek Mexican
performance events, 84, 209n41; gay
men, 120-21, 218n52, 219n54; Nayarit
immigrants, 84; Nayarit, visitors
from, 1-2, 4, 84, 85, 209n43; and the
pan-Latinx identity, 87-88; police,
89; relationships with employees,
110, 121, *122*, 130, 151, 154; service
workers, 82, 139; single women, 84,
129; as unable to cook at home, 80
—CLIENTELE, DIVERSITY OF: overview, 6,
17, 23; celebrities, 17, 65-66; comfort
and casual joy provided to, 17; as
cosmopolitan, 17, 89-90, 134; and
difference, comfort with, 23; location
on Sunset Boulevard as ensuring, 81;
working-class ethnic Mexicans as
core clientele, 17, 36, 80
—PUBLICITY: advertisement in *El Eco de
Nayarit*, 1-2, *3*, 84, 165; flyers on car
windshields at Latin music dances,
84; radio advertisements, 85-86; the
Salas/Aragón fistfight as, 65-66
Nayarit restaurant (original, 1943-52), *37*;
closing of, 39; decor of, 38; DN living
above, 38; location of, 4-5, 35-36;
opening of, 35
Nayarit Segundo ("little Nayarit")
restaurant (1964-68), 1-2, *3*, 5
The Negro Motorist Green Book, 91, 212n62
neighborhoods: fragility of, 180; freeways
and destruction of, 54-55, 203-4n59;
isolation from other neighborhoods,
130; NIMBY (Not In My Backyard)
campaigns and siting of undesirable
projects, 204n65; racial boundaries
of, 146-47; restaurants as both
defining and defined by, 182; as unit
of analysis, 27-28, 197n5. *See also*

ethnic enclaves; gentrification;
housing; multiethnic and multicultural neighborhoods; segregation;
specific neighborhoods
Nervov, Alejandro "Alex," 175
New York (city), 13, 158, 197-98n9
Nikola's restaurant, -63
NIMBY (Not In My Backyard) campaigns,
204n65
normalcy/deviancy, and "good immigrants," 117
Nuestra Señora la Reina de los Ángeles
(church), 36, 178

Olvera Street, 35-36, 67, 69-71
O'Malley, Walter, 57, 63, 139
ONE, Inc., 56
Ontiveros, Lupe, 223n33
Orange County, Mexican restaurants in,
74
Ortega, César, 121, 152
Ortego, Aleríco "Al," 177
Osuna, Guadalupe, 121
Osuna, Steven, 121
others/otherness: progressive and radical
politics of Echo Park and common
cause among, 46, 47, 53, 201-2n40;
and traversing the racialized
landscape of LA, 146-47
Our Lady of Guadalupe, 144

Pack, Evelia Díaz Barraza, 88, 91-92, 120,
125, 126-27, 130, 151, 158-59, *166*,
169, 170, 179
Pack, Ramón, II, 81, 87-88, 90, 116, 120,
127, 151, 158-59, 169
pan-Latinx spaces: and adoption of each
other's accents and slang, 87; and
Latinidad (pan-Latinx identity), 86,
211n56; Mexican identity as default

for, 86, 211n86; shared history of racism and discrimination and, 88; Spanish language and, 86–87. *See also* Latinx people

Pantages Theater, 81

Parker, William, 120

patria chica: overview, 24; advertisement for the Nayarit playing on, 2; and Club Nayarit as celebrating Indigenous identity, 173; definition of, 2; the name of the restaurant as signaling, 84; and the Nayarit's parade float emphasizing Indigenous identity, 93–94, *95*, 173; and respect for others' homelands, 163; and the retirement banquet for Martín Sáizar, 171; as shared sense of place, 98, 99; translocal placemaking efforts and, 24, 162, 168

People's Child Care Center, 61

Perea, Alberto (husband of DN): and Carlos (son), 39; in census records, 31, 32, 34; death of, 32; living separately from DN, 34; marriage to DN, 32, 34

Perea, Carlos (son of DN), 32, *33*, 34, *37*, 38–39

Perea, María (daughter of DN). *See* Molina, María

performance spaces, 10

Picasso, Raquel, 39

Pinto, Jesus "Jesse," 157, 160

Pioneer Market, 62, 155–56, 179

place, and fluidity of identity, 123

placemakers: and continued vulnerability of Latinx residents to powers that be, 57; definition of, 8–9; gay men as, 117, 218n46; honoring, need for, 181; José Inés Jiménez, 174

placemaking: defined by geographers, 188–89n9; defined more expansively

as resistant and oppositional, 9–10, 189n11; extending from LA to Nayarit, 162; "La Noche de Esclavos" (NDE), service workers' night out institution as, 141; and space as political and strategic, 8; white progressive and radical residents making opportunities for Mexican immigrants, 61–62. *See also* resistance; translocal connections; urban anchors

—VIA THE NAYARIT RESTAURANT: overview, 113; as both convivial and political, 67; emotional ties as driving, 99, 100, 113; extended community and, 159–60; and gay male employees, 130–31; and women employees, 130–31. *See also* placetaking by employees of the Nayarit; restaurants and businesses opened by former Nayarit employees

place-taking by employees of the Nayarit: asserting their right to the city, 24, 137; bravery required for, 149, 151; Christmas decor, 136; cultural coalescence enabled by, 136; customers taking an active role in, 136–37; as recent adult immigrants, 134–35; sharing their cultural capital with friends and family, 135, 137, 138–39; tipping and being tipped, 135

police: cross-dressers arrested by, 153; as cultural brokers at the Nayarit, 89; discrimination against ethnic Mexicans, 50, 51; fear of attention from, and DN as moderating gay male workers' appearance and comportment, 117; gay meeting spots and bars as harassed and raided by, 55–56, 117, 120, 150–51, 153, 158, 218n52; gay men entrapped by, 120, 150–51;

police *(continued)*
    hangouts of, 62; violent brutality of,
    50, 146; young ethnic Mexican
    women as criminalized by, 124
Polish people and hierarchy of whiteness,
    41
political resistance: Chicanx movement,
    18–19, 21–22, 142, 148–49, 187–88n4,
    215n19; Civil Rights movement,
    11–12, 18, 141; immigrants who
    sought dignity and belonging despite
    not partaking in, 19; Nayarit workers
    and lack of engagement with, 141–42;
    the postwar era and ethnic Mexicans,
    141. *See also* resistance; social justice
politics: Club Nayarit's goal of strength-
    ening mainstream Los Angeles
    political connections, 176–78; global,
    and differential racialization, 15; lack
    of Latinx representation in public
    office, 177; oral histories and
    omissions of, 21–22, 195n46. *See also*
    Echo Park—progressive and radical
    politics of; labor organizing and labor
    unions; political resistance
politics of respectability: appearance and
    dress of DN and, 79; beauty pageants
    and, 141; definition of, 208n30
Pomona, 209n41
Porras, Carlos, 88, 114, 115–16, 118,
    119–20, *119*, 121, *122*, 151, 155
Porras, David (son of María Molina), 6,
    119, 121, 138–39
Portelli, Allessandro, 22–23
Portillo, Felipe, 121
Porto, Rosa, 211n57
Porto's Bakery, 89, 211n57
postwar era: ethnic Mexicans organizing
    politically for civil rights, 141;
    income inequality in Mexico, 104,

133, 164; INS registration rules, 101;
    "Mexican miracle," 163–64;
    segregation enforced on African
    Americans, 146; white flight as less
    likely to occur in multi-ethnic/
    multicultural neighborhood, 23. *See
    also* Cold War
Preciado, Aurelia Guijarro, 82
press coverage of ethnic Mexicans: as
    inflammatory and racist, 50, 51,
    202–3n49; on the laborer as expected
    mold, 168; "Mexican colony" of East
    Los Angeles, 106. *See also El Eco de
    Nayarit*; *La Opinión*; reviews of
    restaurants
Price, Patricia, 188–89n9
Price, Susan, 188–89n9
Prince Philip of Spain, 156
Progressive Era: perpetuating the
    stereotype of the "dirty Mexican,"
    68–69; and the politics of respect-
    ability, 208n30
public charge, likelihood of becoming:
    affidavit stating an immigrant has a
    job and will not become, 104;
    definition of, 32; immigration
    officers' scrutiny of, 26, 196n50;
    Aimee Semple McPherson and aid
    without question in order to avoid,
    49; mass deportation of Mexicans
    (1931–33), 32, 49; and women
    immigrating alone, 26; and working-
    class Mexican immigrants as steering
    clear of the government, 172. *See also*
    deportation of Mexicans
public health, and perpetuation of
    stereotypes, 68–69
public housing: proposed in Compton and
    stopped by white racists, 146; urban
    renewal and Chavez Ravine, 56–57

public order charges, as punishing those who live their lives in public, 29, 56

public spaces: access to space for Mexican ethnic peoples, limits of, 4; as hostile to marginalized, racialized groups, 9; invisibility in, immigrants as seeking, 66–67; protection of Elysian Park, for access by the working class, 61; Spanish language use and "spatial entitlement," 87; urban anchors as uncontested space, 96

Puente, Tito ("King of Latin Music"), 90

Puerto Ricans, 90

Quinn, Anthony, 48–49, 148

race: as relational concept, 46–47, 51–53; and sexuality, falsely seen as separate areas of inquiry, 116–17, 218nn45–46; as term, 8. *See also* diversity; racial hierarchy; racialized groups

race-making practices: racialized power structures as remaining intact, 29; Spanish colonial rule and, 28, 29; US conquest and, 28–29

racial brokers, 200n28

racial hierarchy: agricultural labor and, 34–35; carceral systems and, 29; differential racialization, 15, 192–93n29; land dispossession and, 147; as naturalized via cultural representation, 148; white establishment and, 14–15; of whiteness/inbetween people, and discrimination, 41. *See also* discrimination—against ethnic Mexicans; race-making practices; racialized groups; racism

racialized groups: defined as constructed and changeable category, 8; public spaces as hostile to, 9; and semipub-

lic spaces, placemaking in, 9–10, 189n11; whites, classification of ethnic Mexicans as, 16–17, 103, 205n72

racially restrictive covenants: overview, 44; defined as enforcement of segregation, 15, 44; Fair Housing Act as prohibiting, but not not requiring removal of covenants from existing deeds (1968), 16; intimidation, harassment, and violence enforcing, 44; neighborhood associations and, 44, 45, 53; private parties allowed to abide by (1948–68), 15–16, 44; real estate agents and and property owners enforcing, 16, 44, 53–54; ruled not enforceable by states (1948), 15–16; segregation previously enforced by law not reversed, 16; white-classification of Mexicans as no protection against, 16

racism: overview, 15; African American experience of, as differing from ethnic Mexicans, 16, 41, 103; Community Service Organization (CSO) fighting, 141; and ethnic Mexican women, 124; pan-Latinx identity and shared experience of, 88. *See also* discrimination; institutional racism and inequality; racialized groups; racially restrictive covenants; segregation; social justice; structural inequalities; violence of racism and discrimination

radio: Club Nayarit dance and, 175; death of DN honored on, 178; Nayarit advertisements on, 85–86; NDE (service workers' night out institution) advertised on, 140; Spanish-language, audience for, 228n40

Radio Express, 178
railroad, 29, 30, 216n29
Rainbow Gardens (Pomona), 209n41
Ralph Story's Los Angeles (TV), 81
Ramírez, Judith, 140
Ramona Gardens, 137
Ramos, Andrea, 154
Ramos, Lupita, 160
Ranger, Isaac, as cultural broker, 38, 40
Rasic, Nikola, 62
Ray, James Earl, 143–44
Reagan, Ronald and Nancy, 82
real estate agents: Latinx, as breaking
    through the color line, 200n28; racial
    covenants enforced by, 16, 44, 53–54
Rechy, John, 152–53
Red Gulch/Red Hill, 49, 202n46
Redhead (bar), 216n35
redlining, 57–58, 205nn68,70
Reina, Joe, 73
religion and churches: Angelus Temple/
    Aimee Semple McPherson, 48–49;
    and DN, 78, 117; First Unitarian
    Church, 49; and placemaking for
    Cuban immigrants, 88–89; and social
    justice, 48–49. *See also* Catholic
    Church
remittances: donations by DN for
    municipal projects, 113, 161, 178;
    employees of the Nayarit not
    pressured to send, 112–13, 129;
    hometown associations providing,
    173; home towns as benefiting by,
    113; Mexican government control of
    funds for local public works, 173; as
    obligation and emotional bond,
    112–13
replenished ethnicity, 85, 209n43
resistance: dressing up as assertion of
    dignity and, 67, 206n3; and "families

of resemblance," forging, 148–49; to
    gentrification, 181; placemaking
    more expansively defined as, 9–10,
    189n11; refusal to whitewash the
    menu as, 14, 73, 207n18; seeking
    dignity and belonging as, 19;
    traditional food preparation as, 69,
    70; urban anchors and, 12. *See also*
    labor organizing and labor unions;
    political resistance; politics of
    respectability
respectability. *See* politics of
    respectability
restaurants: as already economically
    vulnerable, 182; closures and
    complications due to COVID-19,
    182–84; closures due to gentrification,
    131, 181–82; community afforded by,
    loss of, 183; exploration by Nayarit
    employees, encouraged by DN,
    132–33, 136; food journalism and
    movement for visibility and humani-
    zation of back-of-house staff, 13,
    191n19; food trends and difficulty
    cultivating a regular clientele, 182;
    fund-raising on behalf of Mexico, 71;
    gay customers, range of treatment of,
    218n52; high-stakes investors,
    dependence on, 182; immigrant
    restauranteurs hit by COVID-19,
    183–84; as integral parts of people's
    social worlds, 94; "La Noche de
    Esclavos" (NDE, "Night of the
    Slaves"), service workers' night out
    institution, 139–41; Nayarit fictive kin
    visiting, 6–7; refusal to serve ethnic
    Mexicans, 148, 169; service workers as
    clientele of the Nayarit, 82, 139; as
    sites of everyday resistance, 12; as
    urban anchors, 10. *See also* ethnic

transportation: bus line servicing the Nayarit, 81; streetcars, 47, 54. *See also* freeways

Treaty of Guadalupe Hidalgo (1848), 28–29, 213n68

Treviño, Tonny, 140

undocumented workers: costs and risks as higher for, 103–4; COVID-19 toll on, 183; demand for low-wage labor and, 102–3; deportation as constant threat to, 103; DN employing, 107–8; documented family members living with, 103; doing jobs that others reject, 183; exploitation of, 103; illegality as burden for, 103, 104; increase in, and increased difficulty of documented entry, 102; as percentage of California workforce, 183; as percentage of the restaurant workforce, 183; punitive laws against, 101; rate of entry (1942–64), 18; registration with the INS after 1940, 101; Social Security cards legal for (until 1972), 107; taxes paid by, 183. *See also* deportation of Mexicans

United Cannery, Agricultural, Packing and Allied Workers of America (UCAPAWA), 141

United Farm Workers (UFW), 18, 19, 144–45

United States: conquest of Mexico/war with Mexico (1846–48), 14, 28–29, 147, 192n25; Cuban Refugee Program, 87–88; Foreign Service offices, 105; wars of, as factor in differential racialization, 15; working-class Mexican immigrants steering clear of the government except where unavoidable, 162, 172. *See also* Border Patrol; census, US; citizenship status; Cold War; deportation of Mexicans; federal laws; Great Depression; immigration; Immigration and Naturalization Service (INS); institutional racism and inequality; legal system; postwar era; racism; social justice; structural inequalities; US Federal Court of Appeals; US Supreme Court; World War II

urban anchors: African American communities and creation of, 17, 193–94n36; anchor institutions distinguished from, 10, 189–90n12; and belonging, 66, 91; in Boyle Heights, 79, 140; clusters of, 62–63; of Cuban community, 89; definition of, 10; Echo Park Lake as, 47; and ethnic enclaves, 17; everyday resistance and, 12; of gay community, 156–58, 224n53; gentrification and loss of, 160, 182–83; as immigrant-, family-, and gay-spaces all at once, 121; the Nayarit as, 100–101; political resistance and, 11–12; restaurants and businesses opened by former Nayarit employees as, 153, 156, 158, 159–60; in Silver Lake, 89, 211n57; social networks as expanded by, 99; the stable workforce as integral element of, 63; as uncontested public space, 96. *See also* entrepreneurship, ethnic; placemaking

urban renewal: Chavez Ravine destruction, 56–57; Echo Park as largely escaping, 54, 56; siting of garbage dumps, prisons, toxic incinerators, 56, 204n65. *See also* freeways

US Federal Court of Appeals, *Mendez v. Westminster School District* (1946), 16–17

US Foreign Service offices, 105
US Supreme Court: *Brown v. Board of Education*, 15, 16–17; *Hernandez v. State of Texas* (1954), 106; *Loving v. Virginia* (1967), 149; *Plessy v. Ferguson* (1896), 16; *Shelley v. Kraemer* (1948), 15–16, 44
US war with Mexico (1846–48), 14, 28, 192n25

Valenzuela, Elba, 140
Van Doren, Mamie, 65
Vargas, Zaragosa, 147–48
Verdugo Inn, 140
Vidaurri, Soledad (Sally), 16
Vietnamese refugees, 46
Vinton, Bobby "the Polish Prince," 135–36
violence, gentrification as, 180
violence of racism and discrimination: as lived reality, 146; police brutality, 50, 146; segregation and racially restrictive covenants enforced via, 15, 44, 146, 148; for venturing out of designated sphere, 148
visas: application process, 105, 215n16; arrest for homosexual behavior as ending hope for, 150; assistance from DN, 105; attorney assistance with, 107; fees for, 104; green cards, 101, 103, 104, 107, 150; guest worker visas, 101–2; resident visas, 102; waiting list, 104. *See also* documented immigration
voter registration, 142

Warehouse (Marina del Rey), 136
Warren, Earl, 51
Watts, 21–22, 146
Watts uprising (1965), 21–22
wealth accumulation, systematic legal and social barriers to, 15, 58, 205n70

Wells, Wesley, 50
West Hollywood, gay and lesbian community and, 150
Westside: ethnic Mexicans commuting to work in, 146–47; and exploration of the city by Nayarit employees, 137; Hansen's Cakes, 110; as Jewish enclave, 41; Mexican restaurants in, 71–72
West Side Story, 90, 224n53
white flight, 23, 57–60. *See also* racism
whiteness, as hierarchy, 41
white privilege, experiences that complicate, 46. *See also* Echo Park—progressive and radical politics of
white property owners: as enforcing racial covenants, 16, 44, 53–54; techniques used to intimidate buyers of color, 44, *45*, 146. *See also* discrimination; racially restrictive covenants; racism
Wilkerson, Billy, 82
women: autonomy and adventure sought by, 123, 126, 128; as NDE "queen," 140–41; as regular customers, friendships with employees, 121, *122*. *See also* politics of respectability
—AS EMPLOYEES OF THE NAYARIT: appearance and dress of, 126, 128, 129–30; exploration of the city encouraged by DN, 132–33, *138*; opportunities available to, as much greater, 99. *See also* employees of the Nayarit
—MEXICAN IMMIGRANTS: assimilation presumed to be the goal of, 123–24; choosing to return to Mexico, 127; limited options available to, 35; lives of, as difficult to find archival sources about, 24, 123–24, 196n50, 219n59;

women *(continued)*
 parental worries about daughters
 abandoning their culture, 124; racism
 and misogyny as complicating the
 lives of, 124; sponsorship by DN,
 99–100, 123–27, 128, 130; young,
 chaperonage by DN, 124–25, 126–27,
 219n62
—SINGLE OR DIVORCED: DN as, 26, 98, 113;
 immigrating alone, 26–27; immigrating in larger numbers, 124
Wongpec, Irene, *119*, 128–29, 220n69
workers' compensation, 103
working class: as back-of-house kitchen
 staff, 13; child care center to serve,
 61; *El Eco* and in-person contact with,
 169; ethnic Mexicans, as core
 clientele of Barragan's, 156; ethnic
 Mexicans, as core clientele of the
 Nayarit, 17, 23, 36, 80; gay bars, 150,
 216n35; and importance of protecting
 Elysian Park, 61; law center to serve,
 61; Mexican food historically as, 13;
 Mexican immigrants steering clear of
 the government except where
 unavoidable, 162, 172; in Mexico, as
 excluded from the postwar "Mexican
 miracle," 163–64; in Mexico,

 disaffection with the government,
 164; placemakers as, 9; and political
 advocacy as challenging to engage in,
 142; public spaces protected for
 access to, 61; and race as relational
 concept, 46–47. *See also* employees of
 the Nayarit; exploration of the city by
 Nayarit employees, DN's encouragement of
working-class neighborhoods: ethnic
 restaurants as enticing people to,
 13–14. *See also* gentrification;
 neighborhoods; urban renewal;
 specific neighborhoods
Working People's Law Center, 61
World War II: African American community and, 146; economic boom of, 35,
 149–50; gay community and, 149–50;
 internment of Japanese people
 during, 51–52; rationing, 39; and
 scapegoating of ethnic Mexicans,
 51–52. *See also* postwar era

Yorty, Sam, *72*, 176–78
Young, Phoebe, 36, 71

Zeitlin, Jake, 42, 47–48
Zoot Suit riots (1943), 51–52